D1105853

DATE DUE

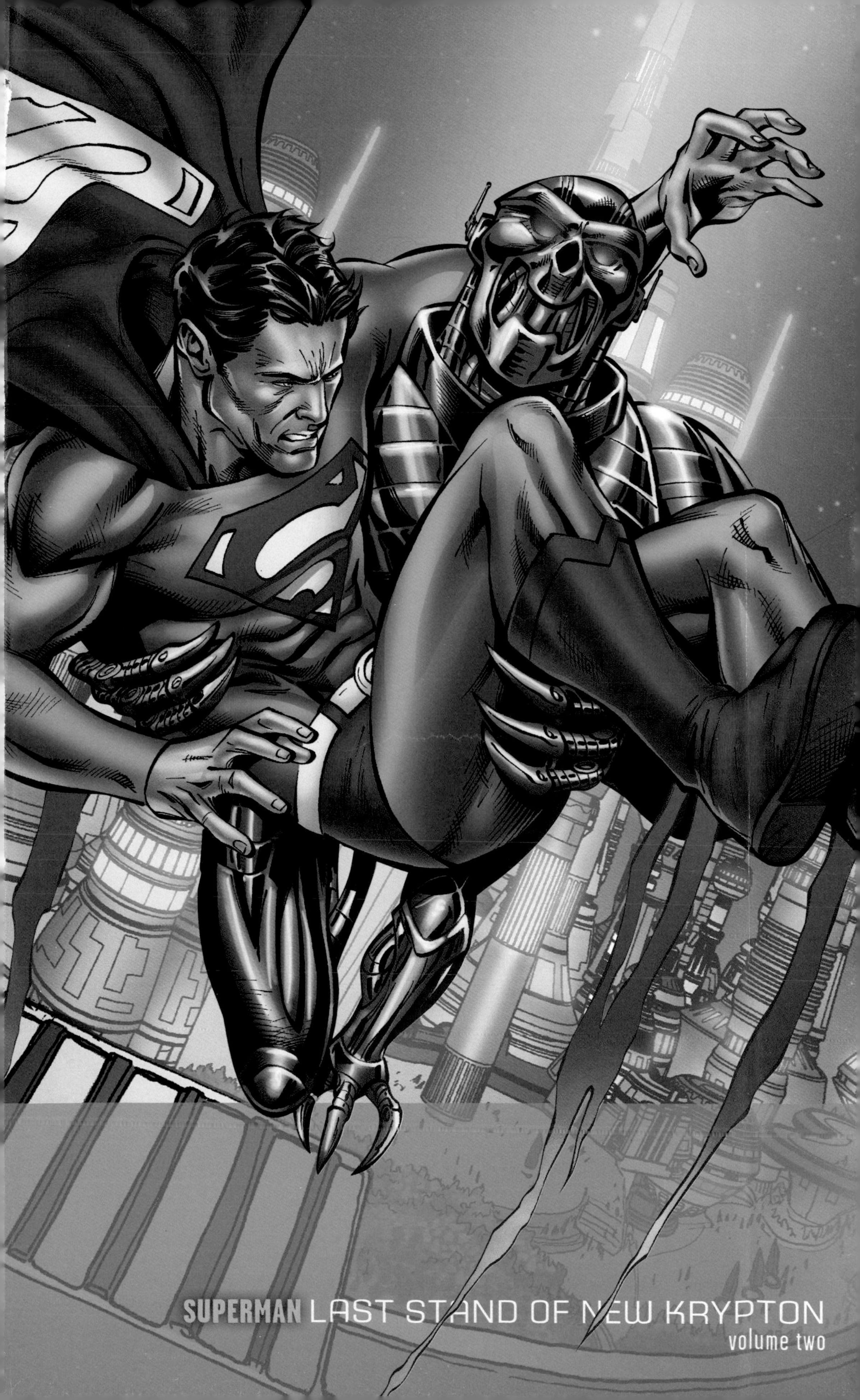
SUPERMAN LAST STAND OF NEW KRYPTON
volume two

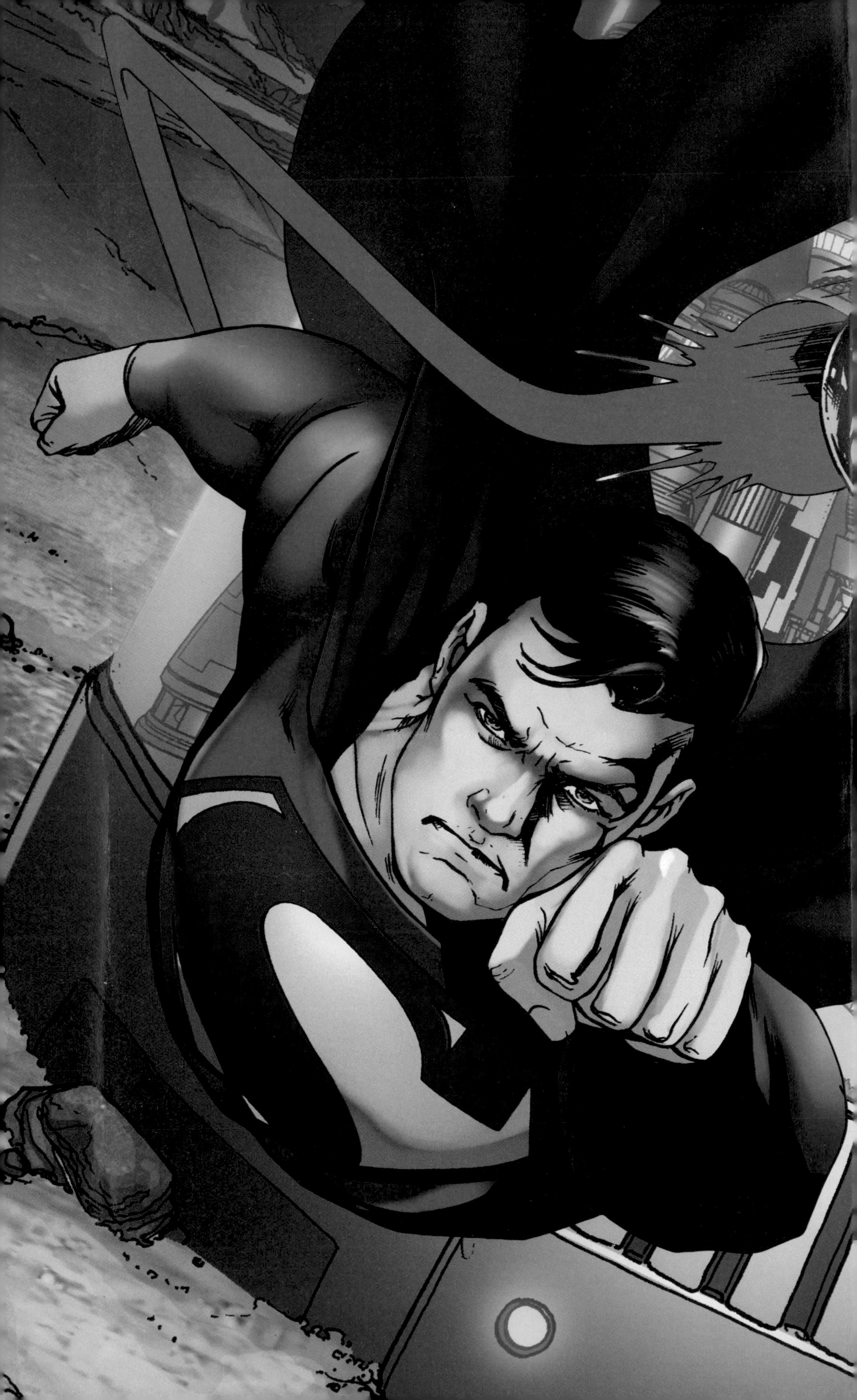

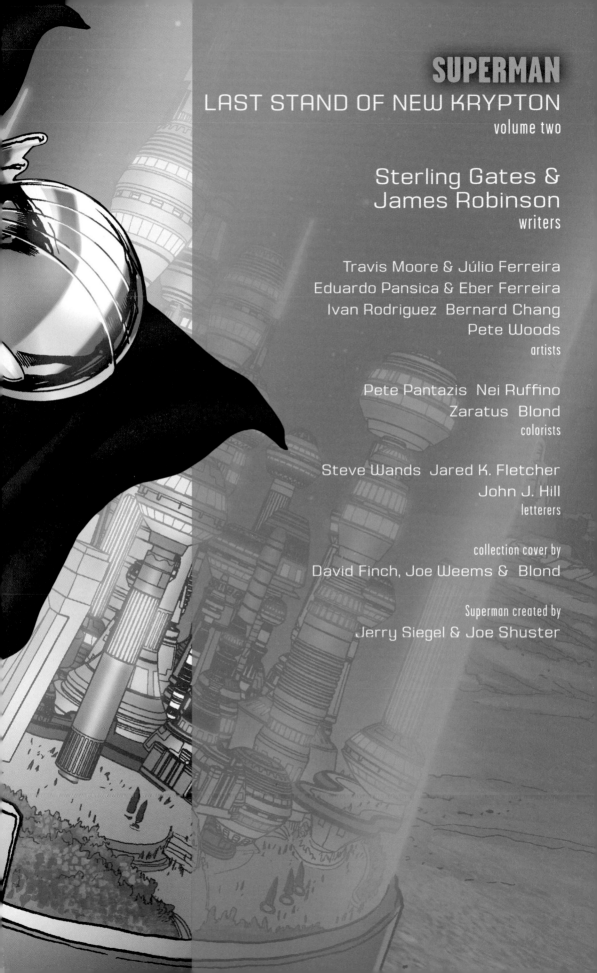

SUPERMAN
LAST STAND OF NEW KRYPTON
volume two

Sterling Gates &
James Robinson
writers

Travis Moore & Júlio Ferreira
Eduardo Pansica & Eber Ferreira
Ivan Rodriguez Bernard Chang
Pete Woods
artists

Pete Pantazis Nei Ruffino
Zaratus Blond
colorists

Steve Wands Jared K. Fletcher
John J. Hill
letterers

collection cover by
David Finch, Joe Weems & Blond

Superman created by
Jerry Siegel & Joe Shuster

MATT IDELSON Editor-original series   WIL MOSS Assistant Editor-original series   BOB HARRAS Group Editor-Collected Editions   SEAN MACKIEWICZ Editor
ROBBIN BROSTERMAN Design Director-Books
DC COMICS
DIANE NELSON President   DAN DIDIO and JIM LEE Co-Publishers   GEOFF JOHNS Chief Creative Officer   PATRICK CALDON EVP-Finance and Administration
JOHN ROOD EVP-Sales, Marketing and Business Development   AMY GENKINS SVP-Business and Legal Affairs   STEVE ROTTERDAM SVP-Sales and Marketing
JOHN CUNNINGHAM VP-Marketing   TERRI CUNNINGHAM VP-Managing Editor   ALISON GILL VP-Manufacturing   DAVID HYDE VP-Publicity   SUE POHJA VP-Book Trade Sales
ALYSSE SOLL VP-Advertising and Custom Publishing   BOB WAYNE VP-Sales   MARK CHIARELLO Art Director

SUPERMAN: LAST STAND OF NEW KRYPTON Volume 2
Published by DC Comics. Cover, text and compilation Copyright © 2011 DC Comics. All Rights Reserved.

Originally published in single magazine form in ADVENTURE COMICS 10, 11, SUPERGIRL 52, SUPERMAN 699, SUPERMAN: LAST STAND OF NEW KRYPTON 3. Copyright ©
2010 DC Comics. All Rights Reserved. All characters, their distinctive likenesses and related elements featured in this publication are trademarks of DC Comics.
The stories, characters and incidents featured in this publication are entirely fictional. DC Comics does not read or accept unsolicited submissions of ideas,
stories or artwork.

DC Comics, 1700 Broadway, New York, NY 10019. A Warner Bros. Entertainment Company
Printed by Quad/Graphics, Versailles, KY, USA. 12/15/10. First printing.
HC ISBN: 978-1-4012-3036-4 SC ISBN: 978-1-4012-3037-1

cover by JOE QUINONES

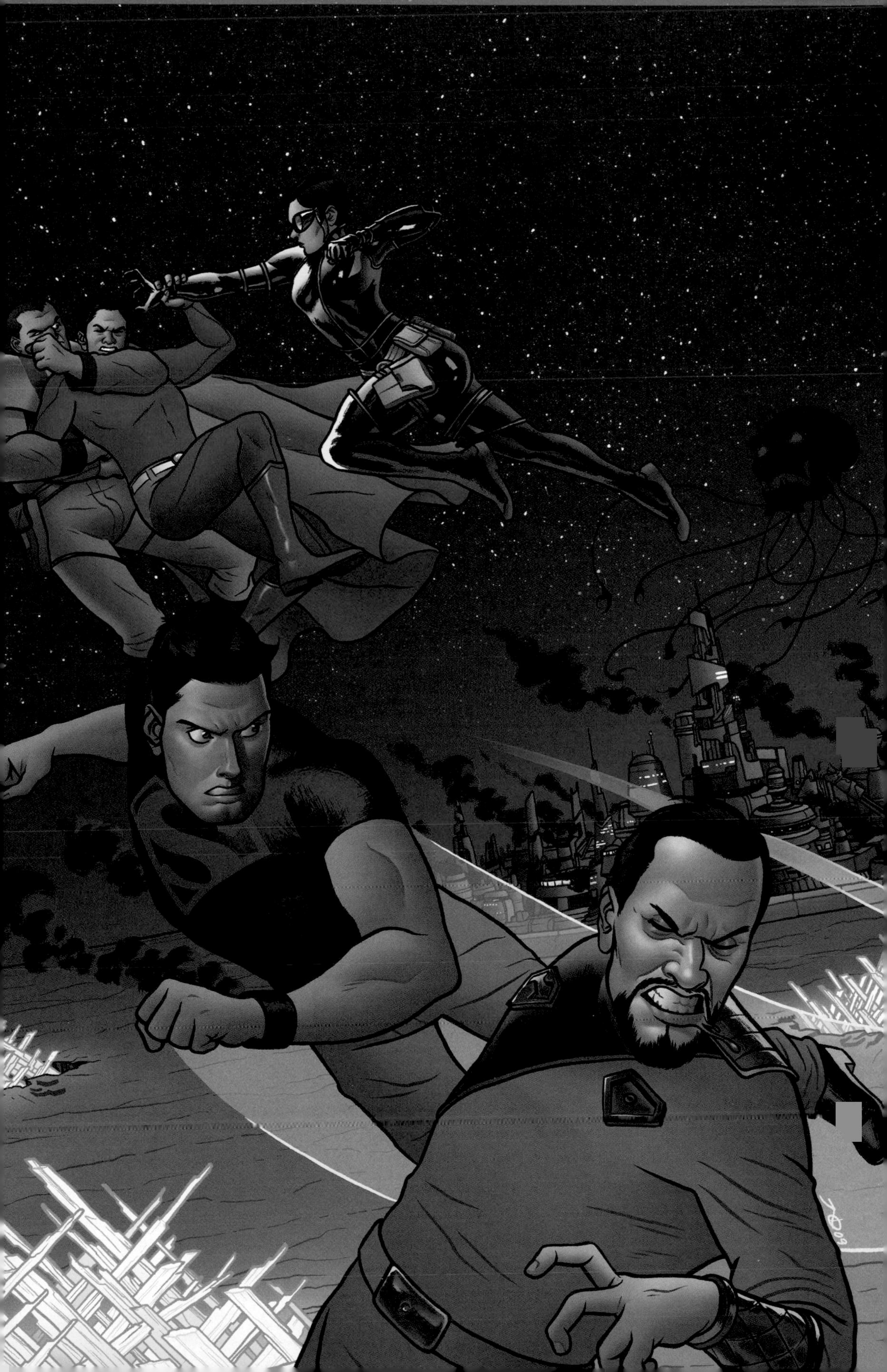

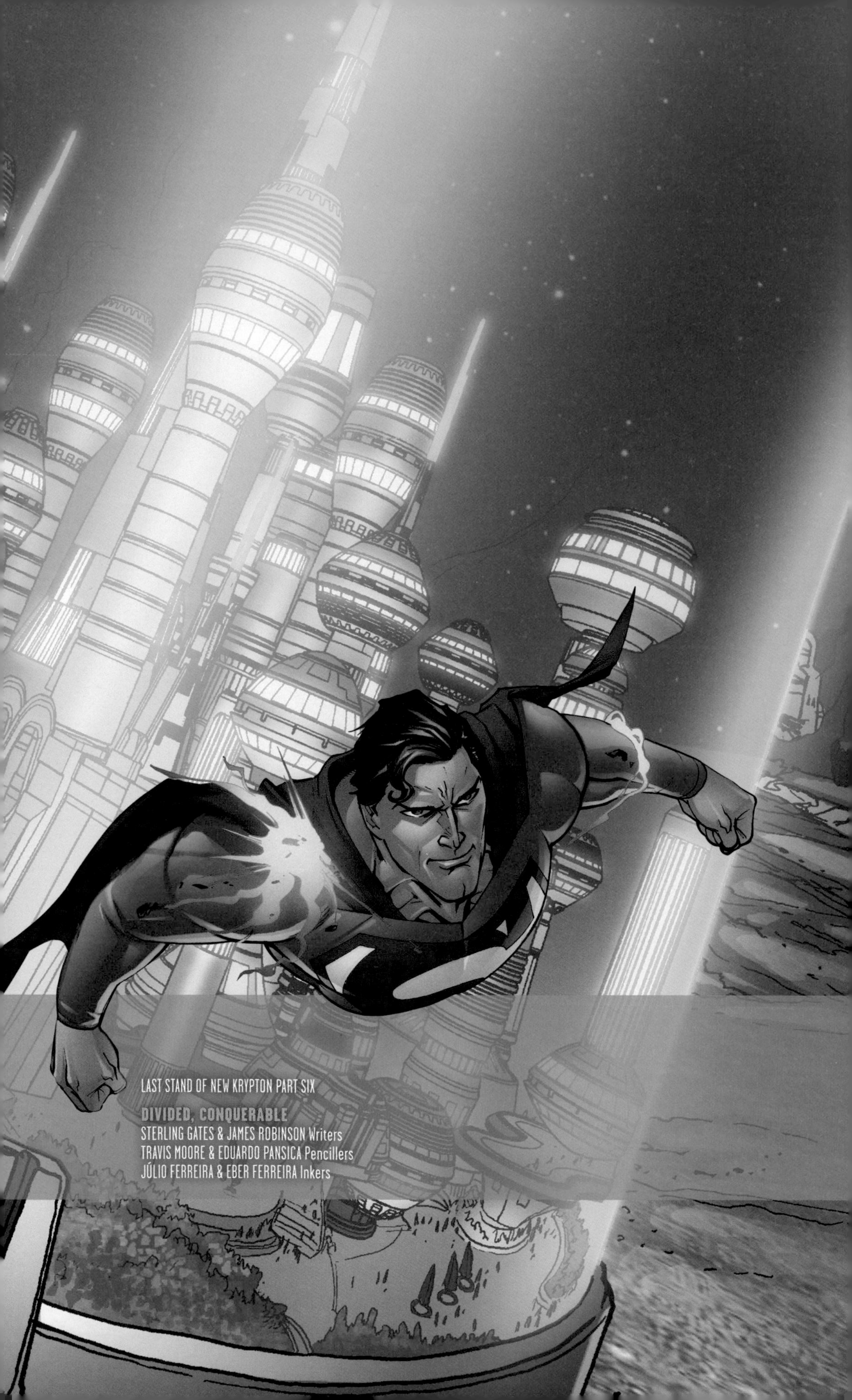

LAST STAND OF NEW KRYPTON PART SIX

DIVIDED, CONQUERABLE

STERLING GATES & JAMES ROBINSON Writers
TRAVIS MOORE & EDUARDO PANSICA Pencillers
JÚLIO FERREIRA & EBER FERREIRA Inkers

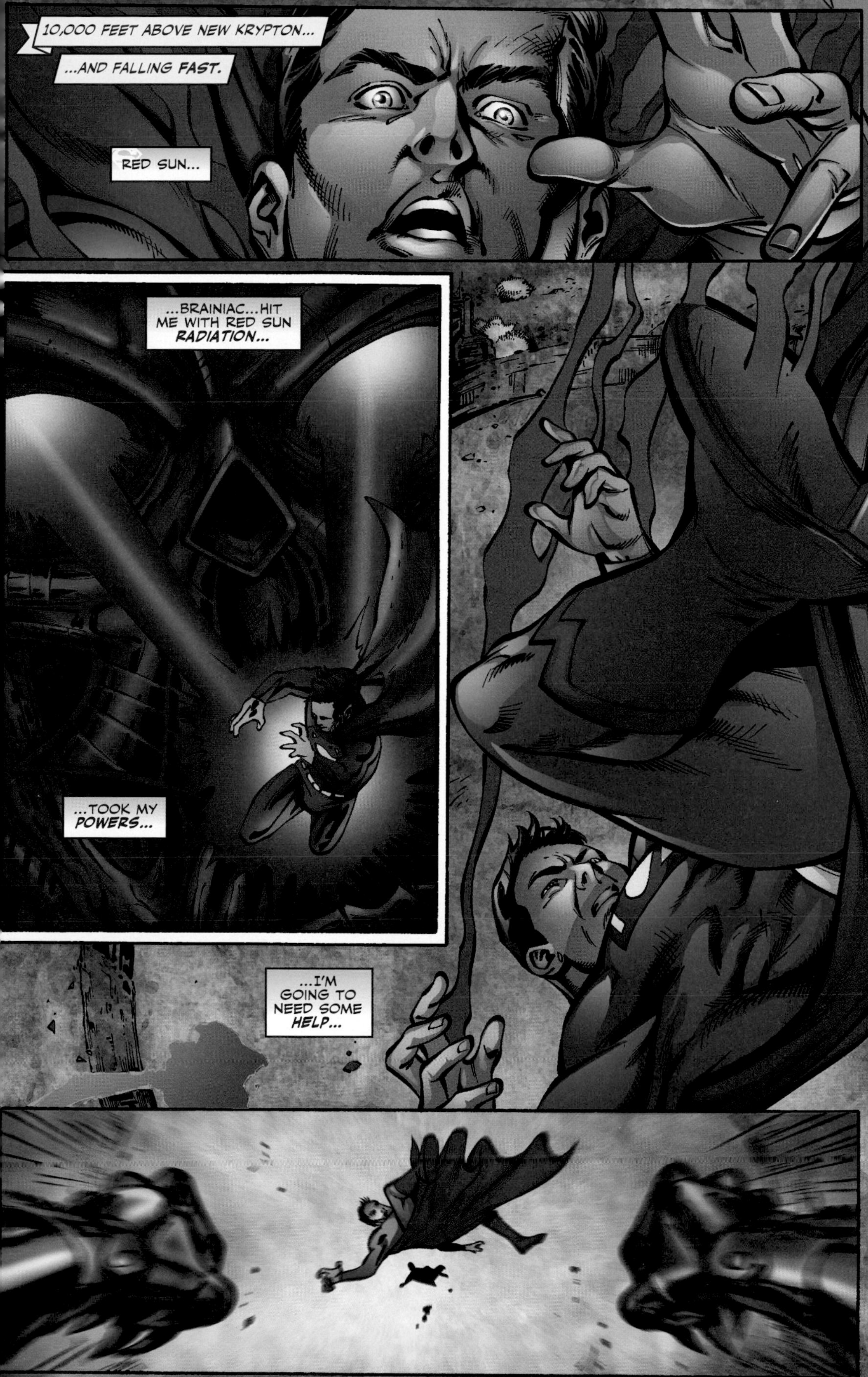
10,000 FEET ABOVE NEW KRYPTON...
...AND FALLING FAST.
RED SUN...
...BRAINIAC...HIT ME WITH RED SUN RADIATION...
...TOOK MY POWERS...
...I'M GOING TO NEED SOME HELP...

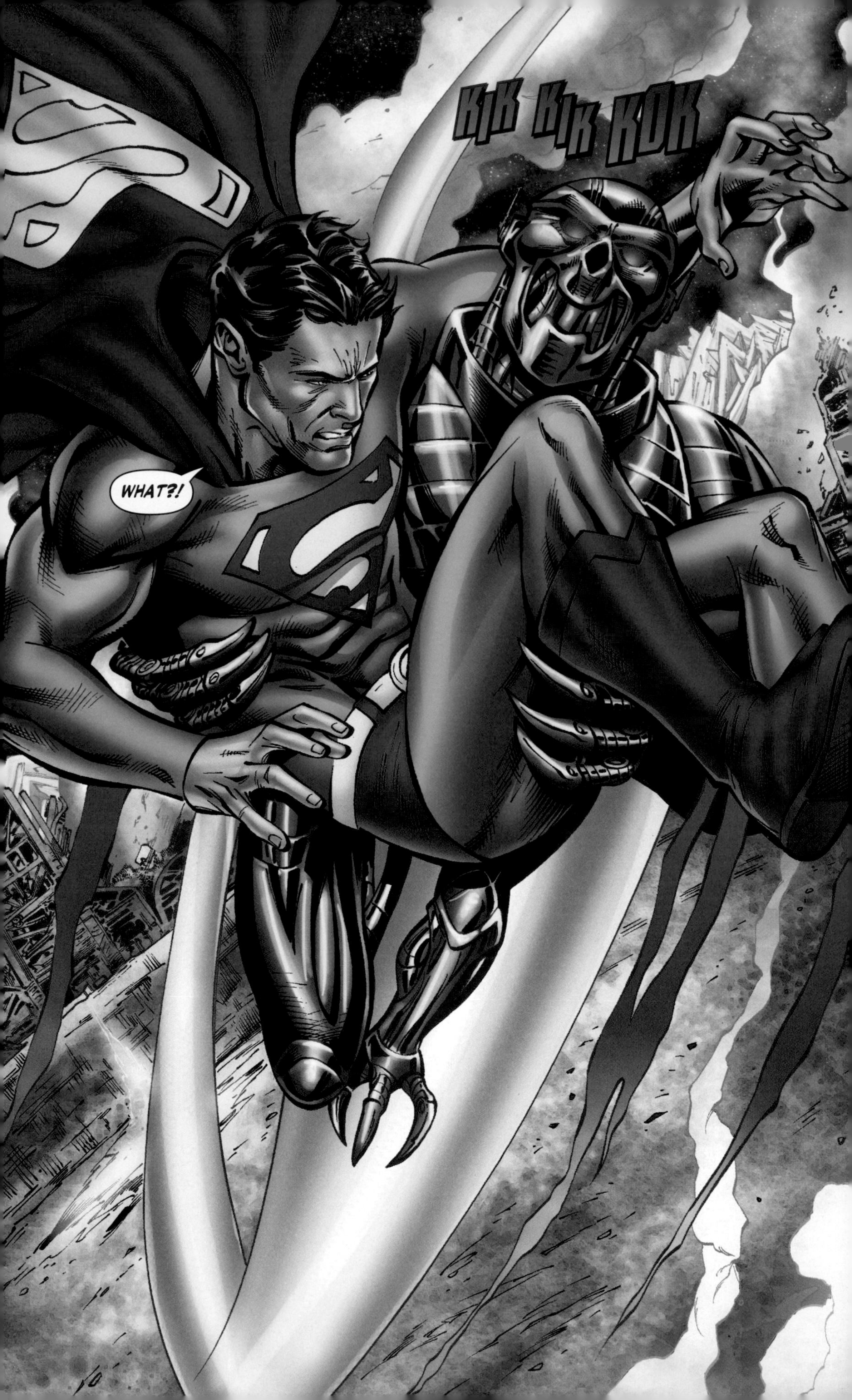
KIK KIK KOK
WHAT?!

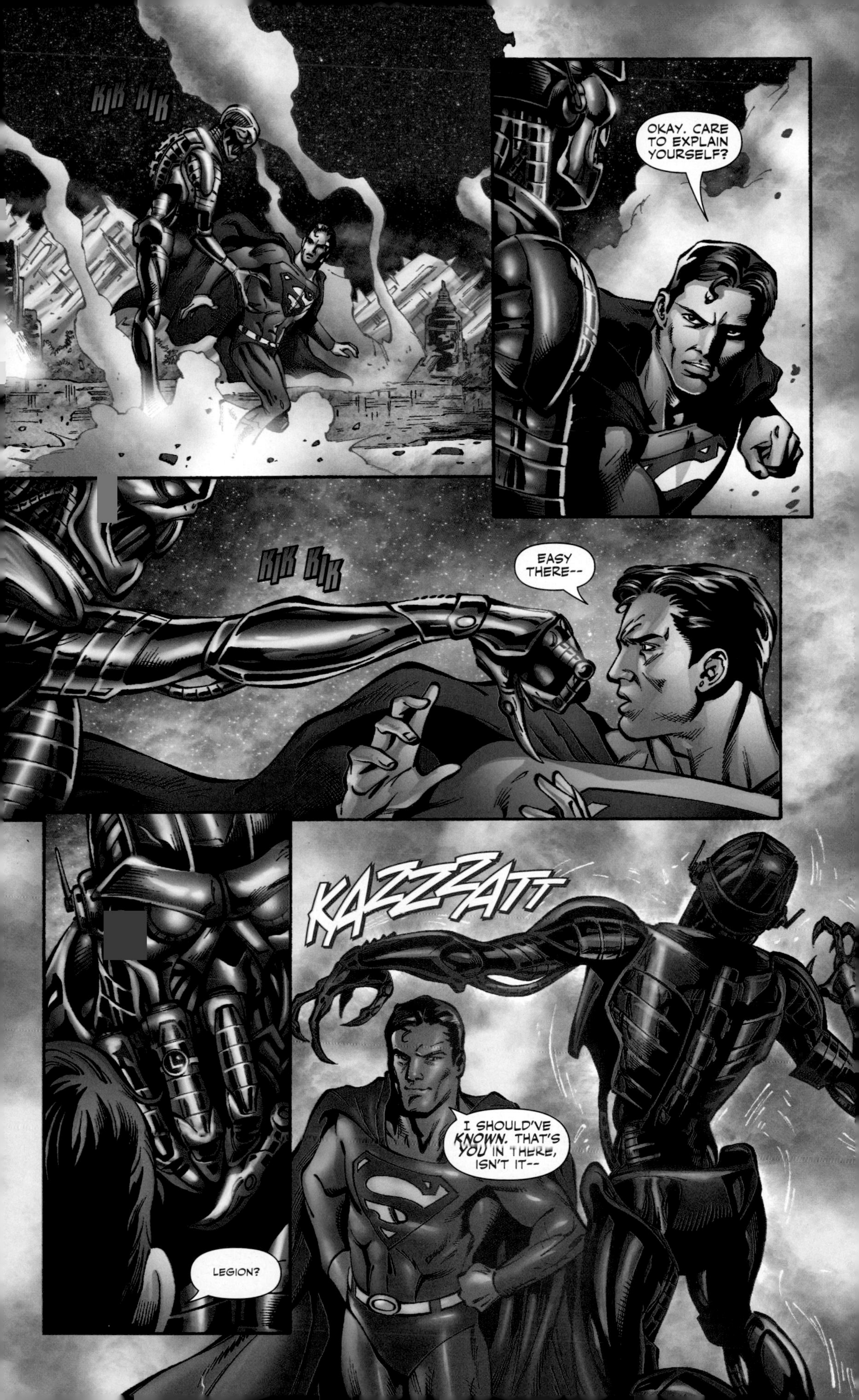
KIK KIK
OKAY. CARE TO EXPLAIN YOURSELF?
KIK KIK
EASY THERE--
KAZZZATT
I SHOULD'VE KNOWN. THAT'S YOU IN THERE, ISN'T IT--
LEGION?

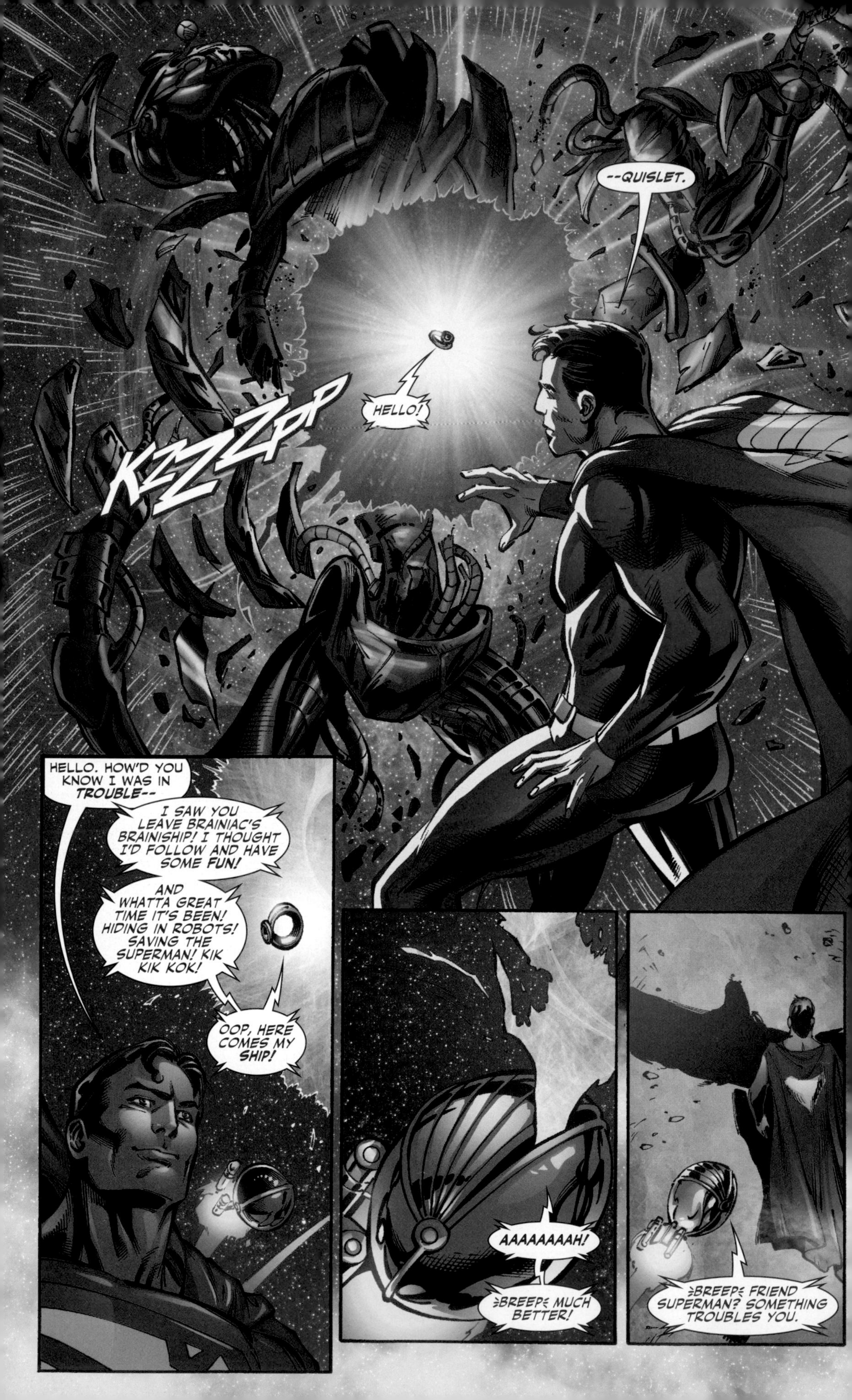
--QUISLET.
HELLO!
KZZZPP
HELLO. HOW'D YOU KNOW I WAS IN TROUBLE--
I SAW YOU LEAVE BRAINIAC'S BRAINISHIP! I THOUGHT I'D FOLLOW AND HAVE SOME FUN!
AND WHATTA GREAT TIME IT'S BEEN! HIDING IN ROBOTS! SAVING THE SUPERMAN! KIK KIK KOK!
OOP, HERE COMES MY SHIP!
AAAAAAAAH!
≥BREEP≤ MUCH BETTER!
≥BREEP≤ FRIEND SUPERMAN? SOMETHING TROUBLES YOU.

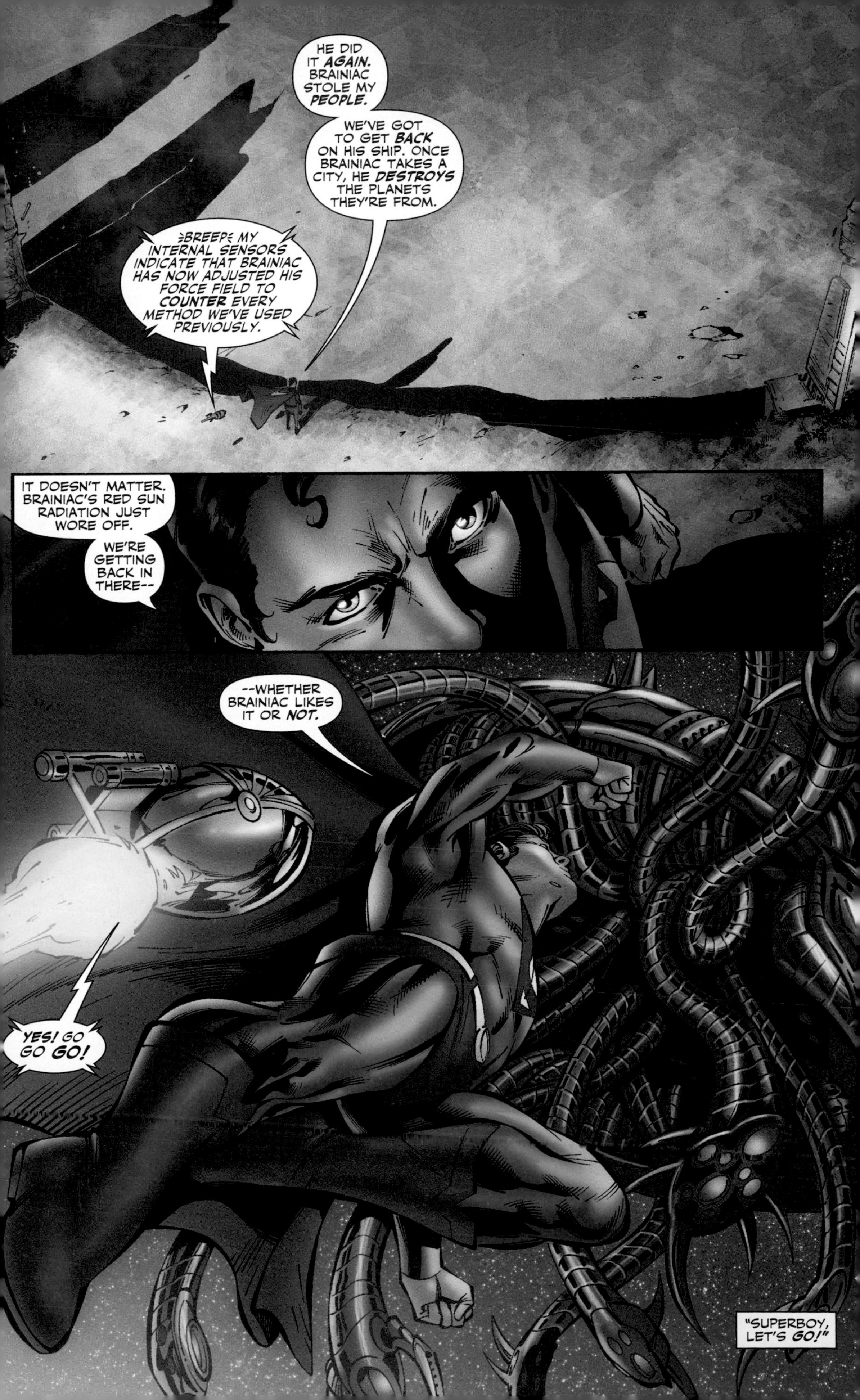
HE DID IT **AGAIN.** BRAINIAC STOLE MY **PEOPLE.**
WE'VE GOT TO GET **BACK** ON HIS SHIP. ONCE BRAINIAC TAKES A CITY, HE **DESTROYS** THE PLANETS THEY'RE FROM.
≥BREEP≤ MY INTERNAL SENSORS INDICATE THAT BRAINIAC HAS NOW ADJUSTED HIS FORCE FIELD TO **COUNTER** EVERY METHOD WE'VE USED PREVIOUSLY.
IT DOESN'T MATTER. BRAINIAC'S RED SUN RADIATION JUST WORE OFF.
WE'RE GETTING BACK IN THERE--
--WHETHER BRAINIAC LIKES IT OR **NOT.**
YES! GO GO **GO!**
"SUPERBOY, LET'S **GO!**"

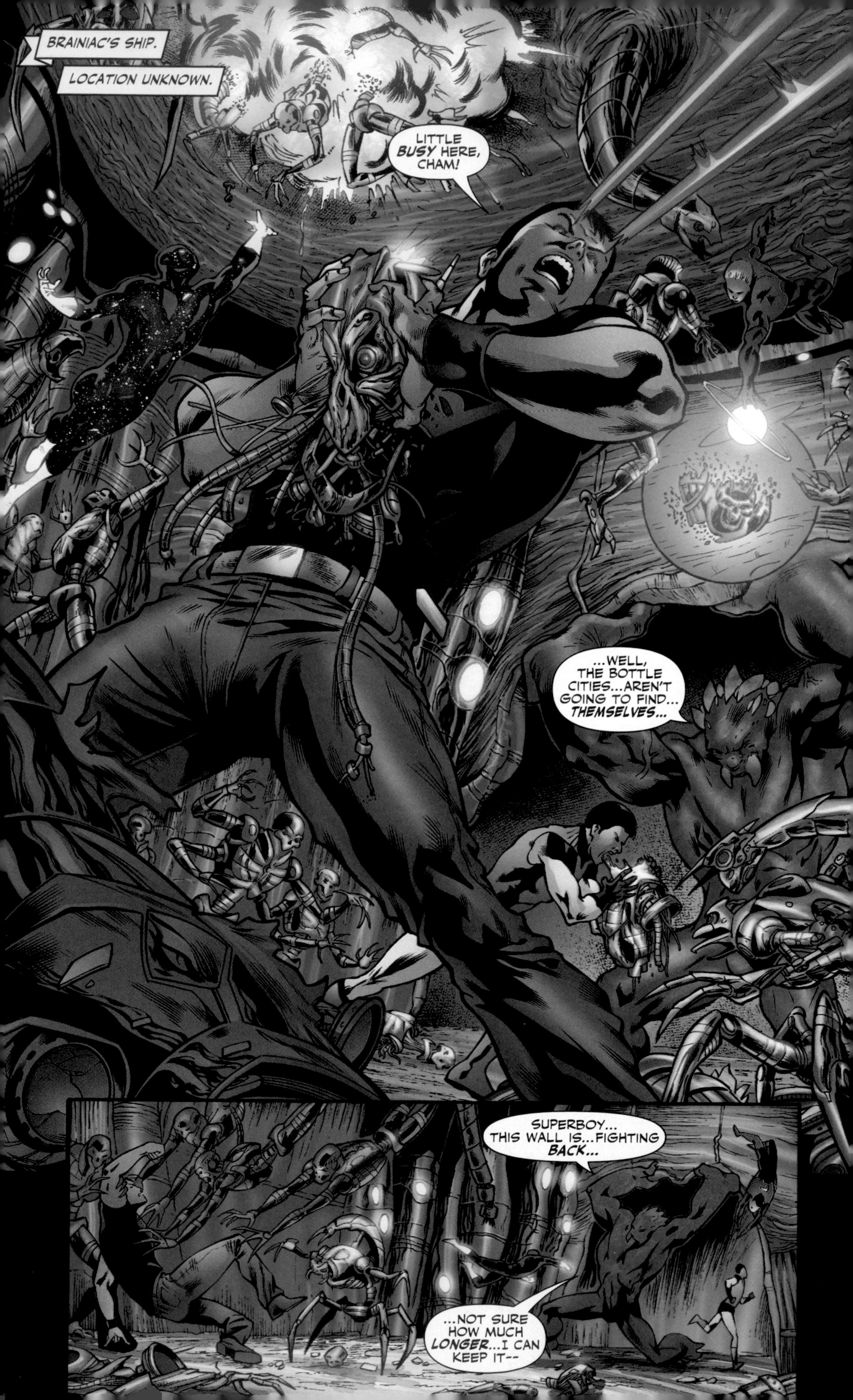
BRAINIAC'S SHIP.
LOCATION UNKNOWN.
LITTLE BUSY HERE, CHAM!
...WELL, THE BOTTLE CITIES...AREN'T GOING TO FIND... THEMSELVES...
SUPERBOY... THIS WALL IS...FIGHTING BACK...
...NOT SURE HOW MUCH LONGER...I CAN KEEP IT--

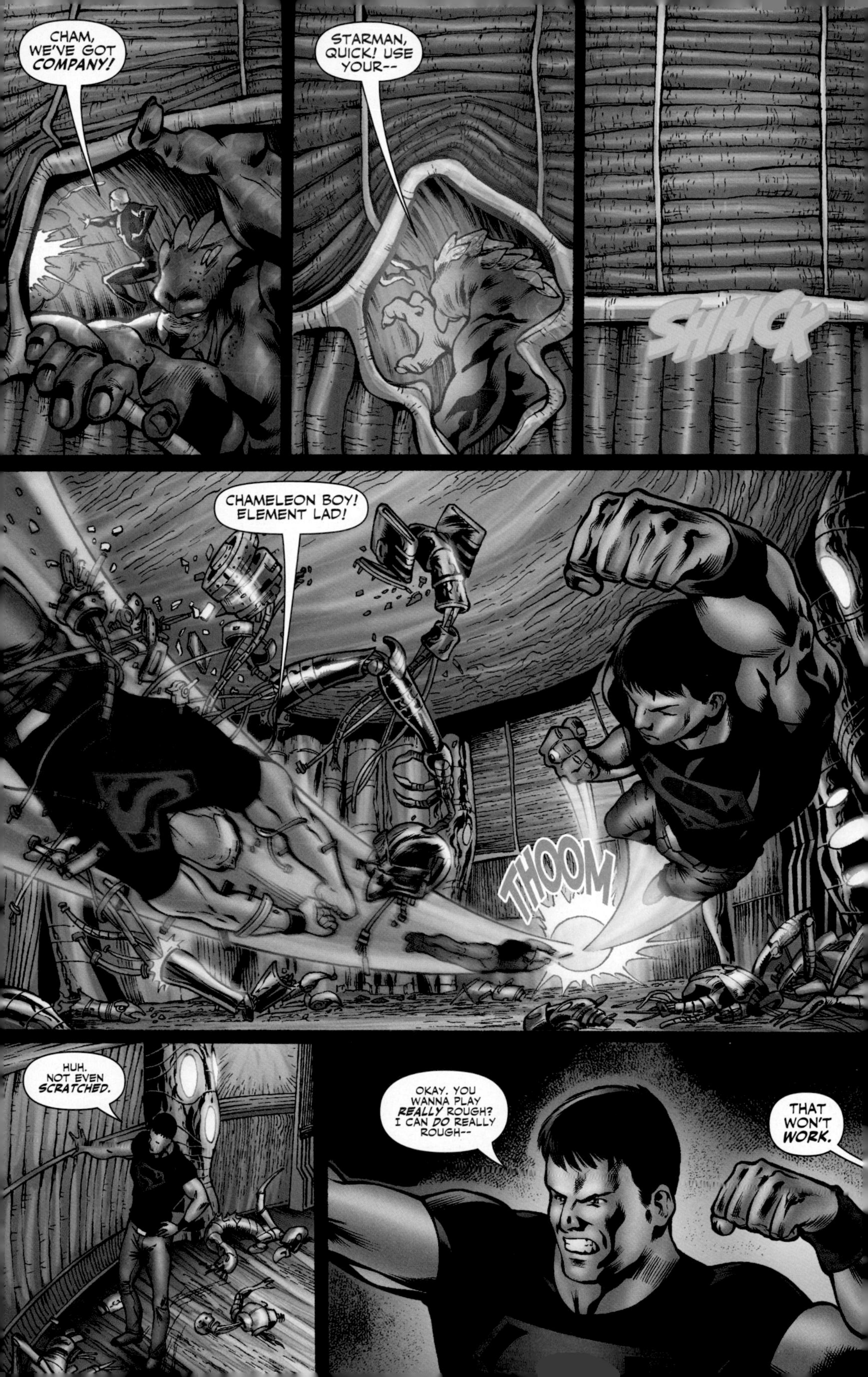
CHAM, WE'VE GOT COMPANY!
STARMAN, QUICK! USE YOUR--
SHHCK
CHAMELEON BOY! ELEMENT LAD!
THOOM
HUH. NOT EVEN SCRATCHED.
OKAY. YOU WANNA PLAY REALLY ROUGH? I CAN DO REALLY ROUGH--
THAT WON'T WORK.

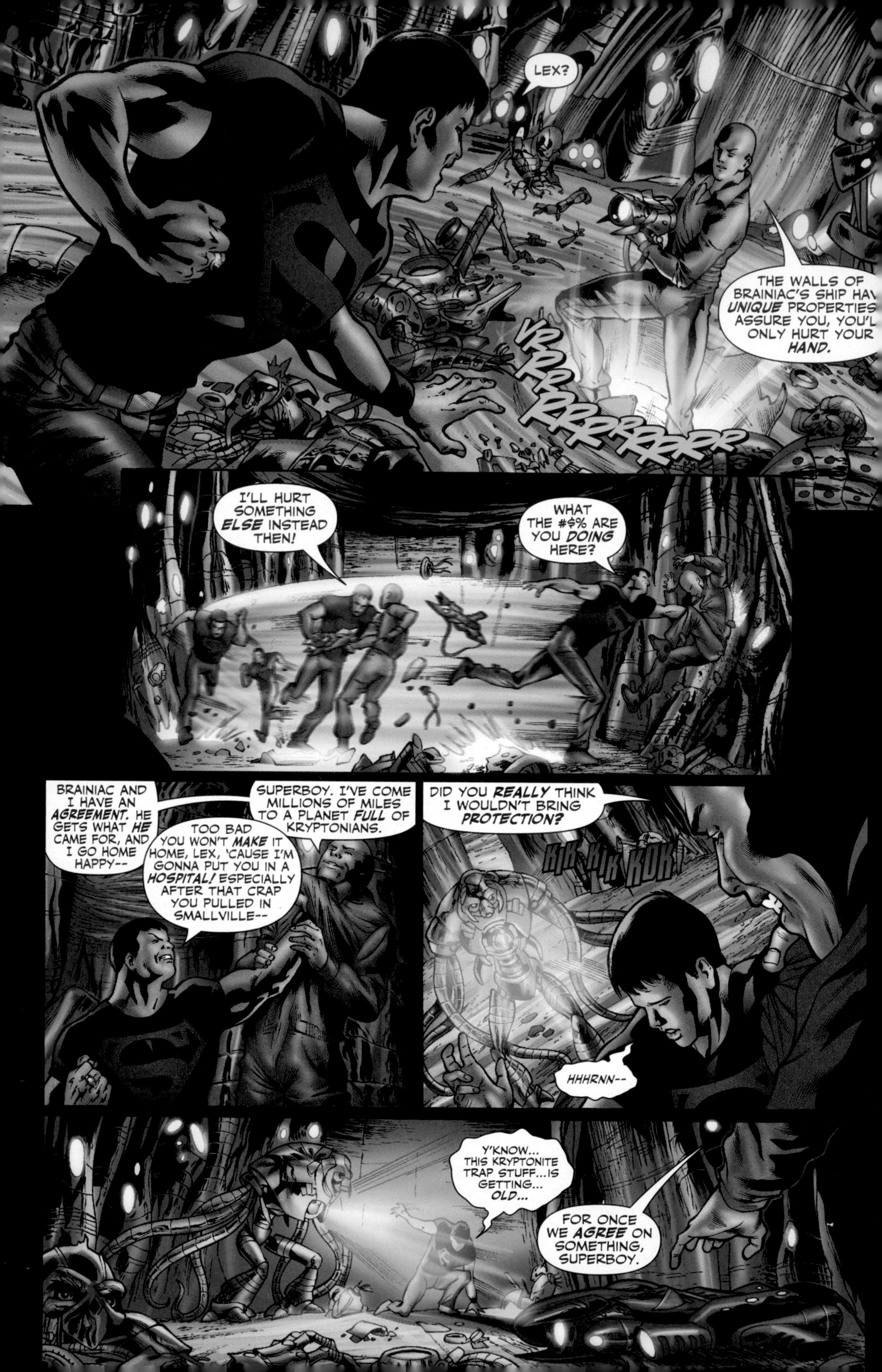
LEX?
THE WALLS OF BRAINIAC'S SHIP HAV UNIQUE PROPERTIES ASSURE YOU, YOU'L ONLY HURT YOUR HAND.
VRRRRRRRRRRRRR
I'LL HURT SOMETHING ELSE INSTEAD THEN!
WHAT THE #$% ARE YOU DOING HERE?
BRAINIAC AND I HAVE AN AGREEMENT. HE GETS WHAT HE CAME FOR, AND I GO HOME HAPPY--
SUPERBOY. I'VE COME MILLIONS OF MILES TO A PLANET FULL OF KRYPTONIANS.
TOO BAD YOU WON'T MAKE IT HOME, LEX, 'CAUSE I'M GONNA PUT YOU IN A HOSPITAL! ESPECIALLY AFTER THAT CRAP YOU PULLED IN SMALLVILLE--
DID YOU REALLY THINK I WOULDN'T BRING PROTECTION?
KIK KIK KOK
HHHRNN--
Y'KNOW... THIS KRYPTONITE TRAP STUFF...IS GETTING... OLD...
FOR ONCE WE AGREE ON SOMETHING, SUPERBOY.

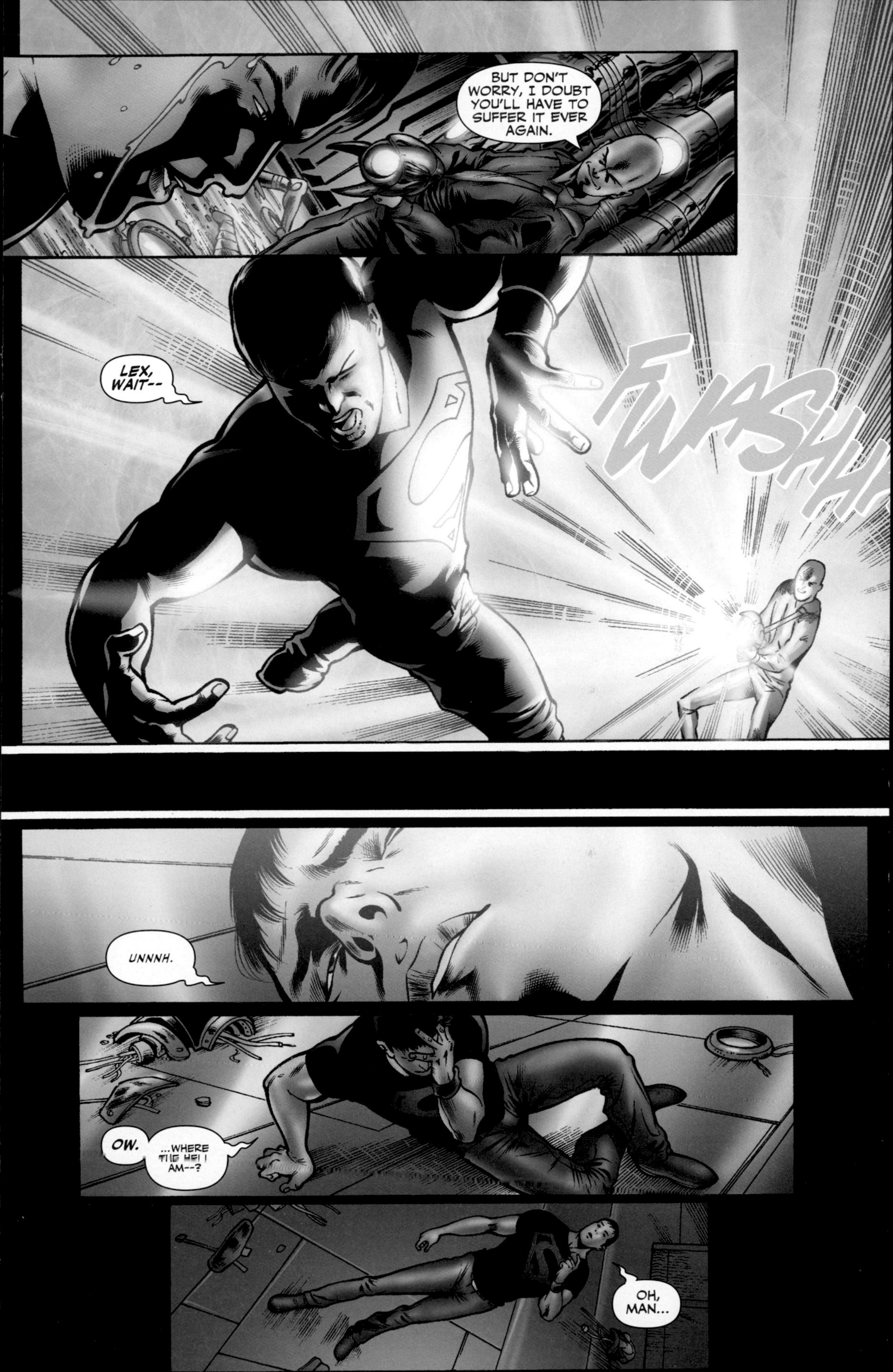
BUT DON'T WORRY, I DOUBT YOU'LL HAVE TO SUFFER IT EVER AGAIN.
LEX, WAIT--
FWASHH
UNNNH.
OW.
...WHERE THE HELL I AM--?
OH, MAN...

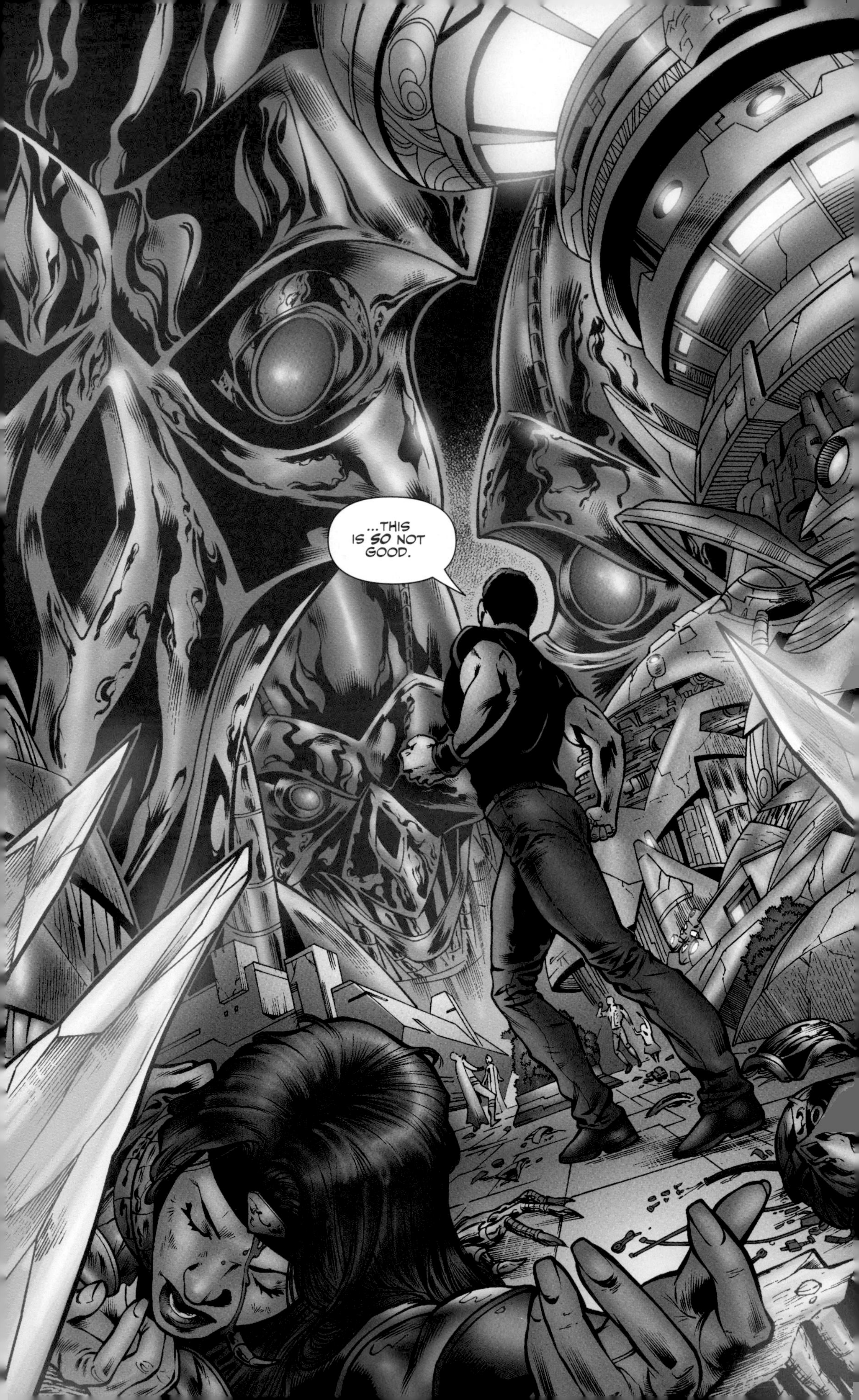
...THIS IS SO NOT GOOD.

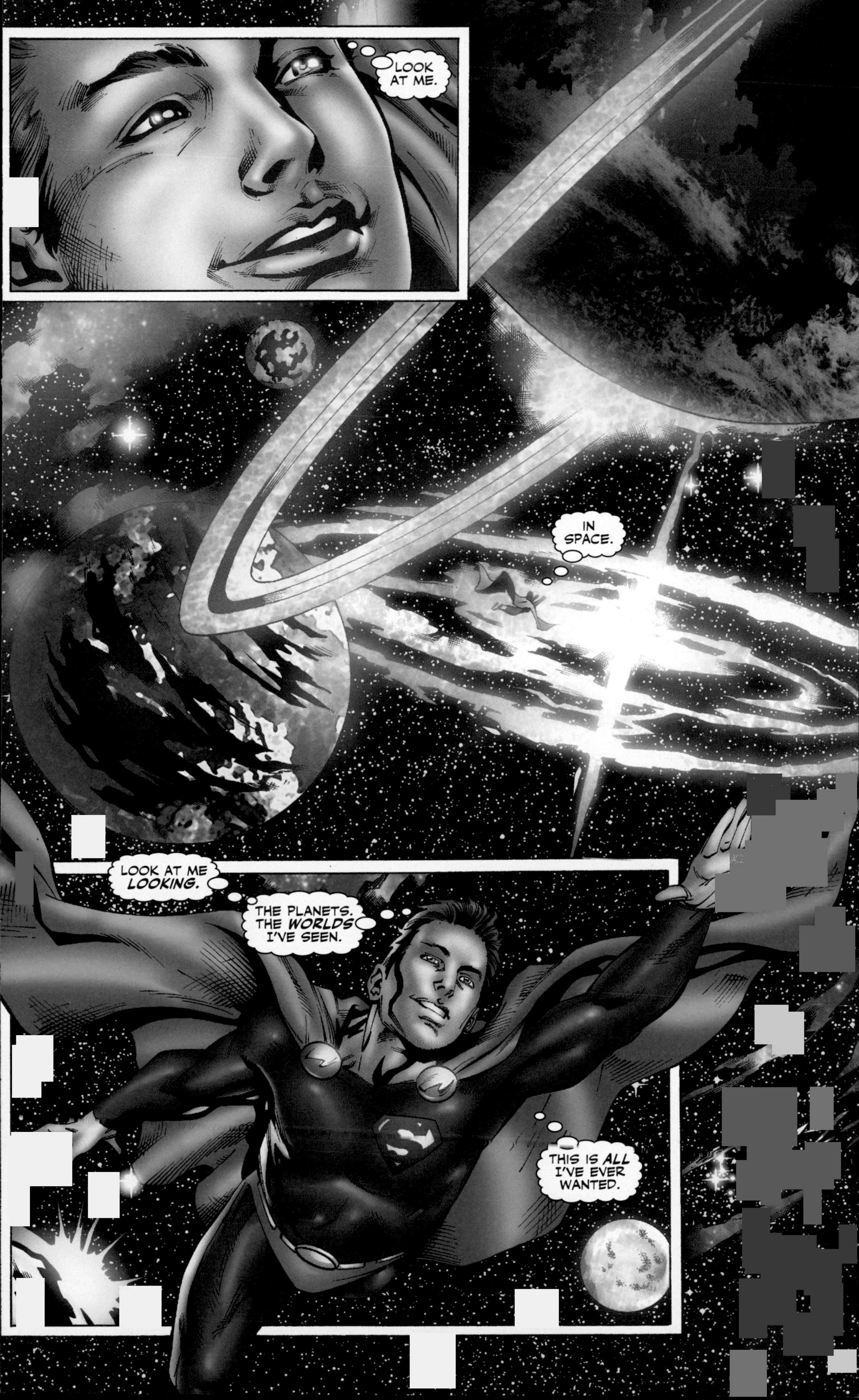
LOOK AT ME.
IN SPACE.
LOOK AT ME LOOKING.
THE PLANETS. THE WORLDS I'VE SEEN.
THIS IS ALL I'VE EVER WANTED.

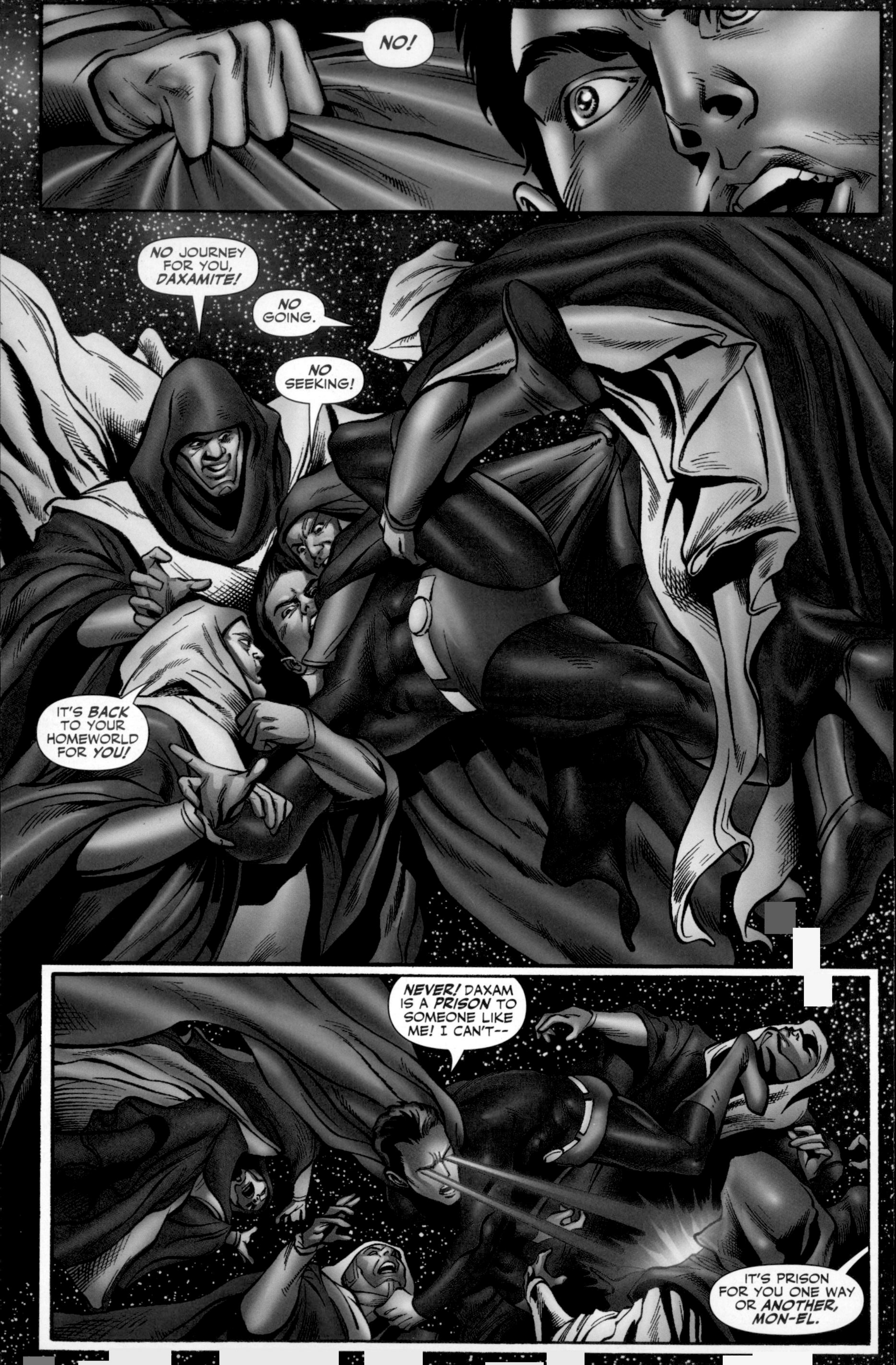
NO!
NO JOURNEY FOR YOU, DAXAMITE!
NO GOING.
NO SEEKING!
IT'S BACK TO YOUR HOMEWORLD FOR YOU!
NEVER! DAXAM IS A PRISON TO SOMEONE LIKE ME! I CAN'T--
IT'S PRISON FOR YOU ONE WAY OR ANOTHER, MON-EL.

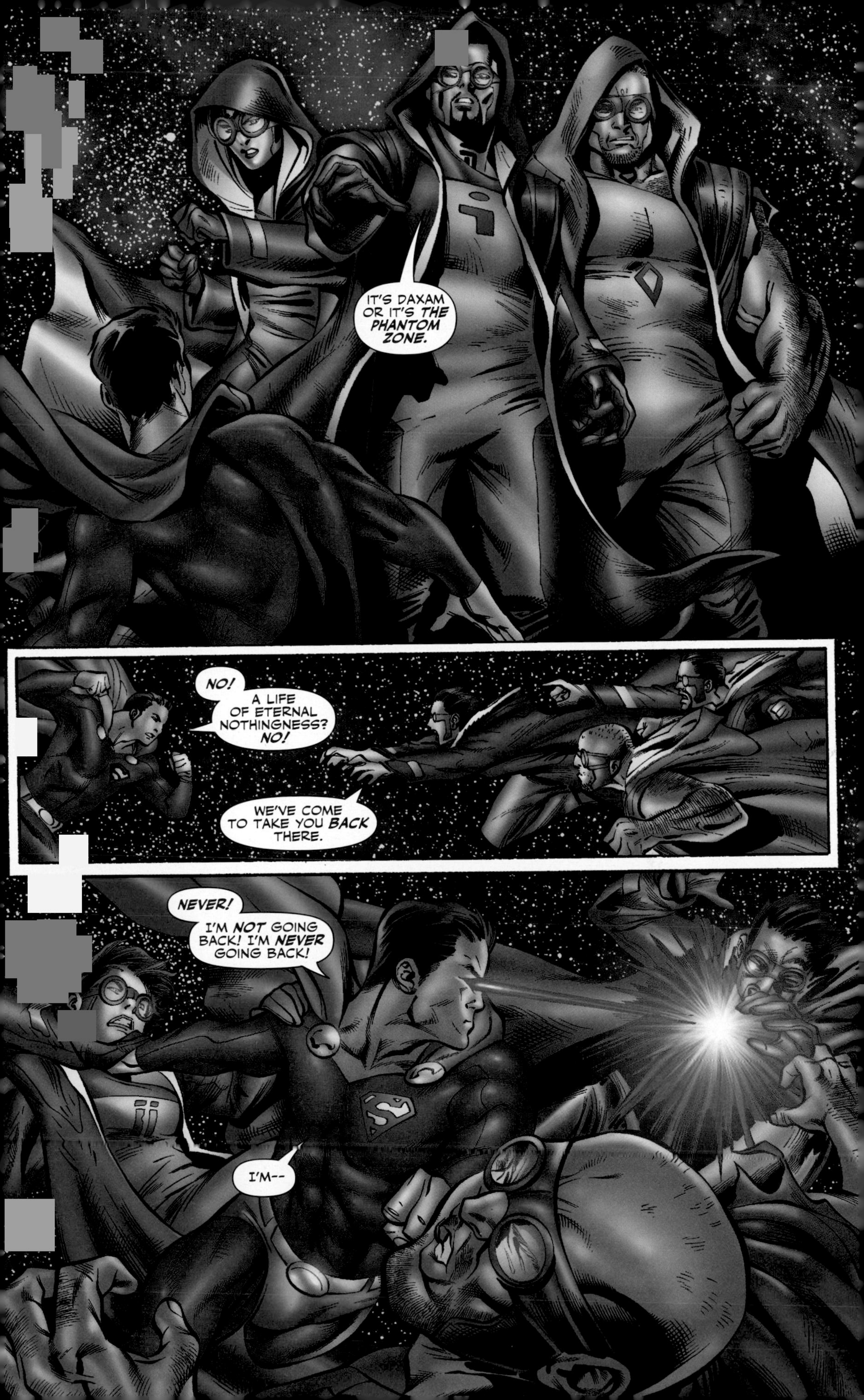

IT'S DAXAM OR IT'S *THE PHANTOM ZONE.*
NO!
A LIFE OF ETERNAL NOTHINGNESS? *NO!*
WE'VE COME TO TAKE YOU *BACK* THERE.
NEVER!
I'M *NOT* GOING BACK! I'M *NEVER* GOING BACK!
I'M--

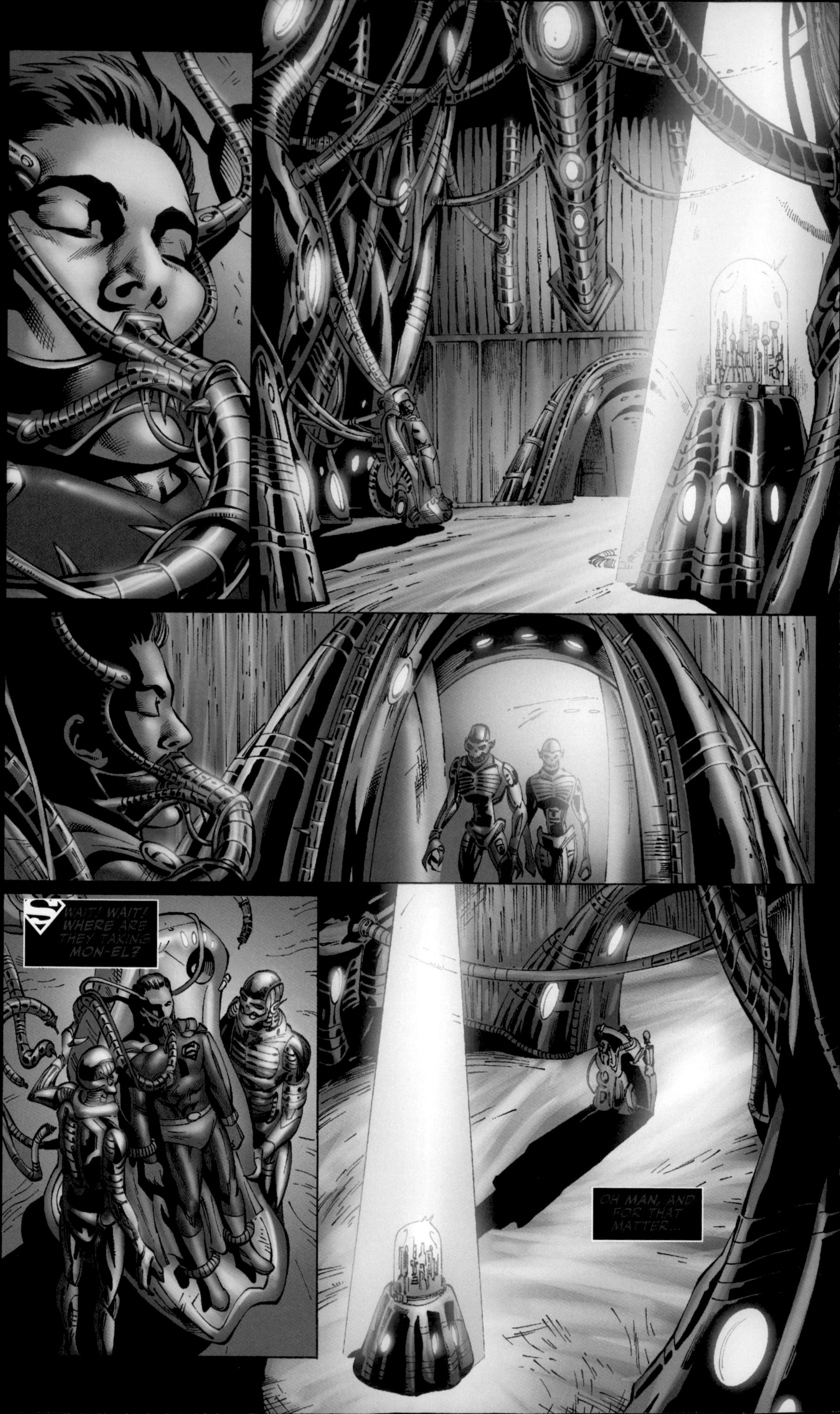
WAIT! WAIT! WHERE ARE THEY TAKING MON-EL?
OH MAN, AND FOR THAT MATTER...

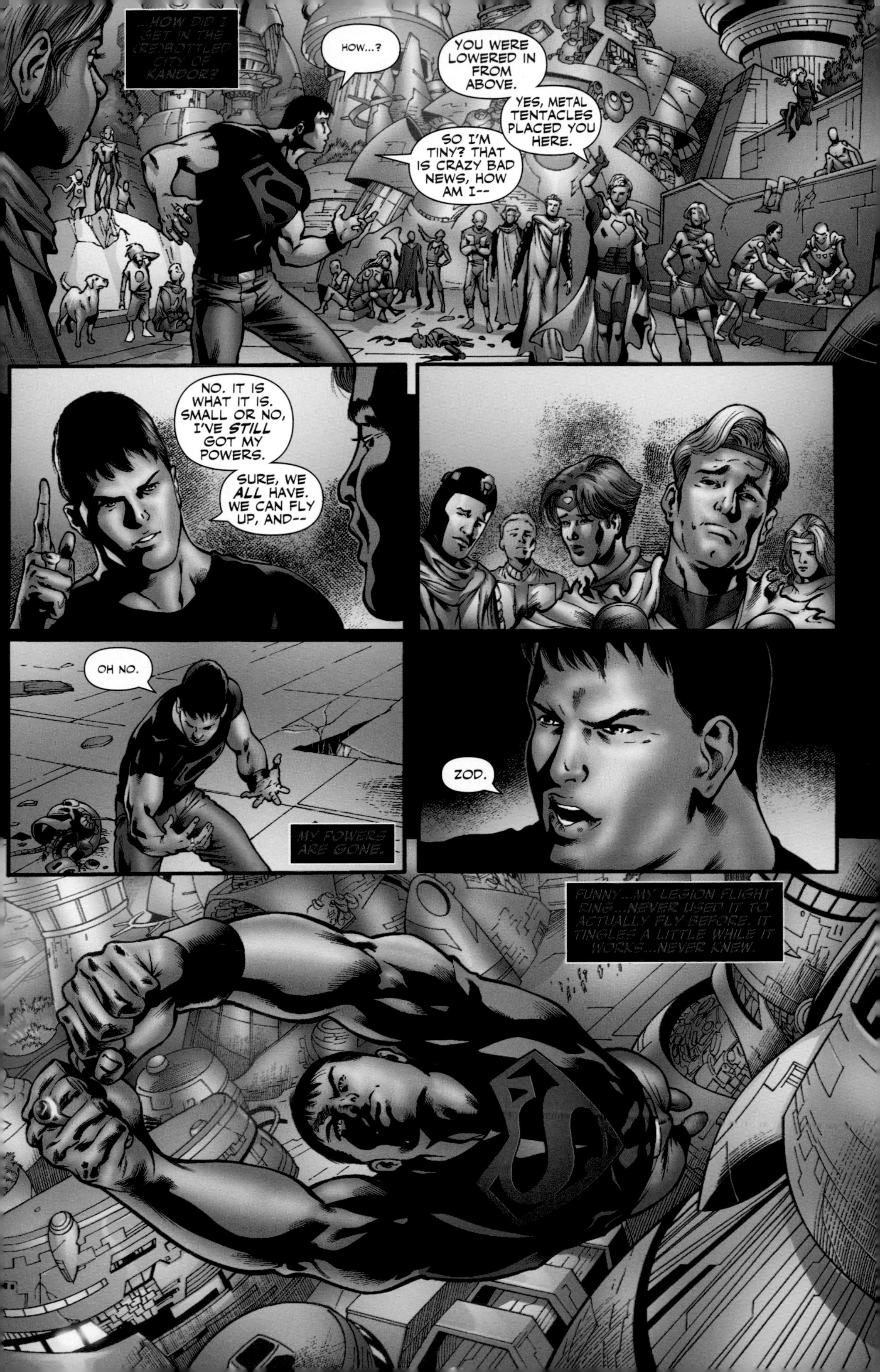
...HOW DID I GET IN THE (RE)BOTTLED CITY OF KANDOR?
HOW...?
YOU WERE LOWERED IN FROM ABOVE.
YES, METAL TENTACLES PLACED YOU HERE.
SO I'M TINY? THAT IS CRAZY BAD NEWS, HOW AM I--
NO. IT IS WHAT IT IS. SMALL OR NO, I'VE STILL GOT MY POWERS.
SURE, WE ALL HAVE. WE CAN FLY UP, AND--
OH NO.
MY POWERS ARE GONE.
ZOD.
FUNNY...MY LEGION FLIGHT RING...NEVER USED IT TO ACTUALLY FLY BEFORE. IT TINGLES A LITTLE WHILE IT WORKS...NEVER KNEW.

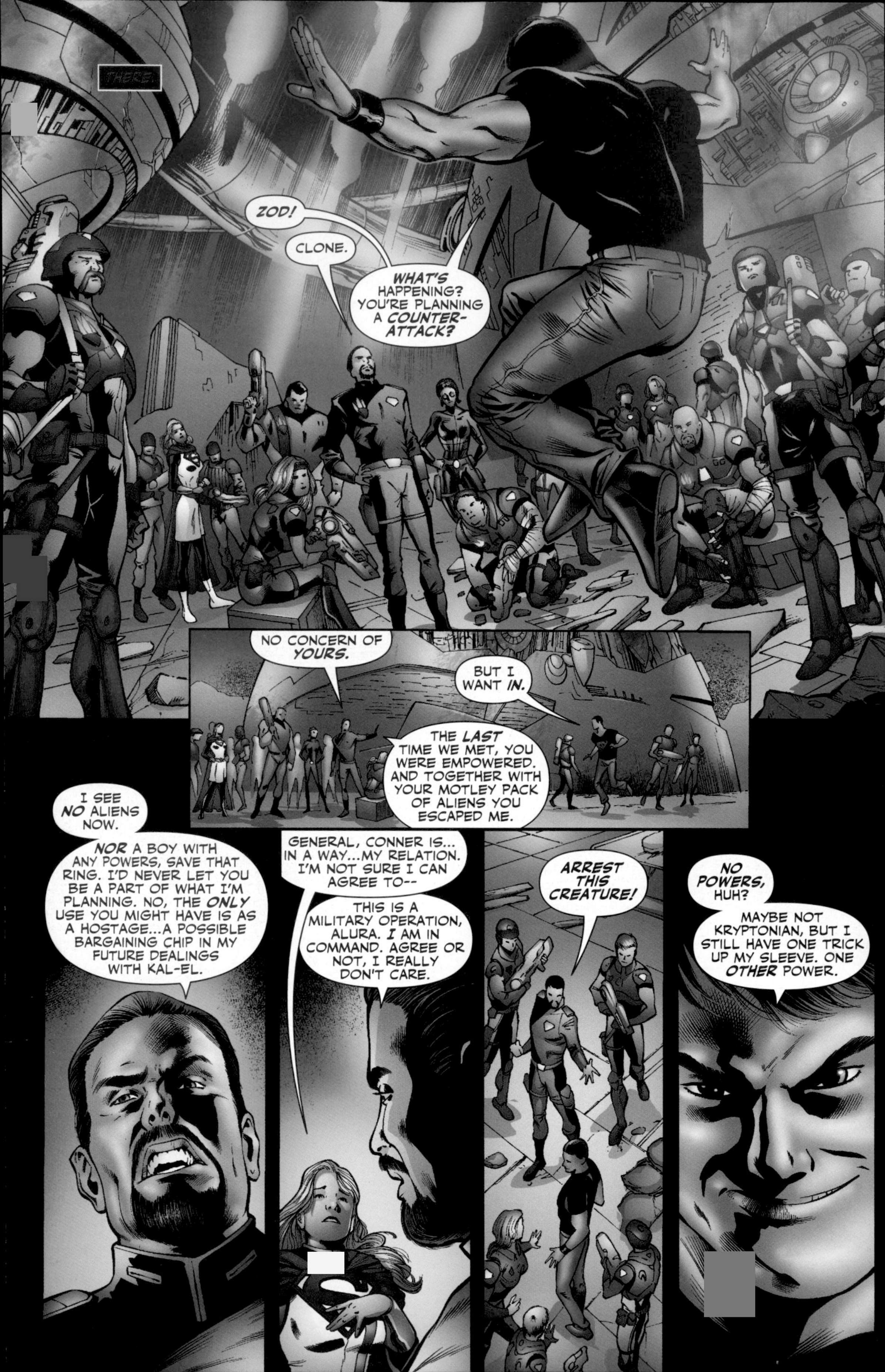
THERE.
ZOD!
CLONE.
WHAT'S HAPPENING? YOU'RE PLANNING A COUNTER-ATTACK?
NO CONCERN OF YOURS.
BUT I WANT IN.
THE LAST TIME WE MET, YOU WERE EMPOWERED. AND TOGETHER WITH YOUR MOTLEY PACK OF ALIENS YOU ESCAPED ME.
I SEE NO ALIENS NOW.
NOR A BOY WITH ANY POWERS, SAVE THAT RING. I'D NEVER LET YOU BE A PART OF WHAT I'M PLANNING. NO, THE ONLY USE YOU MIGHT HAVE IS AS A HOSTAGE...A POSSIBLE BARGAINING CHIP IN MY FUTURE DEALINGS WITH KAL-EL.
GENERAL, CONNER IS... IN A WAY...MY RELATION. I'M NOT SURE I CAN AGREE TO--
THIS IS A MILITARY OPERATION, ALURA. I AM IN COMMAND. AGREE OR NOT, I REALLY DON'T CARE.
ARREST THIS CREATURE!
NO POWERS, HUH?
MAYBE NOT KRYPTONIAN, BUT I STILL HAVE ONE TRICK UP MY SLEEVE. ONE OTHER POWER.

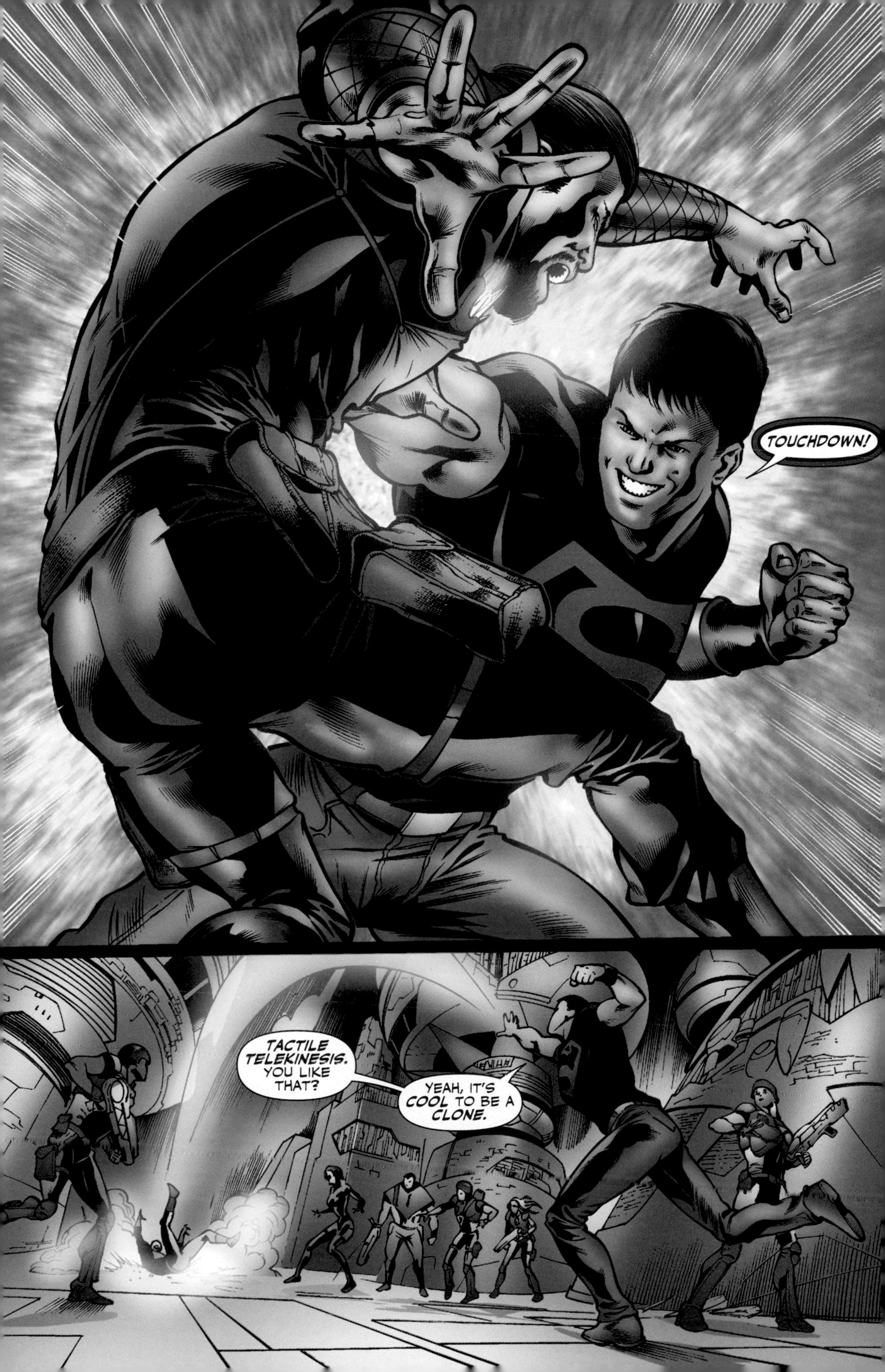
TOUCHDOWN!
TACTILE TELEKINESIS. YOU LIKE THAT?
YEAH, IT'S COOL TO BE A CLONE.

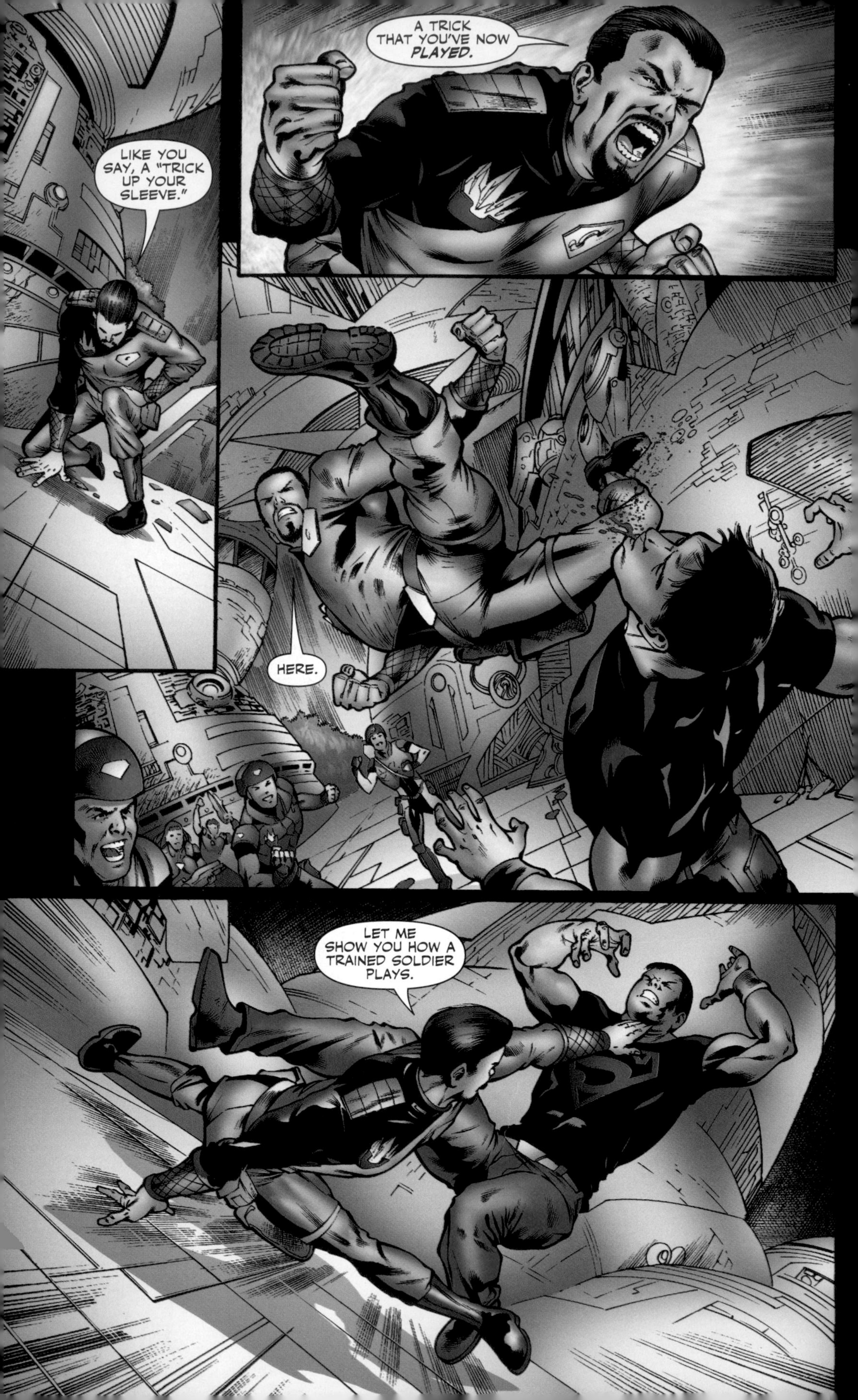
LIKE YOU SAY, A "TRICK UP YOUR SLEEVE."
A TRICK THAT YOU'VE NOW *PLAYED.*
HERE.
LET ME SHOW YOU HOW A TRAINED SOLDIER PLAYS.

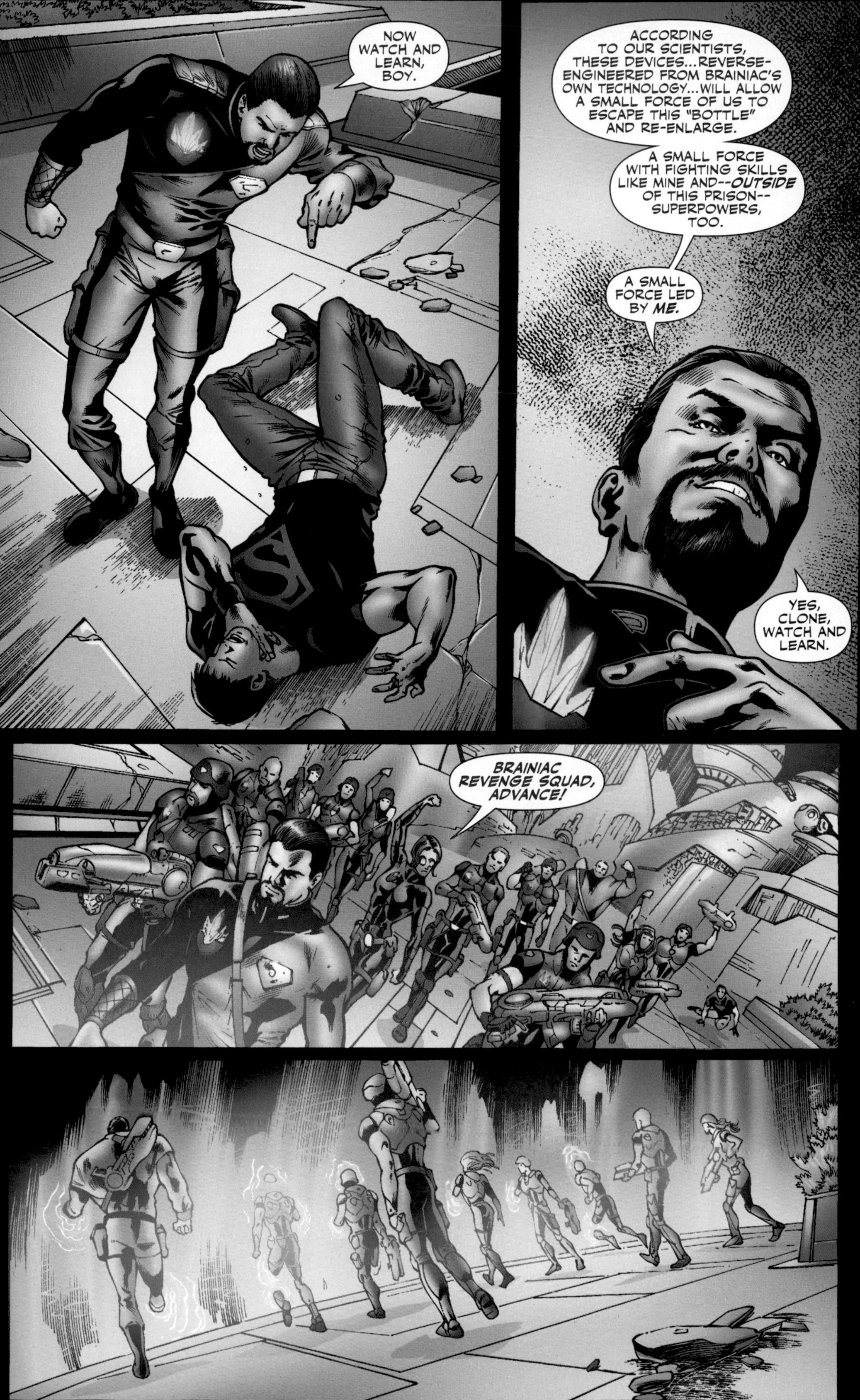
NOW WATCH AND LEARN, BOY.
ACCORDING TO OUR SCIENTISTS, THESE DEVICES...REVERSE-ENGINEERED FROM BRAINIAC'S OWN TECHNOLOGY...WILL ALLOW A SMALL FORCE OF US TO ESCAPE THIS "BOTTLE" AND RE-ENLARGE.
A SMALL FORCE WITH FIGHTING SKILLS LIKE MINE AND--*OUTSIDE* OF THIS PRISON--SUPERPOWERS, TOO.
A SMALL FORCE LED BY ***ME.***
YES, CLONE, WATCH AND LEARN.
BRAINIAC REVENGE SQUAD, ADVANCE!

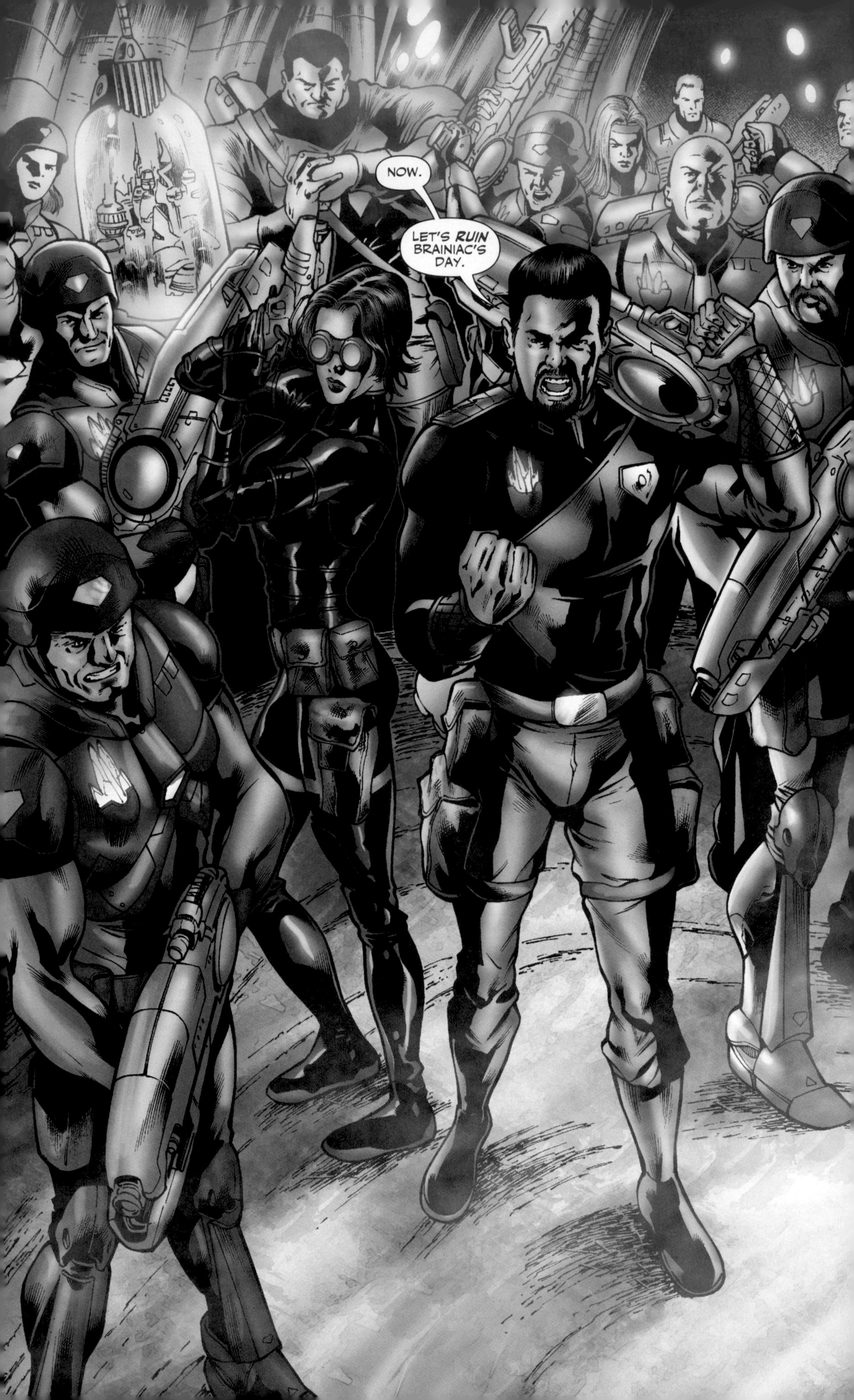
NOW.
LET'S RUIN BRAINIAC'S DAY.

cover by **MATT CAMP** & **NEI RUFFINO**

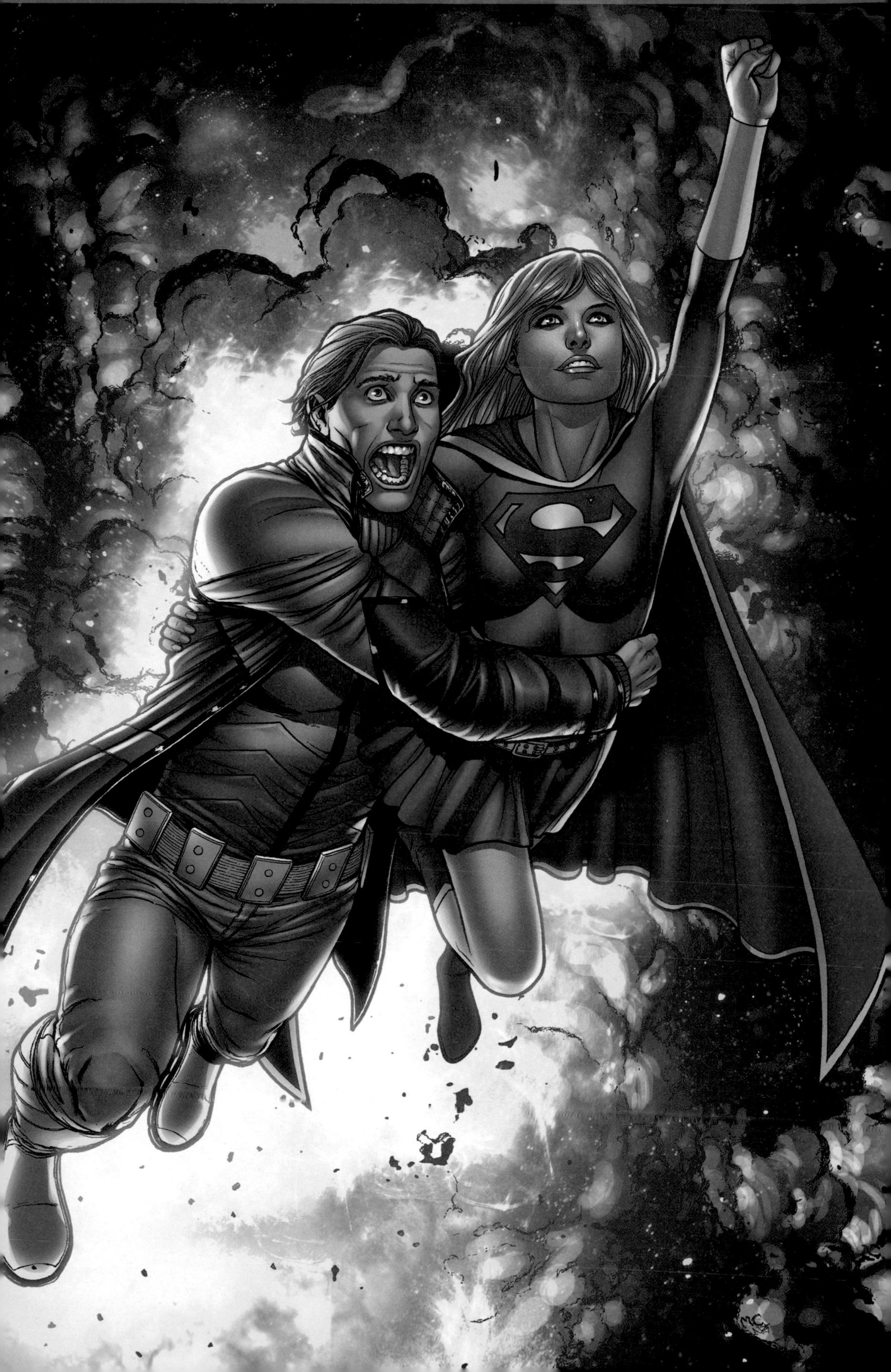

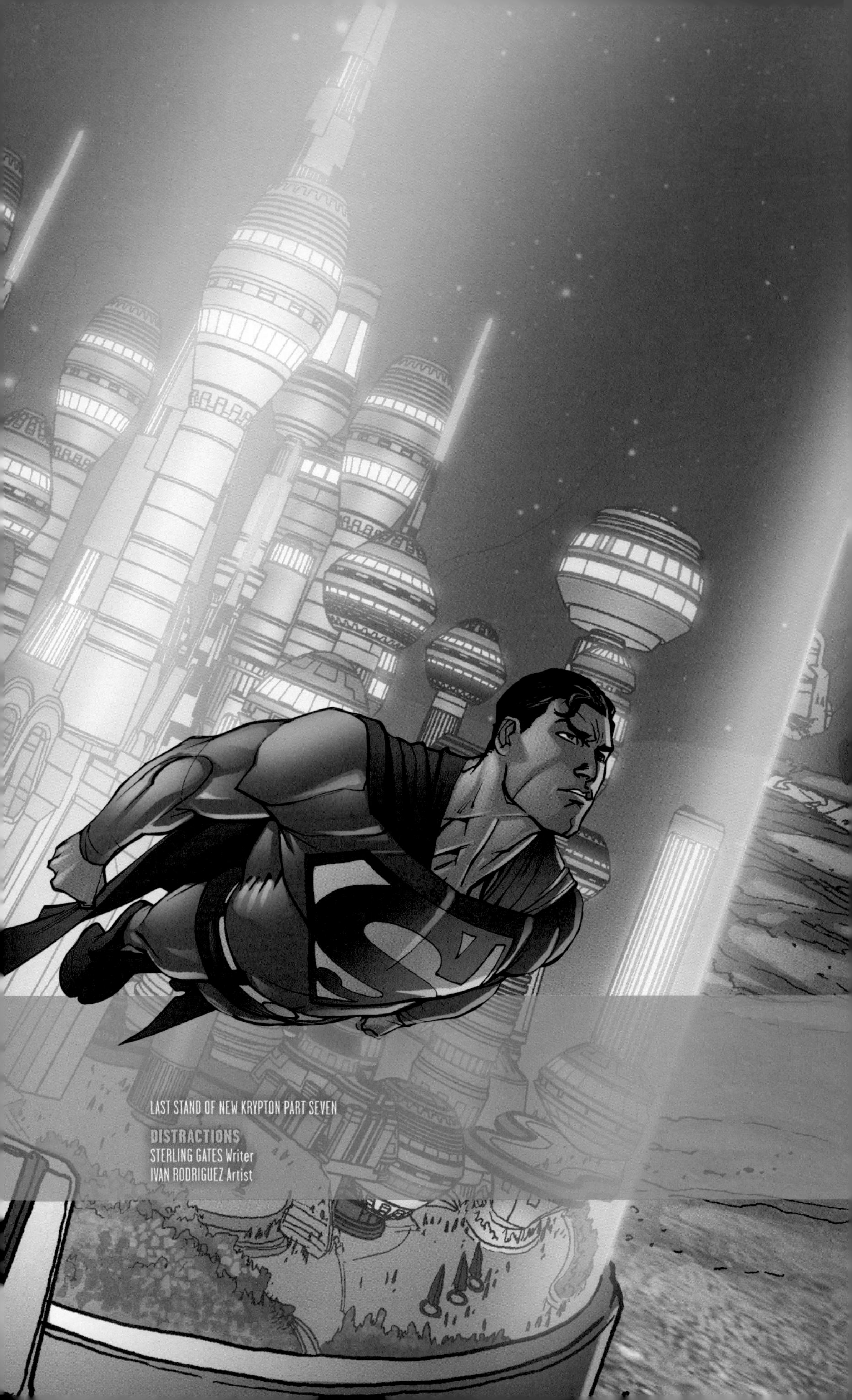
LAST STAND OF NEW KRYPTON PART SEVEN
DISTRACTIONS
STERLING GATES Writer
IVAN RODRIGUEZ Artist

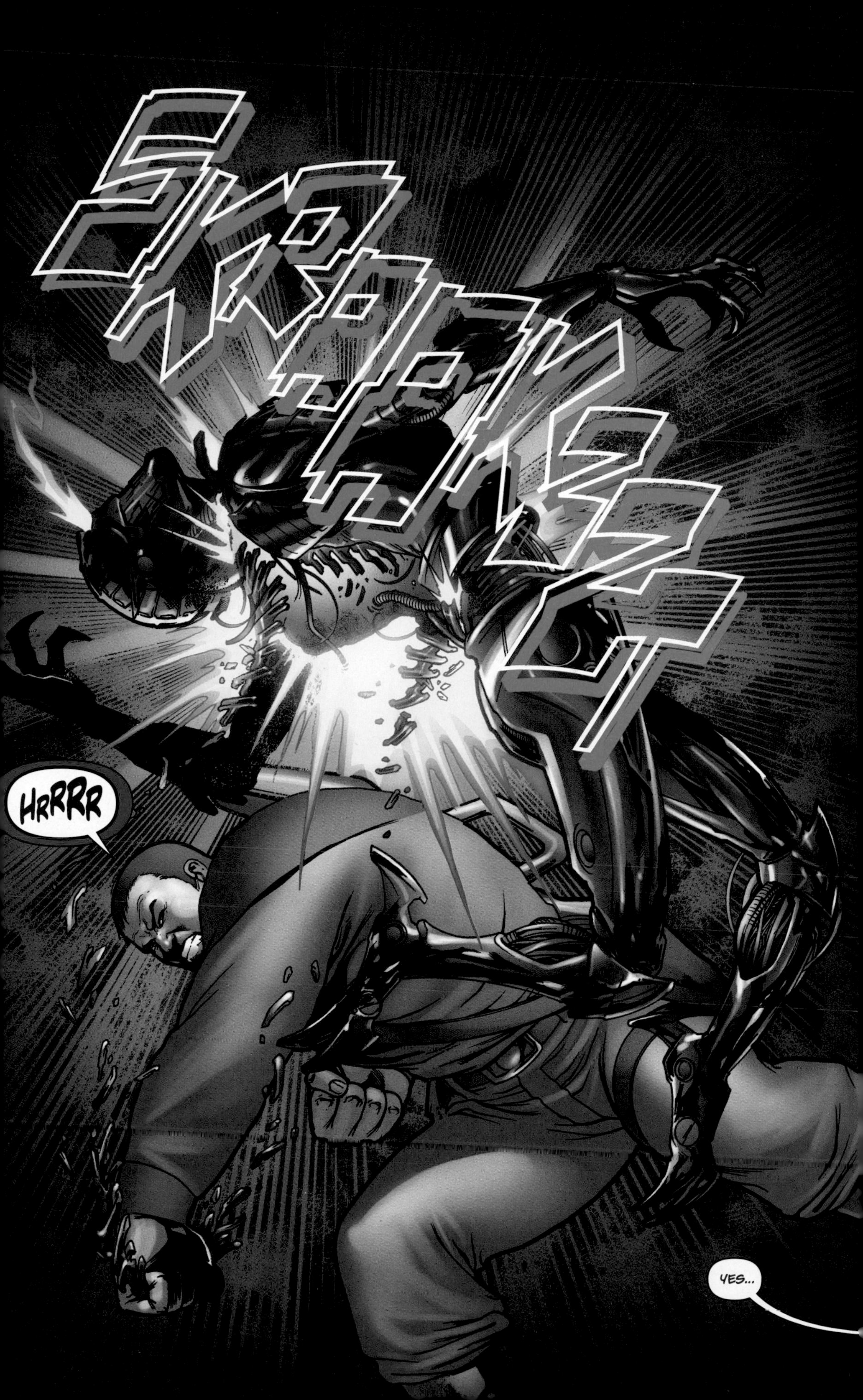
HRRRR
YES...

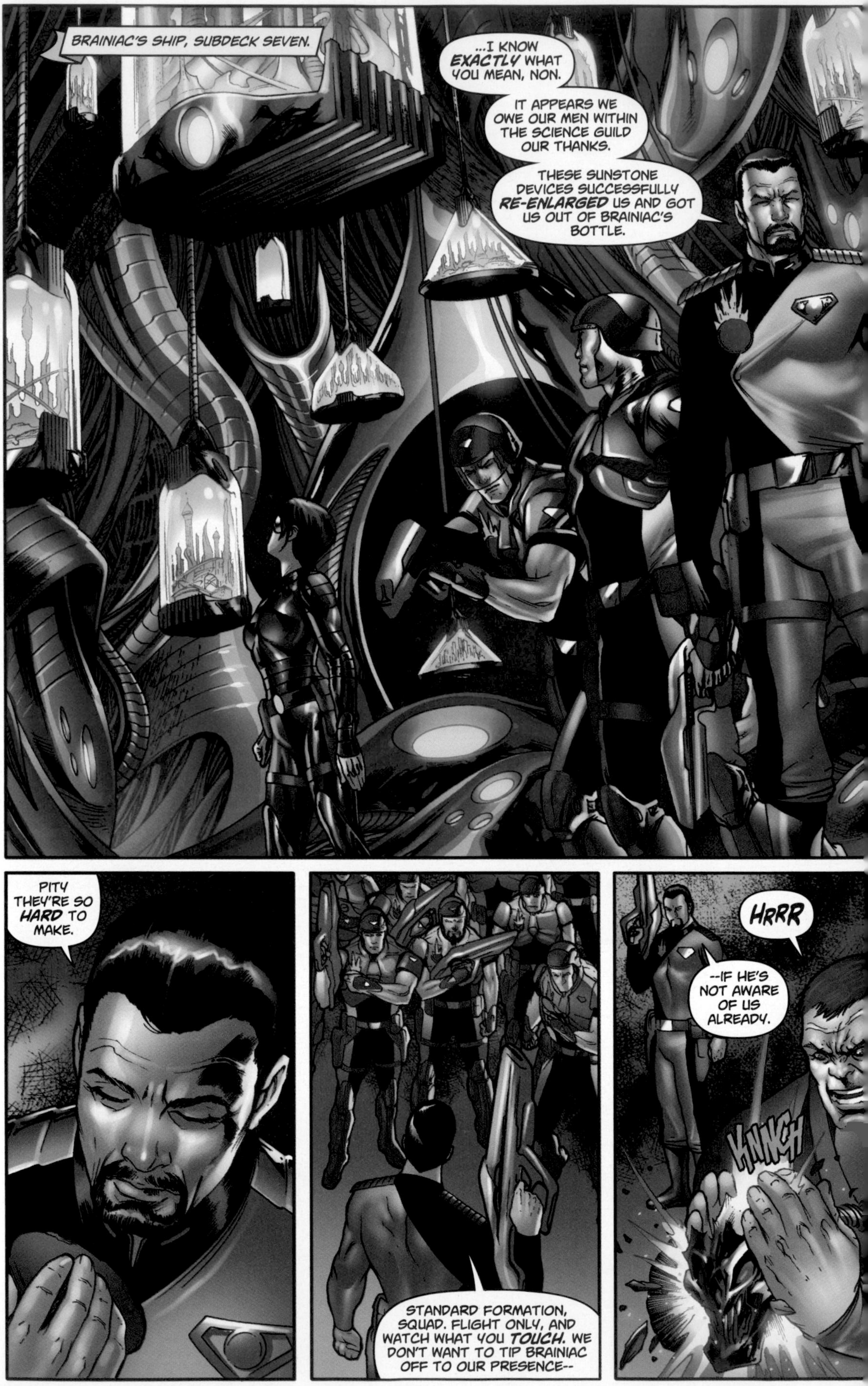
BRAINIAC'S SHIP, SUBDECK SEVEN.
...I KNOW EXACTLY WHAT YOU MEAN, NON.
IT APPEARS WE OWE OUR MEN WITHIN THE SCIENCE GUILD OUR THANKS.
THESE SUNSTONE DEVICES SUCCESSFULLY RE-ENLARGED US AND GOT US OUT OF BRAINIAC'S BOTTLE.
PITY THEY'RE SO HARD TO MAKE.
STANDARD FORMATION, SQUAD. FLIGHT ONLY, AND WATCH WHAT YOU TOUCH. WE DON'T WANT TO TIP BRAINIAC OFF TO OUR PRESENCE--
HRRR
--IF HE'S NOT AWARE OF US ALREADY.
KNNCH

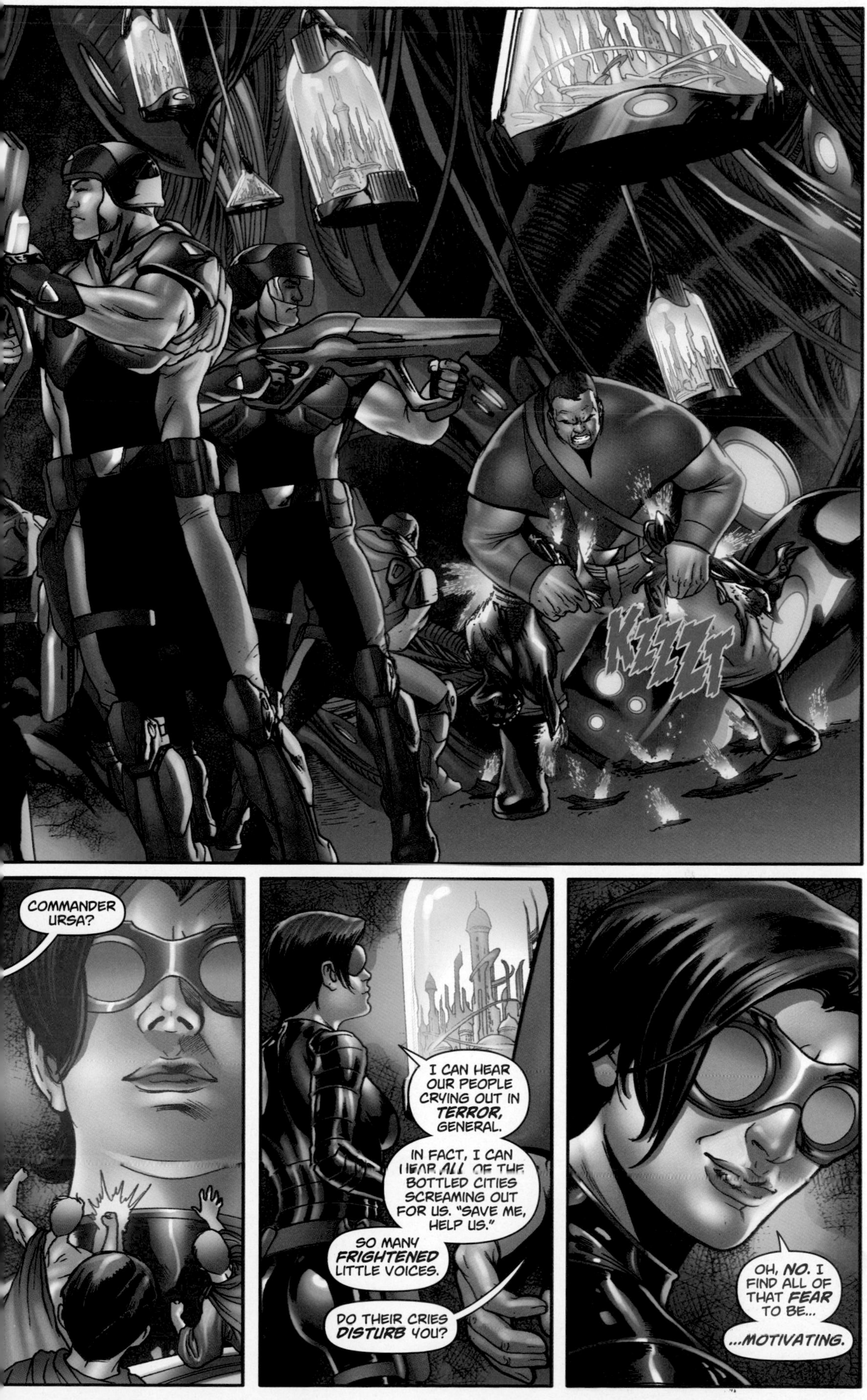
KZZZT
COMMANDER URSA?
I CAN HEAR OUR PEOPLE CRYING OUT IN TERROR, GENERAL.
IN FACT, I CAN HEAR ALL OF THE BOTTLED CITIES SCREAMING OUT FOR US. "SAVE ME, HELP US."
SO MANY FRIGHTENED LITTLE VOICES.
DO THEIR CRIES DISTURB YOU?
OH, NO. I FIND ALL OF THAT FEAR TO BE...
...MOTIVATING.

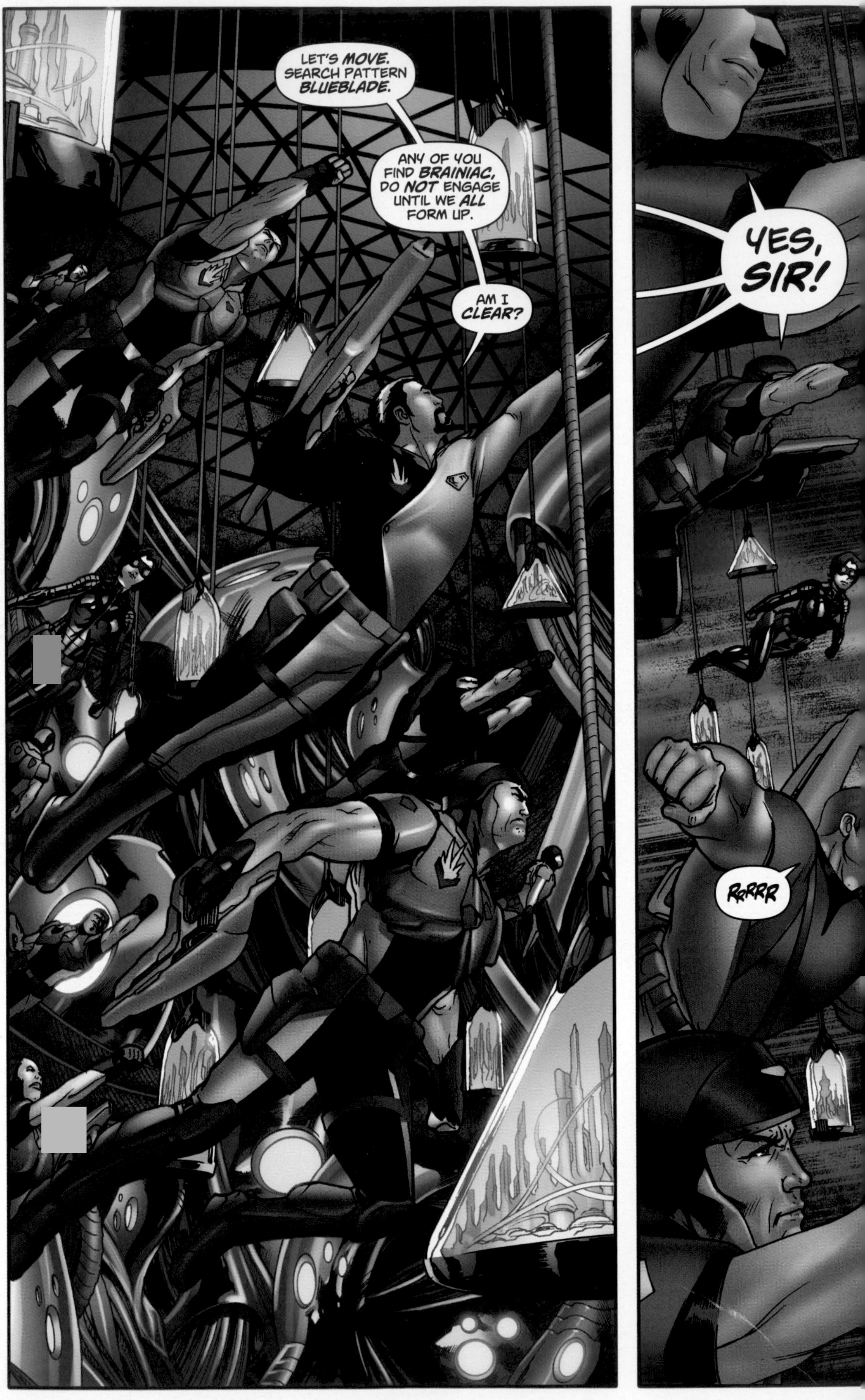
LET'S MOVE. SEARCH PATTERN BLUEBLADE.
ANY OF YOU FIND BRAINIAC, DO NOT ENGAGE UNTIL WE ALL FORM UP.
AM I CLEAR?
YES, SIR!
RRRRR

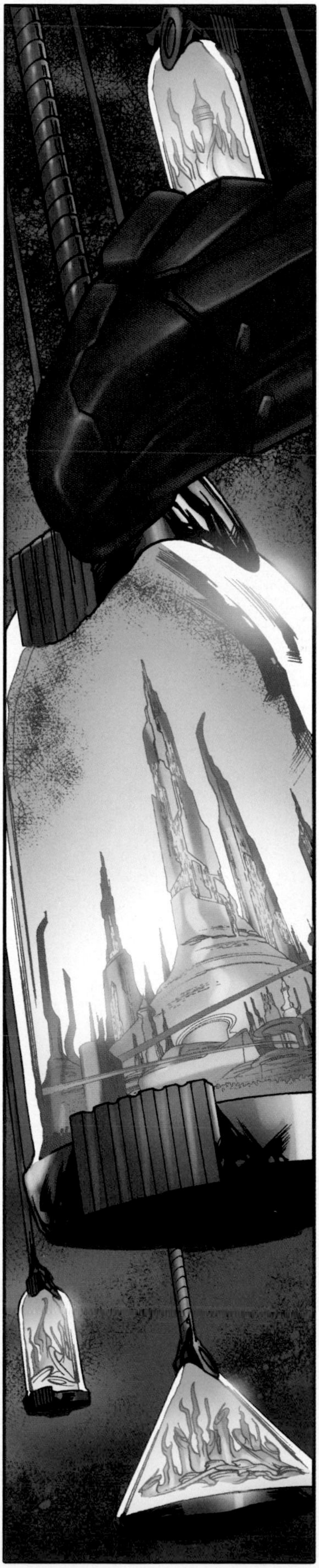

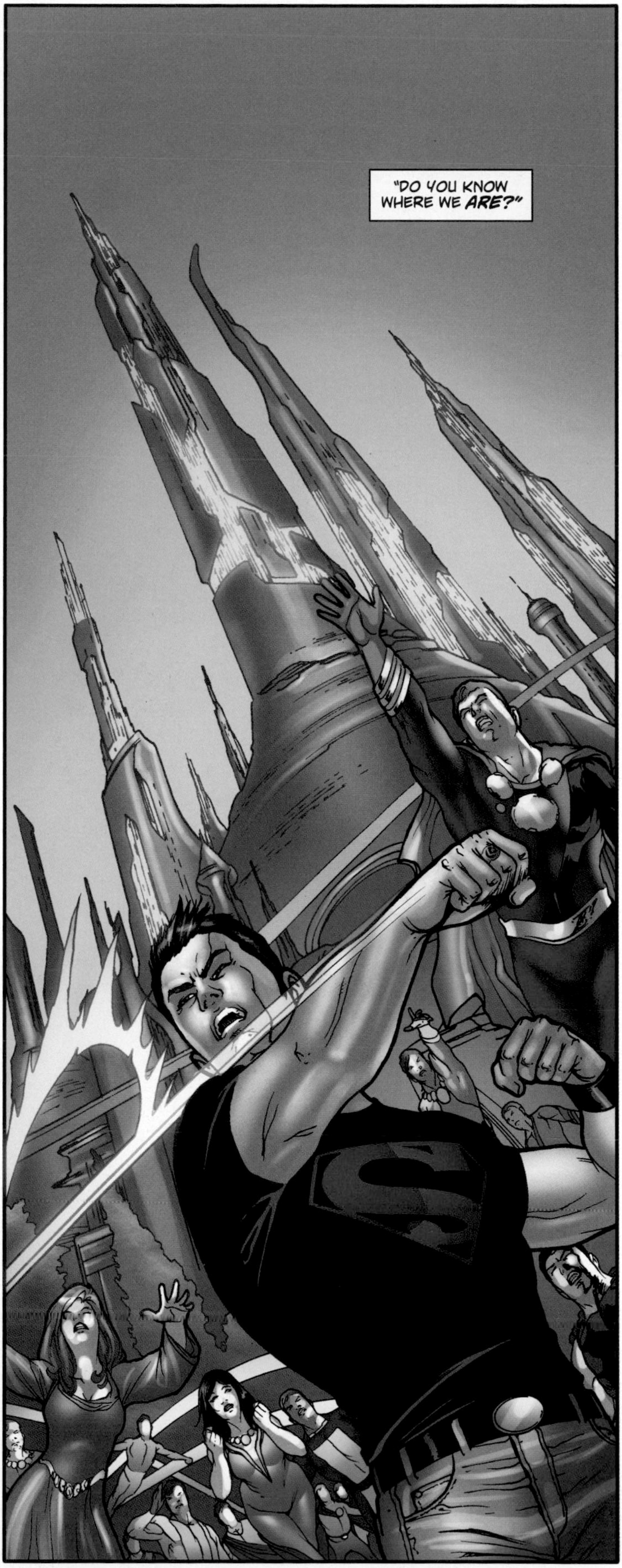
"DO YOU KNOW WHERE WE ARE?"

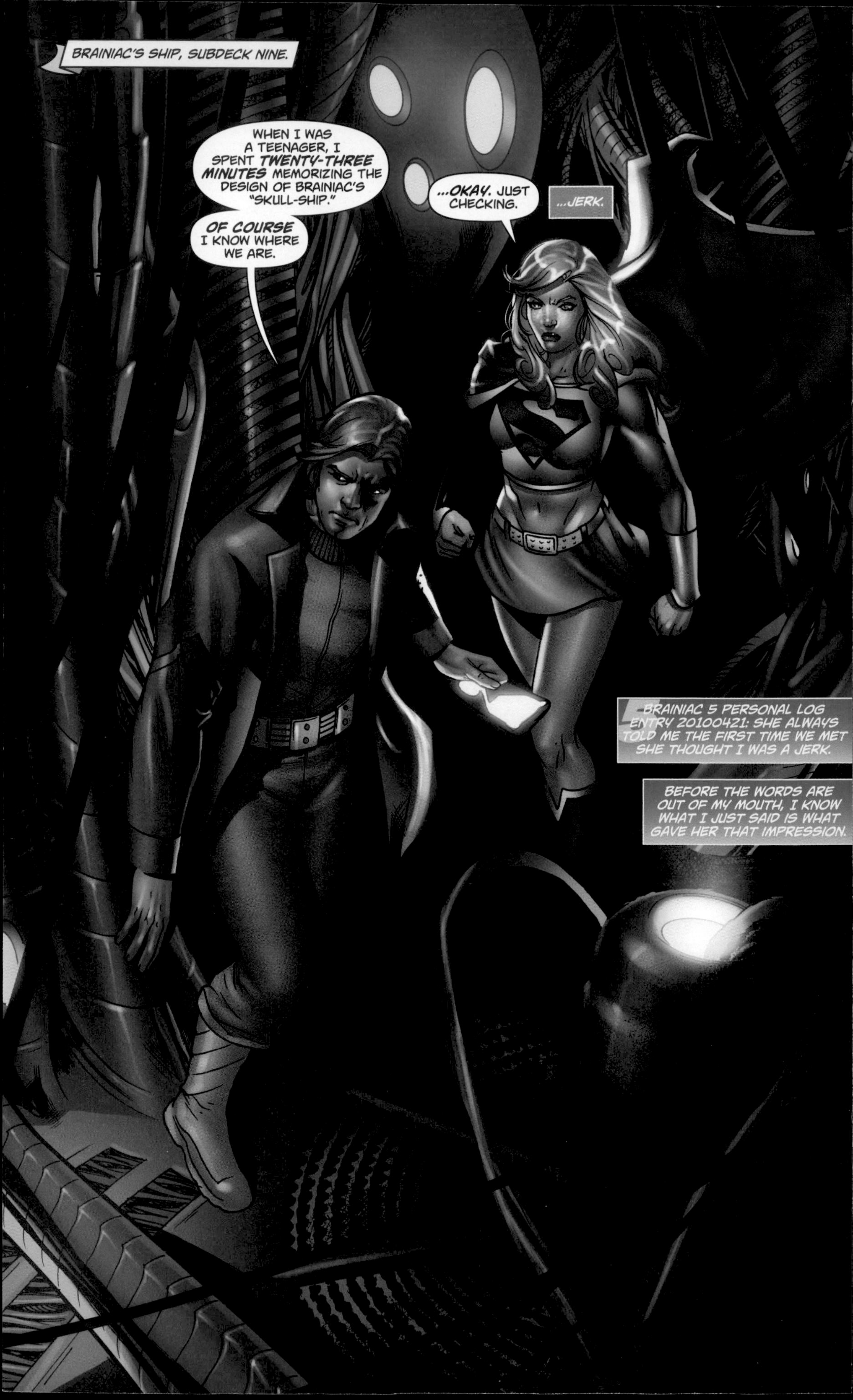
BRAINIAC'S SHIP, SUBDECK NINE.
WHEN I WAS A TEENAGER, I SPENT TWENTY-THREE MINUTES MEMORIZING THE DESIGN OF BRAINIAC'S "SKULL-SHIP."
OF COURSE I KNOW WHERE WE ARE.
...OKAY. JUST CHECKING.
...JERK.
BRAINIAC 5 PERSONAL LOG ENTRY 20100421: SHE ALWAYS TOLD ME THE FIRST TIME WE MET SHE THOUGHT I WAS A JERK.
BEFORE THE WORDS ARE OUT OF MY MOUTH, I KNOW WHAT I JUST SAID IS WHAT GAVE HER THAT IMPRESSION.

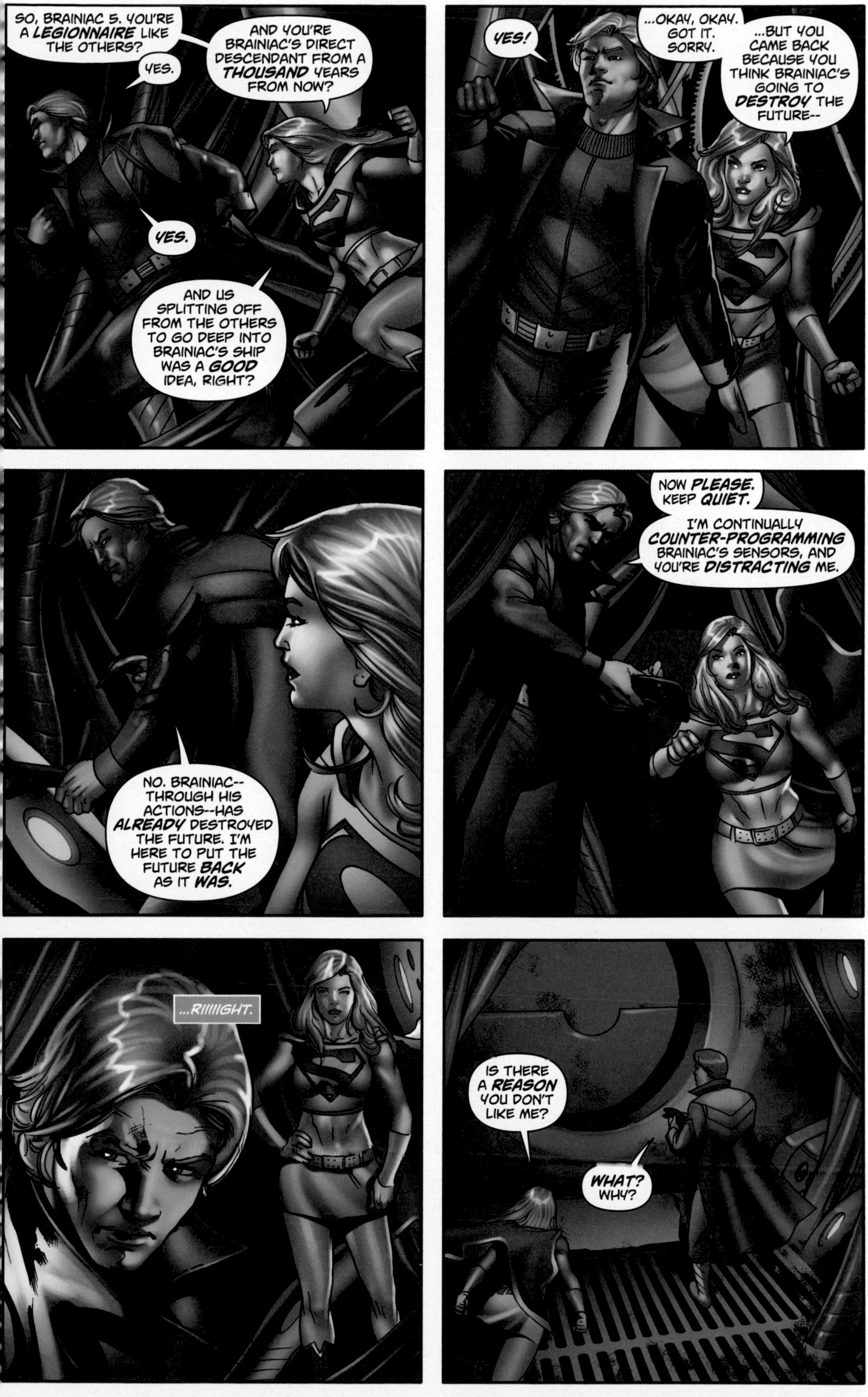
SO, BRAINIAC 5. YOU'RE A LEGIONNAIRE LIKE THE OTHERS?
YES.
AND YOU'RE BRAINIAC'S DIRECT DESCENDANT FROM A THOUSAND YEARS FROM NOW?
YES.
AND US SPLITTING OFF FROM THE OTHERS TO GO DEEP INTO BRAINIAC'S SHIP WAS A GOOD IDEA, RIGHT?
YES!
...OKAY, OKAY. GOT IT. SORRY.
...BUT YOU CAME BACK BECAUSE YOU THINK BRAINIAC'S GOING TO DESTROY THE FUTURE--
NO. BRAINIAC--THROUGH HIS ACTIONS--HAS ALREADY DESTROYED THE FUTURE. I'M HERE TO PUT THE FUTURE BACK AS IT WAS.
NOW PLEASE. KEEP QUIET.
I'M CONTINUALLY COUNTER-PROGRAMMING BRAINIAC'S SENSORS, AND YOU'RE DISTRACTING ME.
...RIIIIGHT.
IS THERE A REASON YOU DON'T LIKE ME?
WHAT? WHY?

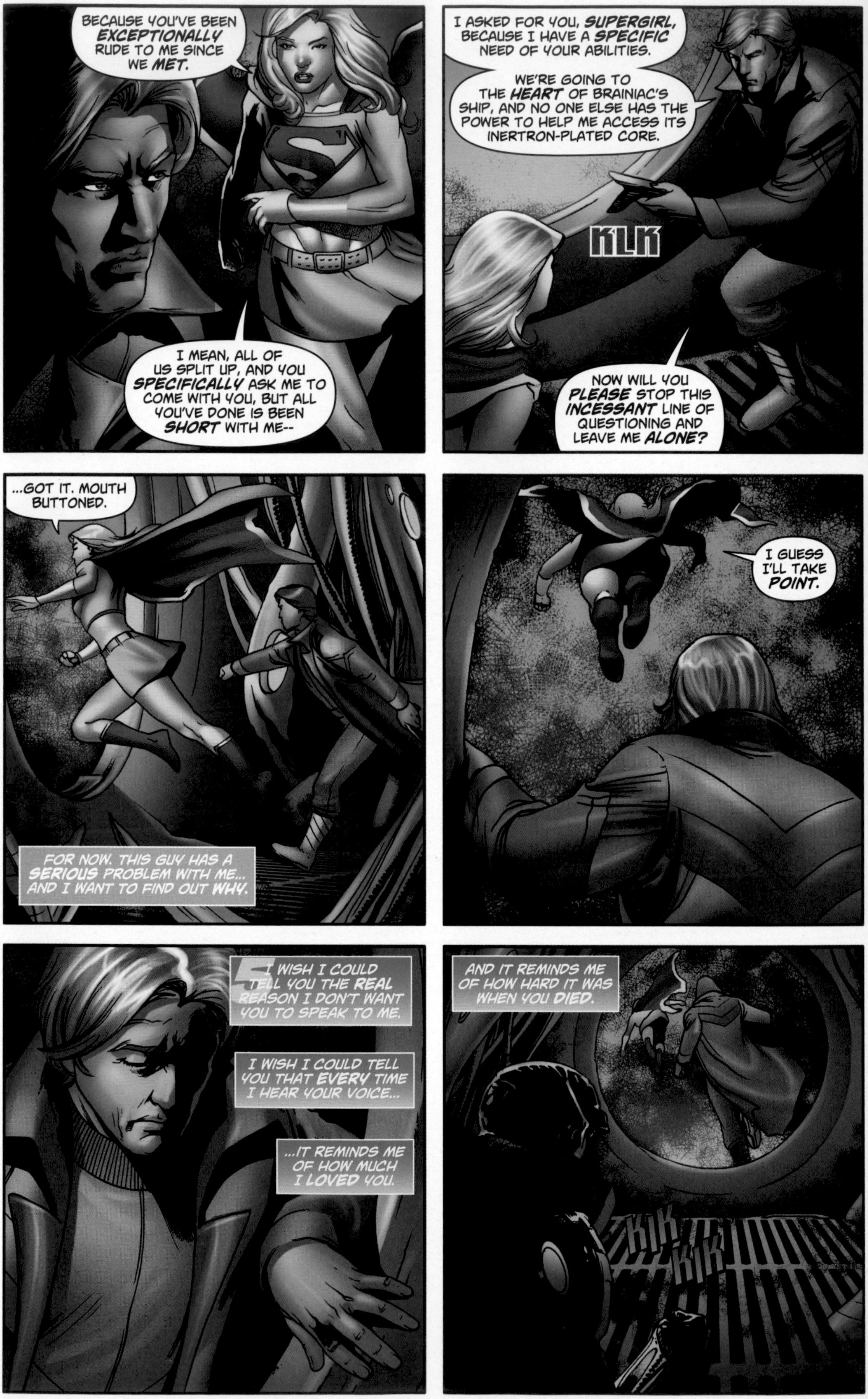

BECAUSE YOU'VE BEEN EXCEPTIONALLY RUDE TO ME SINCE WE MET.
I MEAN, ALL OF US SPLIT UP, AND YOU SPECIFICALLY ASK ME TO COME WITH YOU, BUT ALL YOU'VE DONE IS BEEN SHORT WITH ME--
I ASKED FOR YOU, SUPERGIRL, BECAUSE I HAVE A SPECIFIC NEED OF YOUR ABILITIES.
WE'RE GOING TO THE HEART OF BRAINIAC'S SHIP, AND NO ONE ELSE HAS THE POWER TO HELP ME ACCESS ITS INERTRON-PLATED CORE.
KLK
NOW WILL YOU PLEASE STOP THIS INCESSANT LINE OF QUESTIONING AND LEAVE ME ALONE?
...GOT IT. MOUTH BUTTONED.
FOR NOW. THIS GUY HAS A SERIOUS PROBLEM WITH ME... AND I WANT TO FIND OUT WHY.
I GUESS I'LL TAKE POINT.
I WISH I COULD TELL YOU THE REAL REASON I DON'T WANT YOU TO SPEAK TO ME.
I WISH I COULD TELL YOU THAT EVERY TIME I HEAR YOUR VOICE...
...IT REMINDS ME OF HOW MUCH I LOVED YOU.
AND IT REMINDS ME OF HOW HARD IT WAS WHEN YOU DIED.
KLK KLK

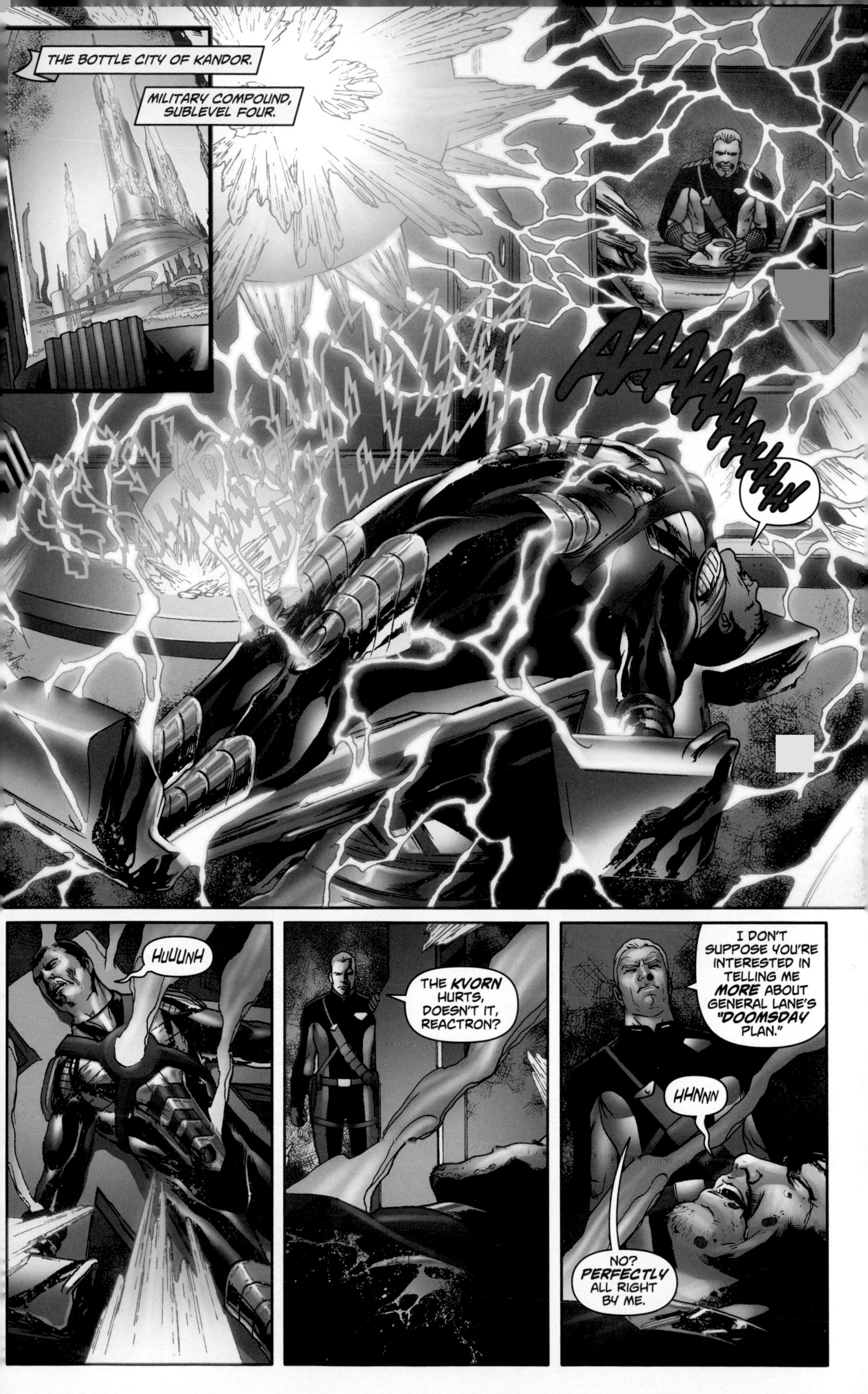
THE BOTTLE CITY OF KANDOR.
MILITARY COMPOUND, SUBLEVEL FOUR.
AAAAAAAAHHH!
HUUUNH
THE KVORN HURTS, DOESN'T IT, REACTRON?
I DON'T SUPPOSE YOU'RE INTERESTED IN TELLING ME MORE ABOUT GENERAL LANE'S "DOOMSDAY PLAN."
HHNNN
NO? PERFECTLY ALL RIGHT BY ME.

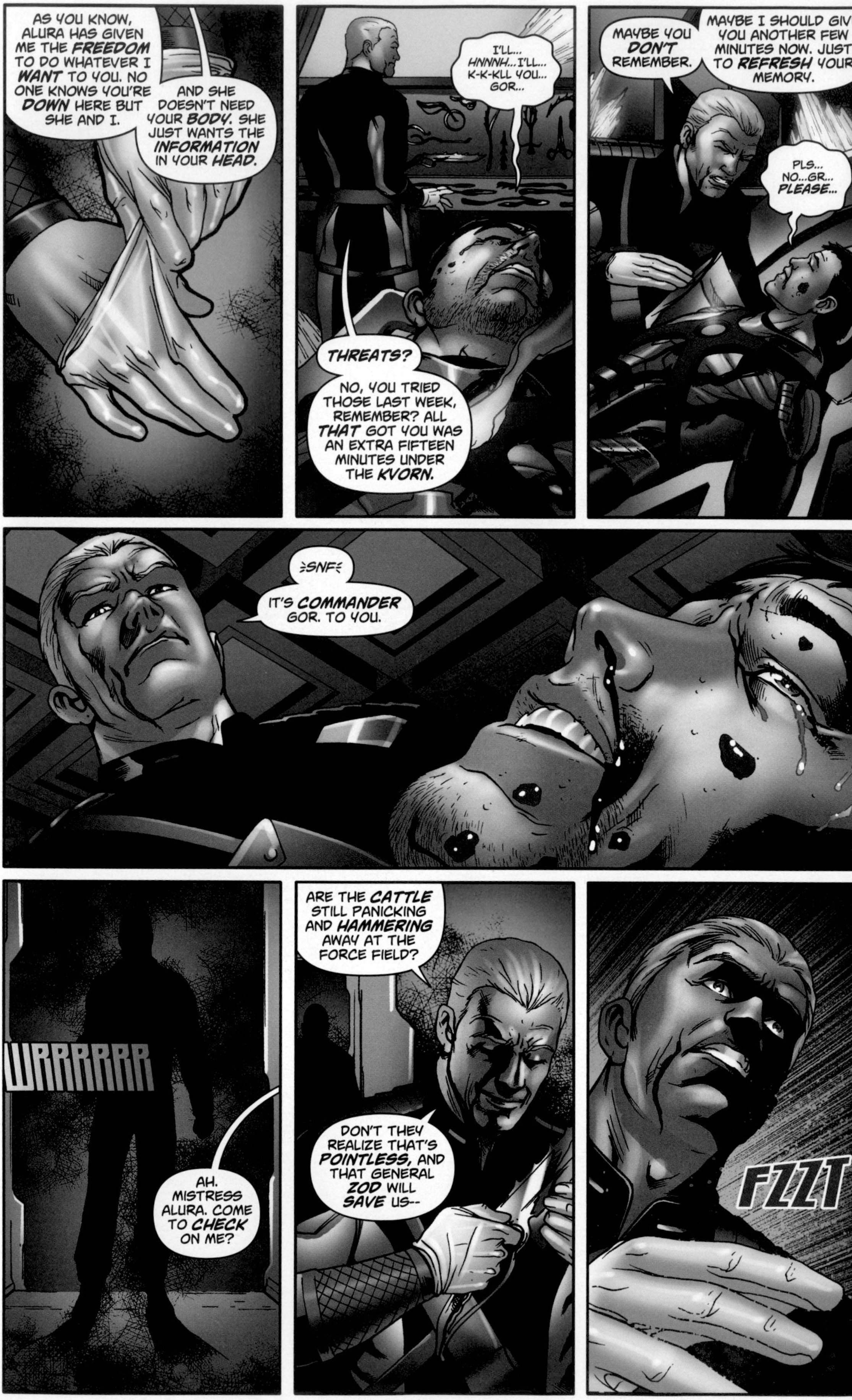
AS YOU KNOW, ALURA HAS GIVEN ME THE FREEDOM TO DO WHATEVER I WANT TO YOU. NO ONE KNOWS YOU'RE DOWN HERE BUT SHE AND I.
AND SHE DOESN'T NEED YOUR BODY. SHE JUST WANTS THE INFORMATION IN YOUR HEAD.
I'LL... HNNNH... I'LL... K-K-KLL YOU... GOR...
THREATS?
NO, YOU TRIED THOSE LAST WEEK, REMEMBER? ALL THAT GOT YOU WAS AN EXTRA FIFTEEN MINUTES UNDER THE KVORN.
MAYBE YOU DON'T REMEMBER.
MAYBE I SHOULD GIVE YOU ANOTHER FEW MINUTES NOW. JUST TO REFRESH YOUR MEMORY.
PLS... NO...GR... PLEASE...
SNF
IT'S COMMANDER GOR. TO YOU.
WRRRRRR
AH. MISTRESS ALURA. COME TO CHECK ON ME?
ARE THE CATTLE STILL PANICKING AND HAMMERING AWAY AT THE FORCE FIELD?
DON'T THEY REALIZE THAT'S POINTLESS, AND THAT GENERAL ZOD WILL SAVE US--
FZZT

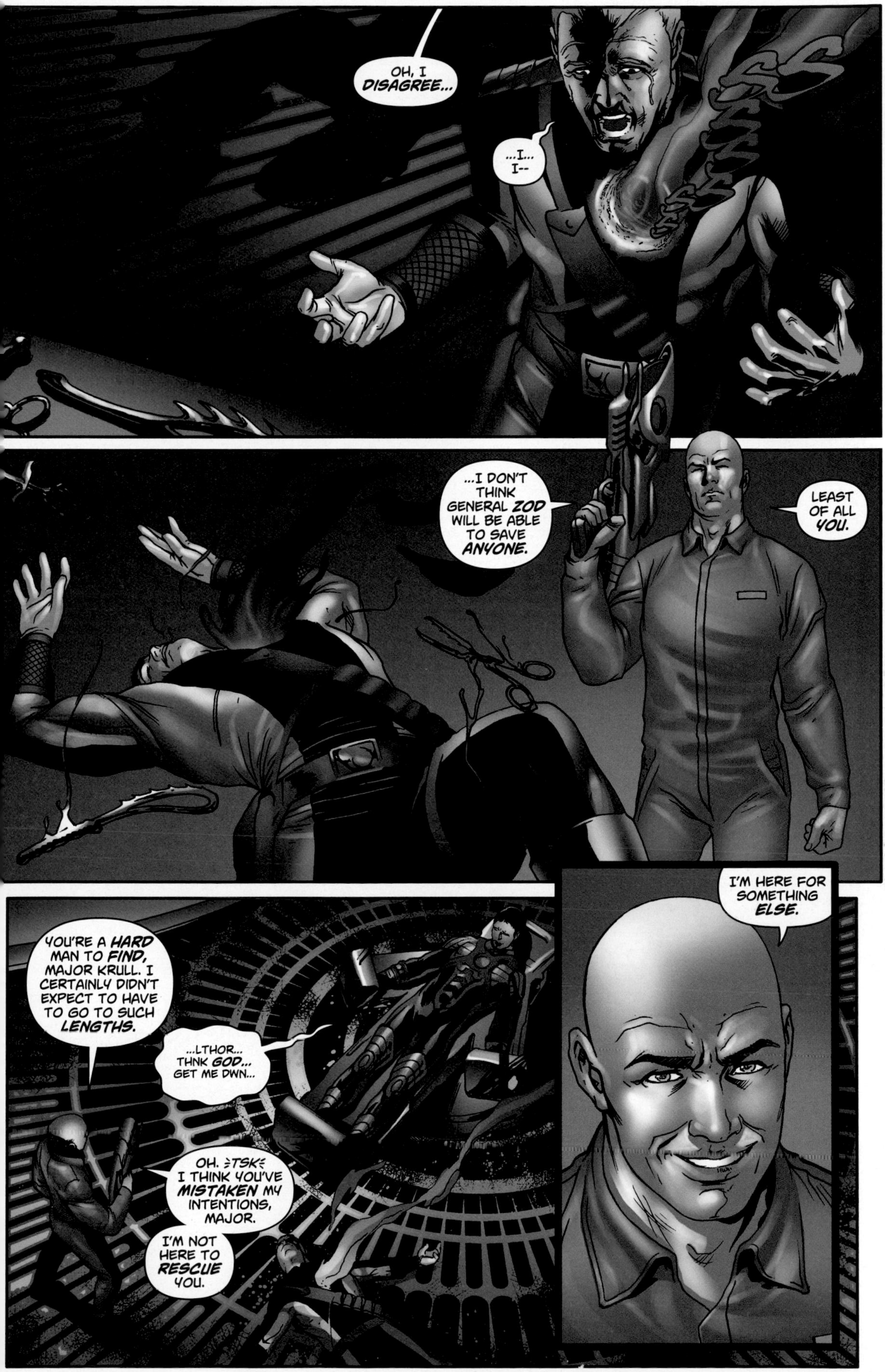
OH, I DISAGREE...
...I... I--
...I DON'T THINK GENERAL ZOD WILL BE ABLE TO SAVE ANYONE.
LEAST OF ALL YOU.
YOU'RE A HARD MAN TO FIND, MAJOR KRULL. I CERTAINLY DIDN'T EXPECT TO HAVE TO GO TO SUCH LENGTHS.
...LTHOR... THNK GOD... GET ME DWN...
OH. ≶TSK≷ I THINK YOU'VE MISTAKEN MY INTENTIONS, MAJOR.
I'M NOT HERE TO RESCUE YOU.
I'M HERE FOR SOMETHING ELSE.

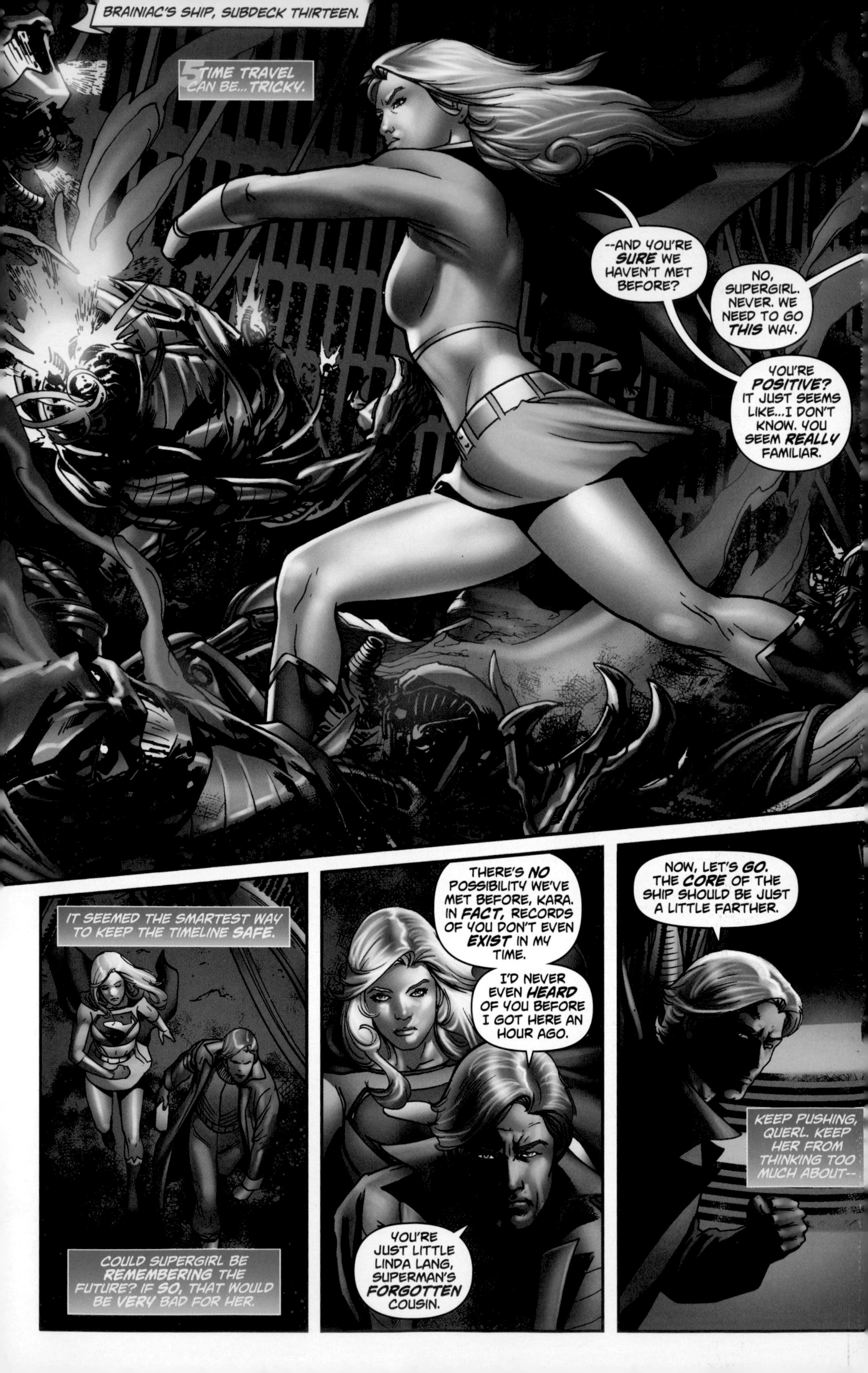
BRAINIAC'S SHIP, SUBDECK THIRTEEN.
TIME TRAVEL CAN BE...TRICKY.
--AND YOU'RE SURE WE HAVEN'T MET BEFORE?
NO, SUPERGIRL. NEVER. WE NEED TO GO THIS WAY.
YOU'RE POSITIVE? IT JUST SEEMS LIKE...I DON'T KNOW. YOU SEEM REALLY FAMILIAR.
IT SEEMED THE SMARTEST WAY TO KEEP THE TIMELINE SAFE.
COULD SUPERGIRL BE REMEMBERING THE FUTURE? IF SO, THAT WOULD BE VERY BAD FOR HER.
THERE'S NO POSSIBILITY WE'VE MET BEFORE, KARA. IN FACT, RECORDS OF YOU DON'T EVEN EXIST IN MY TIME.
I'D NEVER EVEN HEARD OF YOU BEFORE I GOT HERE AN HOUR AGO.
YOU'RE JUST LITTLE LINDA LANG, SUPERMAN'S FORGOTTEN COUSIN.
NOW, LET'S GO. THE CORE OF THE SHIP SHOULD BE JUST A LITTLE FARTHER.
KEEP PUSHING, QUERL. KEEP HER FROM THINKING TOO MUCH ABOUT--

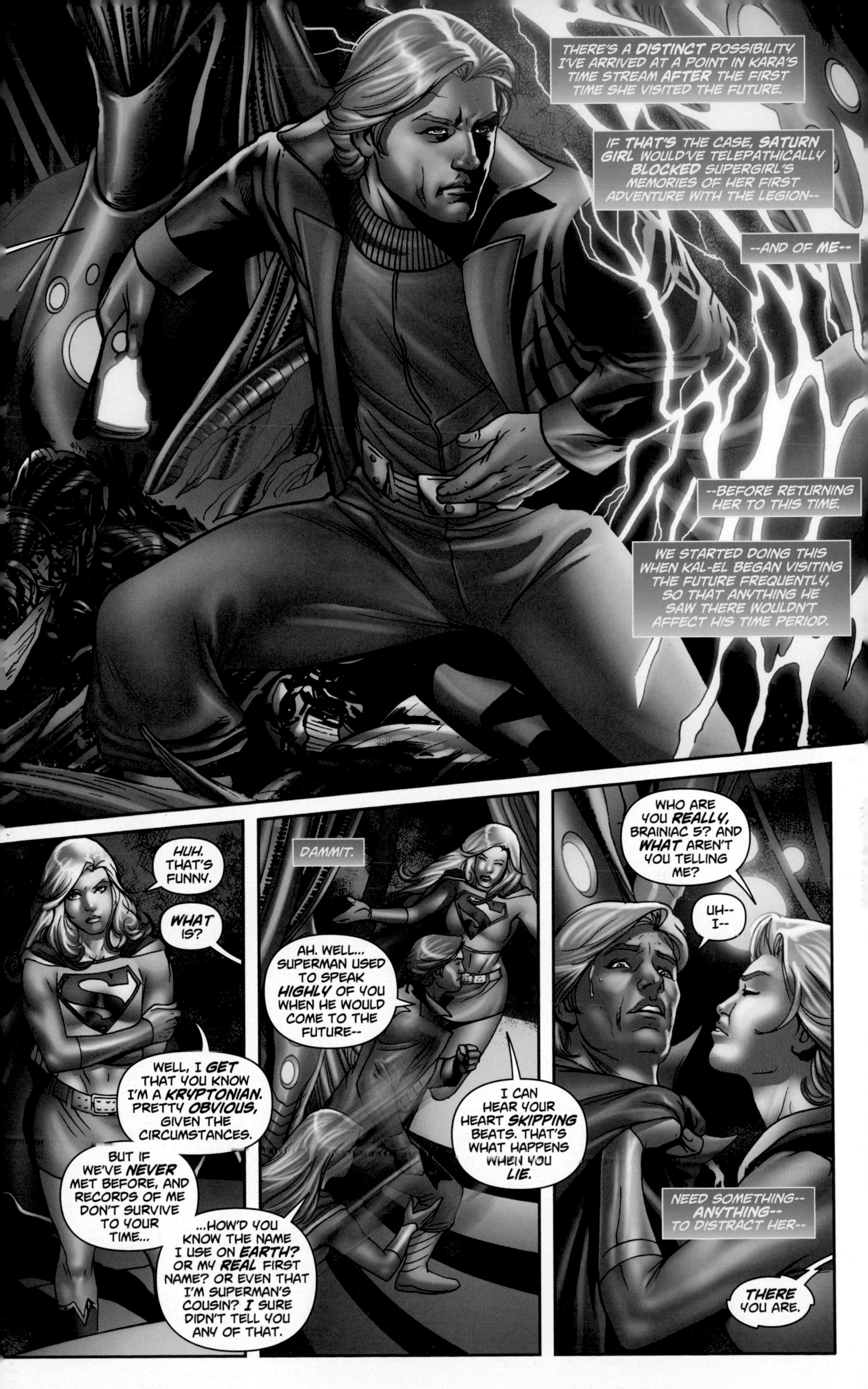
THERE'S A DISTINCT POSSIBILITY I'VE ARRIVED AT A POINT IN KARA'S TIME STREAM AFTER THE FIRST TIME SHE VISITED THE FUTURE.
IF THAT'S THE CASE, SATURN GIRL WOULD'VE TELEPATHICALLY BLOCKED SUPERGIRL'S MEMORIES OF HER FIRST ADVENTURE WITH THE LEGION--
--AND OF ME--
--BEFORE RETURNING HER TO THIS TIME.
WE STARTED DOING THIS WHEN KAL-EL BEGAN VISITING THE FUTURE FREQUENTLY, SO THAT ANYTHING HE SAW THERE WOULDN'T AFFECT HIS TIME PERIOD.
HUH. THAT'S FUNNY.
WHAT IS?
WELL, I GET THAT YOU KNOW I'M A KRYPTONIAN. PRETTY OBVIOUS, GIVEN THE CIRCUMSTANCES.
BUT IF WE'VE NEVER MET BEFORE, AND RECORDS OF ME DON'T SURVIVE TO YOUR TIME...
...HOW'D YOU KNOW THE NAME I USE ON EARTH? OR MY REAL FIRST NAME? OR EVEN THAT I'M SUPERMAN'S COUSIN? I SURE DIDN'T TELL YOU ANY OF THAT.
DAMMIT.
AH. WELL... SUPERMAN USED TO SPEAK HIGHLY OF YOU WHEN HE WOULD COME TO THE FUTURE--
I CAN HEAR YOUR HEART SKIPPING BEATS. THAT'S WHAT HAPPENS WHEN YOU LIE.
WHO ARE YOU REALLY, BRAINIAC 5? AND WHAT AREN'T YOU TELLING ME?
UH-- I--
NEED SOMETHING-- ANYTHING-- TO DISTRACT HER--
THERE YOU ARE.

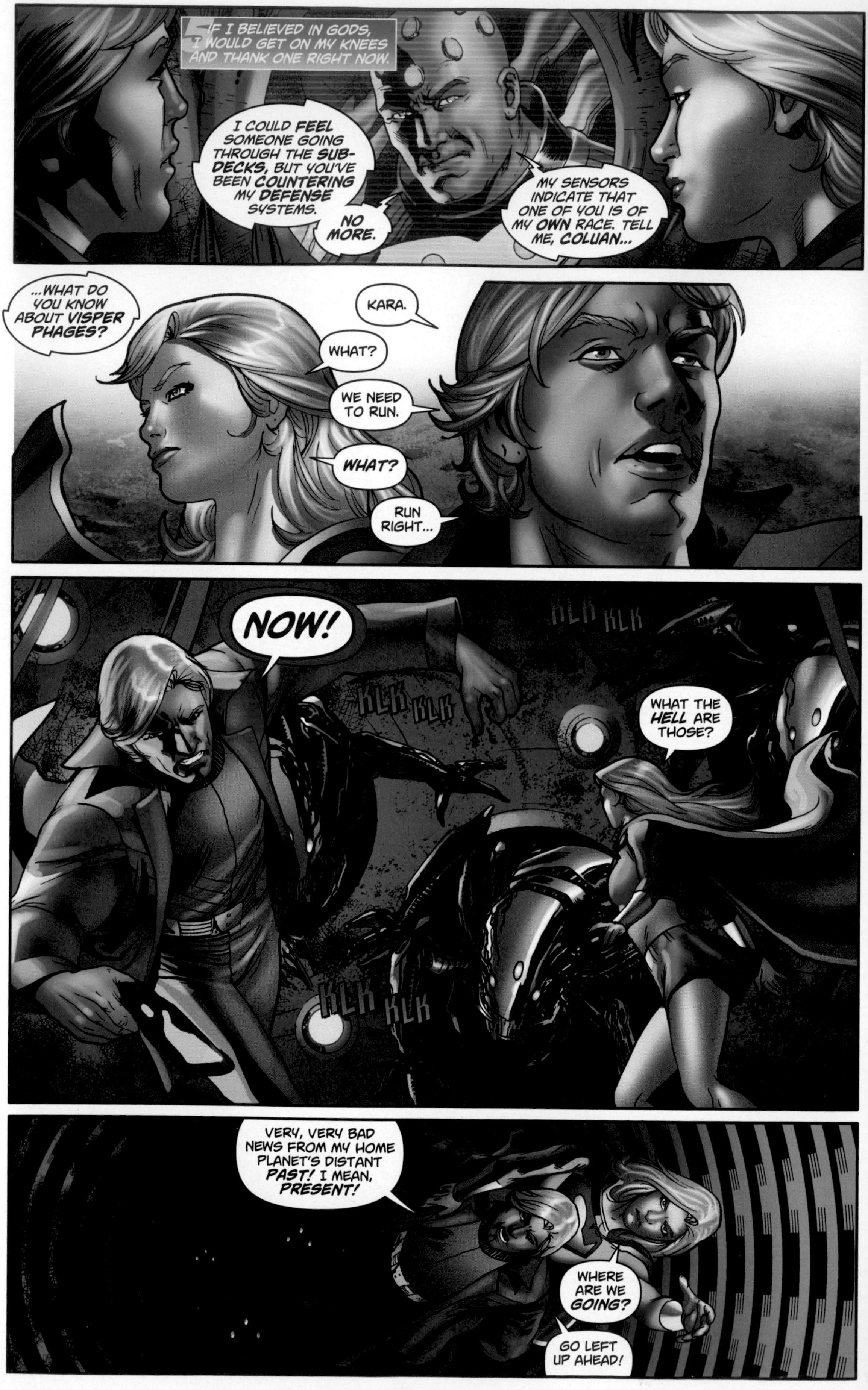
5
IF I BELIEVED IN GODS, I WOULD GET ON MY KNEES AND THANK ONE RIGHT NOW.
I COULD FEEL SOMEONE GOING THROUGH THE SUB-DECKS, BUT YOU'VE BEEN COUNTERING MY DEFENSE SYSTEMS.
NO MORE.
MY SENSORS INDICATE THAT ONE OF YOU IS OF MY OWN RACE. TELL ME, COLUAN...
...WHAT DO YOU KNOW ABOUT VISPER PHAGES?
KARA.
WHAT?
WE NEED TO RUN.
WHAT?
RUN RIGHT...
NOW!
KLK KLK
KLK KLK
WHAT THE HELL ARE THOSE?
KLK KLK
VERY, VERY BAD NEWS FROM MY HOME PLANET'S DISTANT PAST! I MEAN, PRESENT!
WHERE ARE WE GOING?
GO LEFT UP AHEAD!

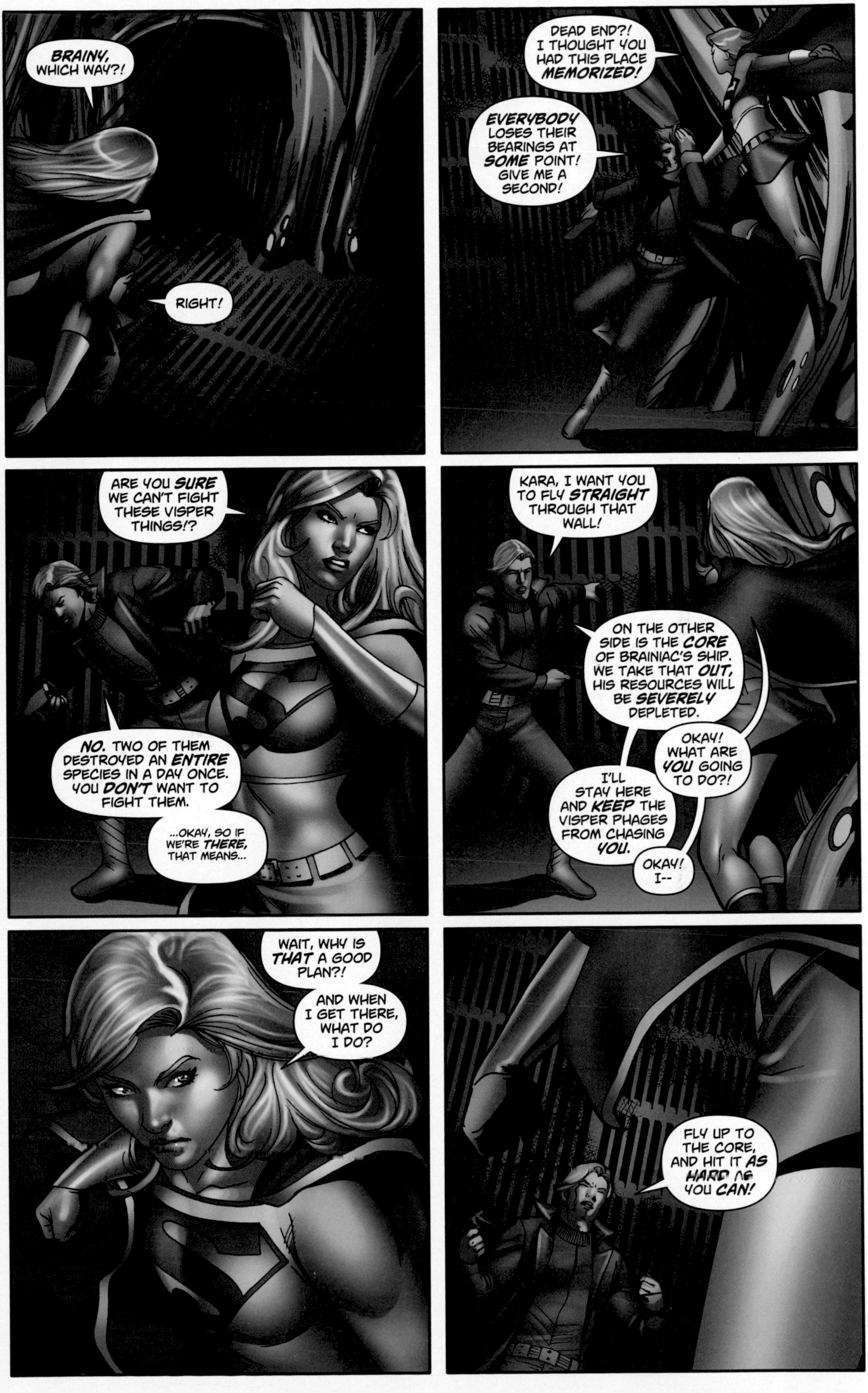
BRAINY, WHICH WAY?!
RIGHT!
DEAD END?! I THOUGHT YOU HAD THIS PLACE MEMORIZED!
EVERYBODY LOSES THEIR BEARINGS AT SOME POINT! GIVE ME A SECOND!
ARE YOU SURE WE CAN'T FIGHT THESE VISPER THINGS!?
NO. TWO OF THEM DESTROYED AN ENTIRE SPECIES IN A DAY ONCE. YOU DON'T WANT TO FIGHT THEM.
...OKAY, SO IF WE'RE THERE, THAT MEANS...
KARA, I WANT YOU TO FLY STRAIGHT THROUGH THAT WALL!
ON THE OTHER SIDE IS THE CORE OF BRAINIAC'S SHIP. WE TAKE THAT OUT, HIS RESOURCES WILL BE SEVERELY DEPLETED.
OKAY! WHAT ARE YOU GOING TO DO?!
I'LL STAY HERE AND KEEP THE VISPER PHAGES FROM CHASING YOU.
OKAY! I--
WAIT, WHY IS THAT A GOOD PLAN?!
AND WHEN I GET THERE, WHAT DO I DO?
FLY UP TO THE CORE, AND HIT IT AS HARD AS YOU CAN!

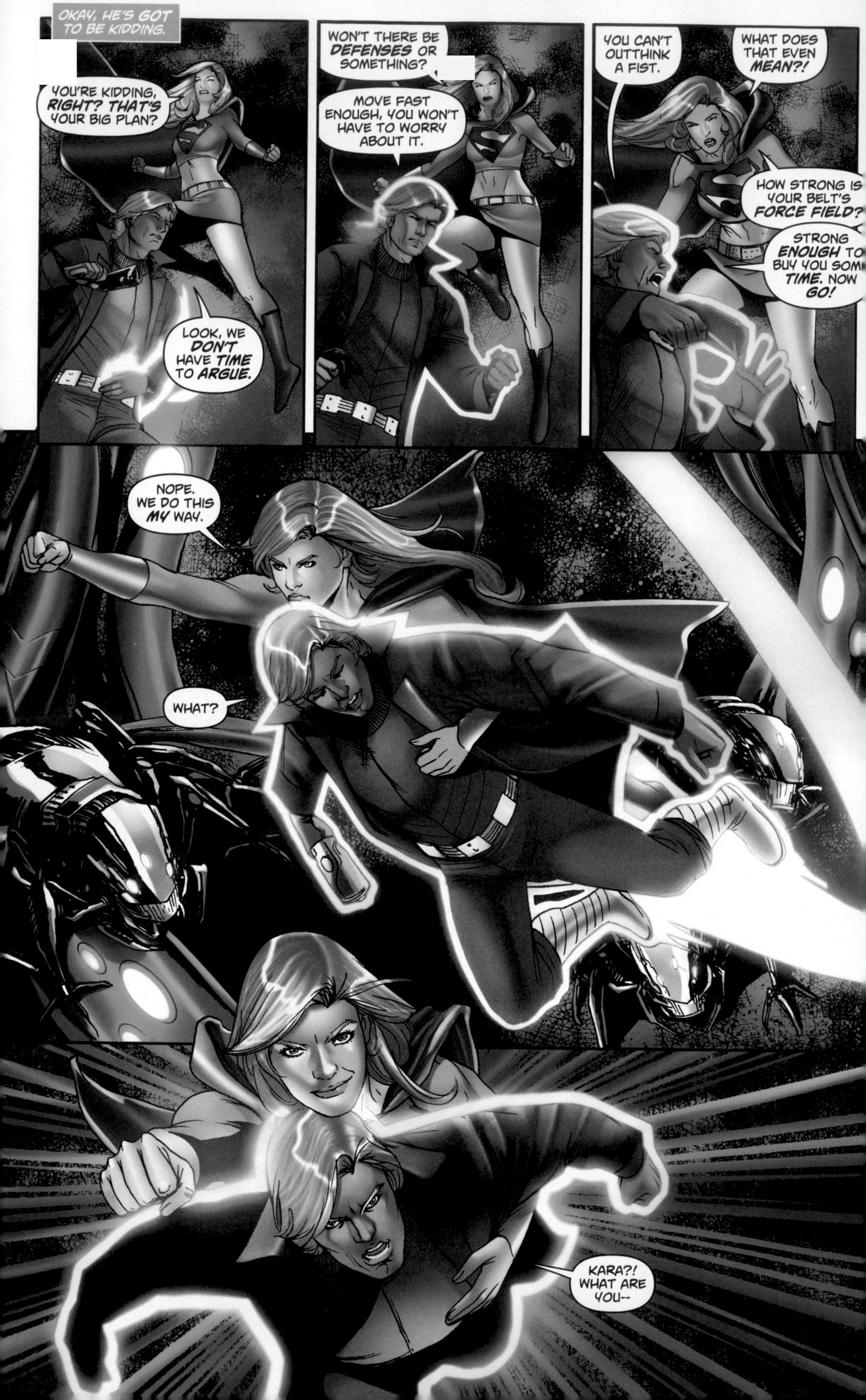
OKAY, HE'S GOT TO BE KIDDING.
YOU'RE KIDDING, RIGHT? THAT'S YOUR BIG PLAN?
LOOK, WE DON'T HAVE TIME TO ARGUE.
WON'T THERE BE DEFENSES OR SOMETHING?
MOVE FAST ENOUGH, YOU WON'T HAVE TO WORRY ABOUT IT.
YOU CAN'T OUTTHINK A FIST.
WHAT DOES THAT EVEN MEAN?!
HOW STRONG IS YOUR BELT'S FORCE FIELD?
STRONG ENOUGH TO BUY YOU SOM TIME. NOW GO!
NOPE. WE DO THIS MY WAY.
WHAT?
KARA?! WHAT ARE YOU--

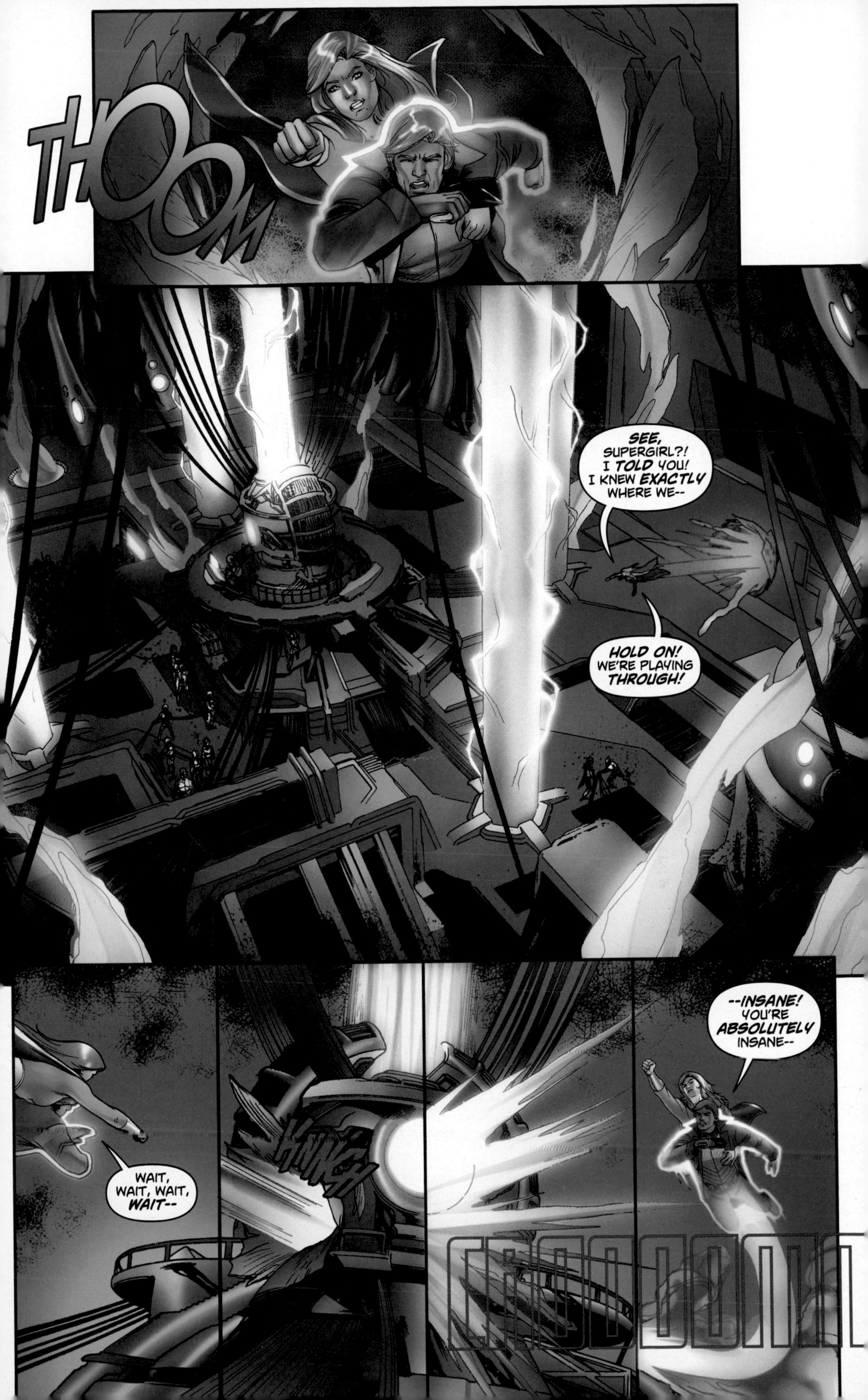
THOOM
SEE, SUPERGIRL?! I TOLD YOU! I KNEW EXACTLY WHERE WE--
HOLD ON! WE'RE PLAYING THROUGH!
WAIT, WAIT, WAIT, WAIT--
--INSANE! YOU'RE ABSOLUTELY INSANE--

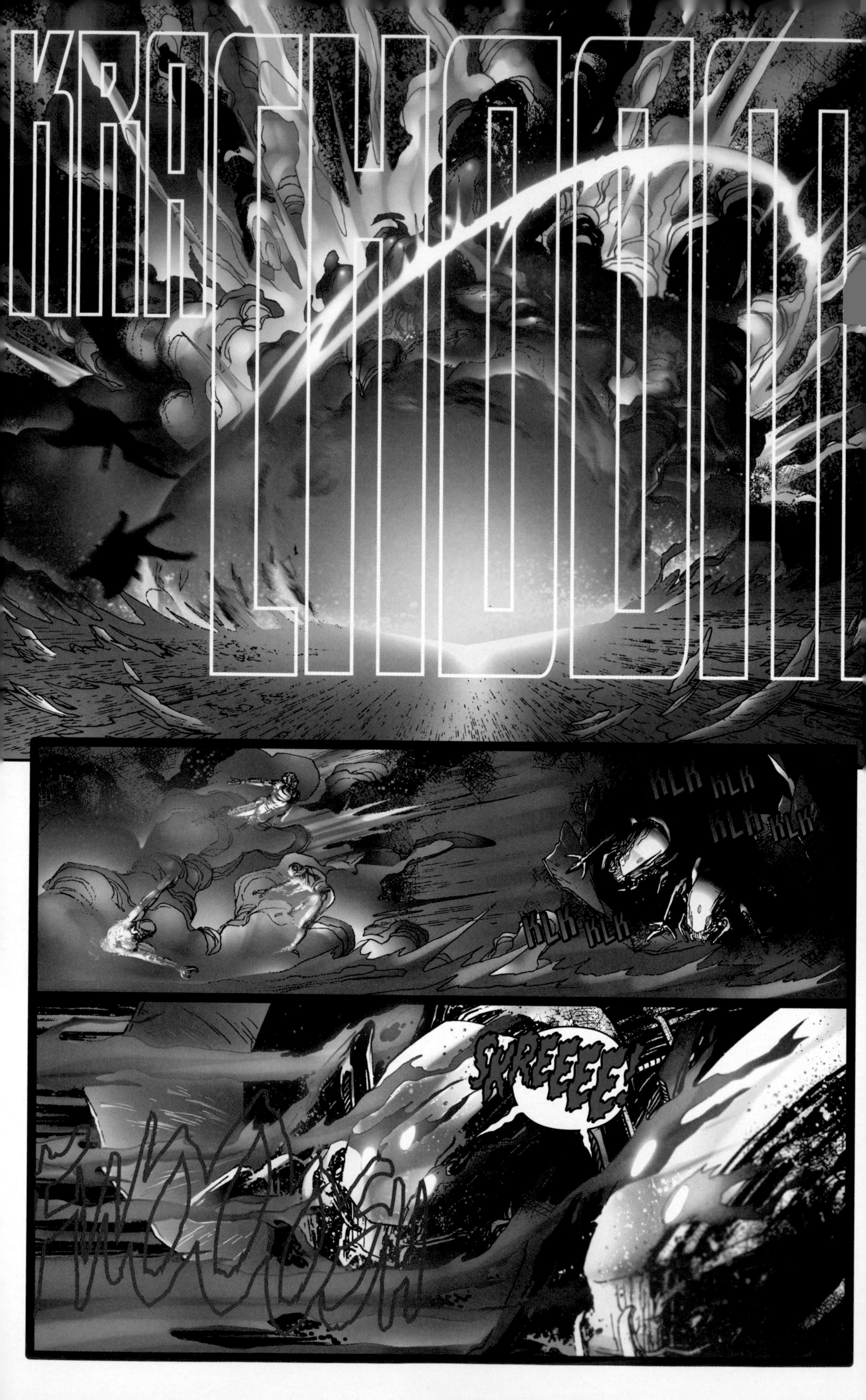
KLK KLK
KLK KLK
KLK KLK
SKREEEE!

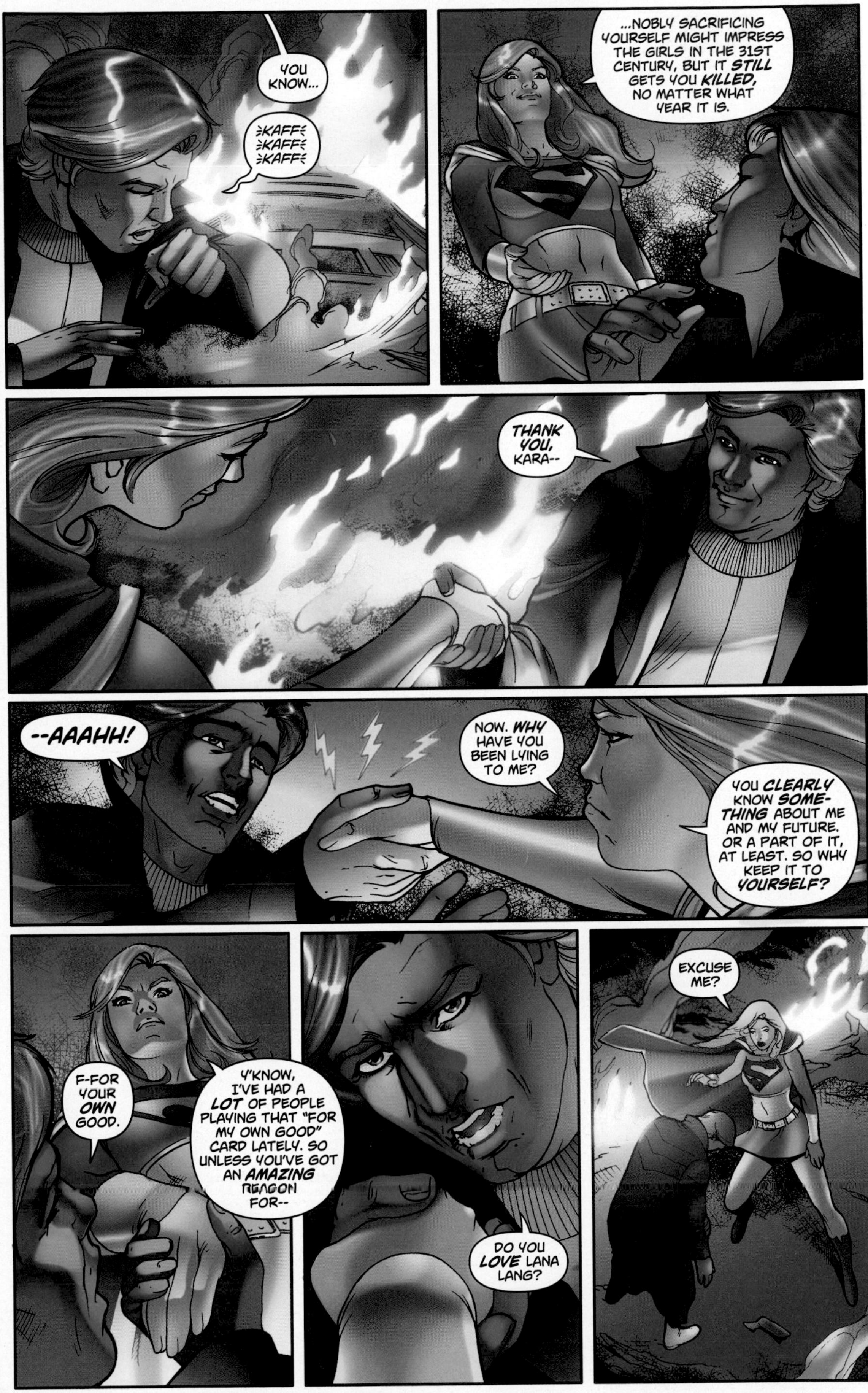
YOU KNOW...
KAFF KAFF KAFF
...NOBLY SACRIFICING YOURSELF MIGHT IMPRESS THE GIRLS IN THE 31ST CENTURY, BUT IT STILL GETS YOU KILLED, NO MATTER WHAT YEAR IT IS.
THANK YOU, KARA--
--AAAHH!
NOW. WHY HAVE YOU BEEN LYING TO ME?
YOU CLEARLY KNOW SOME-THING ABOUT ME AND MY FUTURE. OR A PART OF IT, AT LEAST. SO WHY KEEP IT TO YOURSELF?
F-FOR YOUR OWN GOOD.
Y'KNOW, I'VE HAD A LOT OF PEOPLE PLAYING THAT "FOR MY OWN GOOD" CARD LATELY. SO UNLESS YOU'VE GOT AN AMAZING REASON FOR--
DO YOU LOVE LANA LANG?
EXCUSE ME?

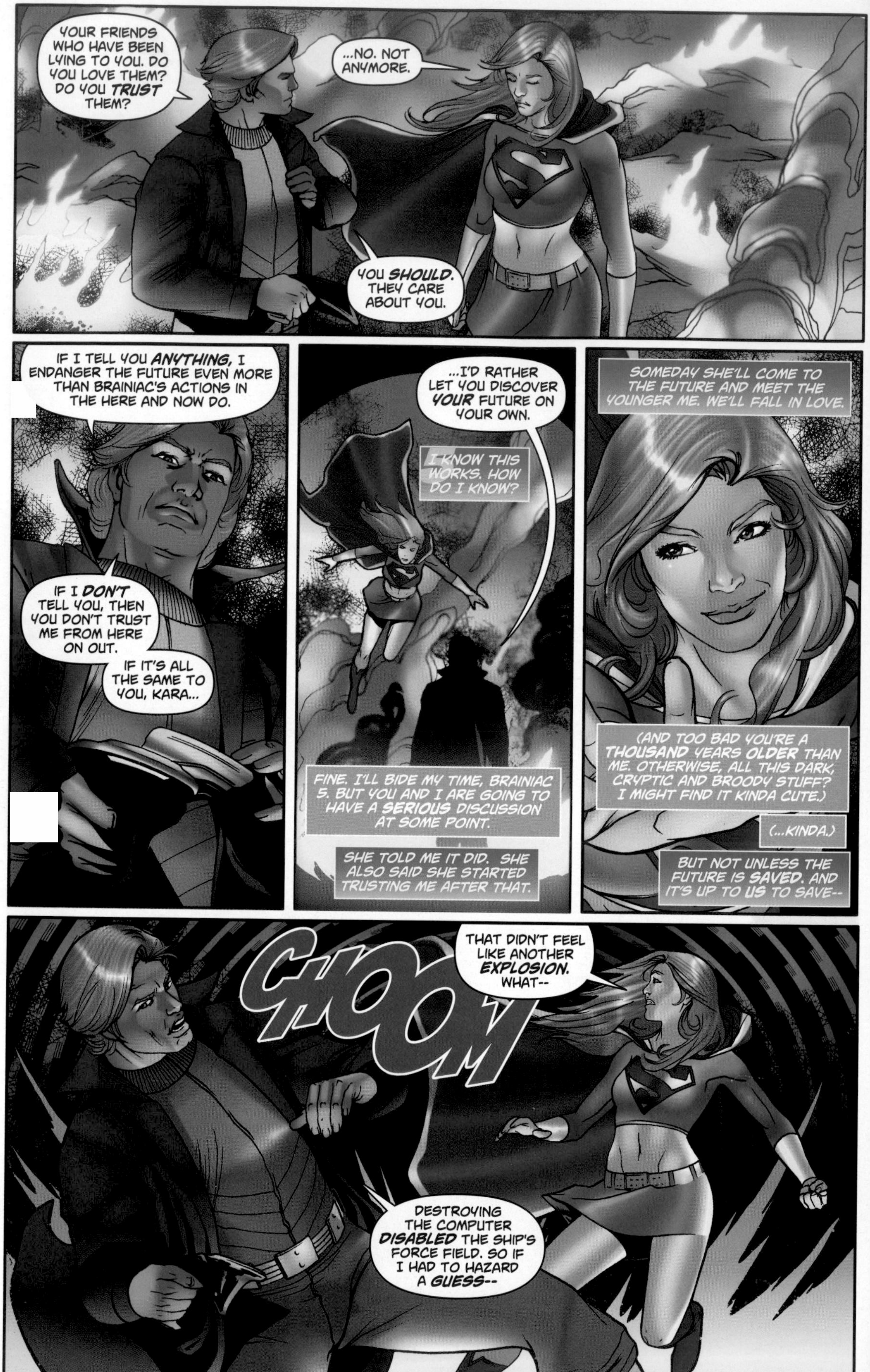
YOUR FRIENDS WHO HAVE BEEN LYING TO YOU. DO YOU LOVE THEM? DO YOU TRUST THEM?
...NO. NOT ANYMORE.
YOU SHOULD. THEY CARE ABOUT YOU.
IF I TELL YOU ANYTHING, I ENDANGER THE FUTURE EVEN MORE THAN BRAINIAC'S ACTIONS IN THE HERE AND NOW DO.
IF I DON'T TELL YOU, THEN YOU DON'T TRUST ME FROM HERE ON OUT.
IF IT'S ALL THE SAME TO YOU, KARA...
...I'D RATHER LET YOU DISCOVER YOUR FUTURE ON YOUR OWN.
I KNOW THIS WORKS. HOW DO I KNOW?
FINE. I'LL BIDE MY TIME, BRAINIAC 5. BUT YOU AND I ARE GOING TO HAVE A SERIOUS DISCUSSION AT SOME POINT.
SHE TOLD ME IT DID. SHE ALSO SAID SHE STARTED TRUSTING ME AFTER THAT.
SOMEDAY SHE'LL COME TO THE FUTURE AND MEET THE YOUNGER ME. WE'LL FALL IN LOVE.
(AND TOO BAD YOU'RE A THOUSAND YEARS OLDER THAN ME. OTHERWISE, ALL THIS DARK, CRYPTIC AND BROODY STUFF? I MIGHT FIND IT KINDA CUTE.)
(...KINDA.)
BUT NOT UNLESS THE FUTURE IS SAVED. AND IT'S UP TO US TO SAVE--
CHOOM
THAT DIDN'T FEEL LIKE ANOTHER EXPLOSION. WHAT--
DESTROYING THE COMPUTER DISABLED THE SHIP'S FORCE FIELD. SO IF I HAD TO HAZARD A GUESS--

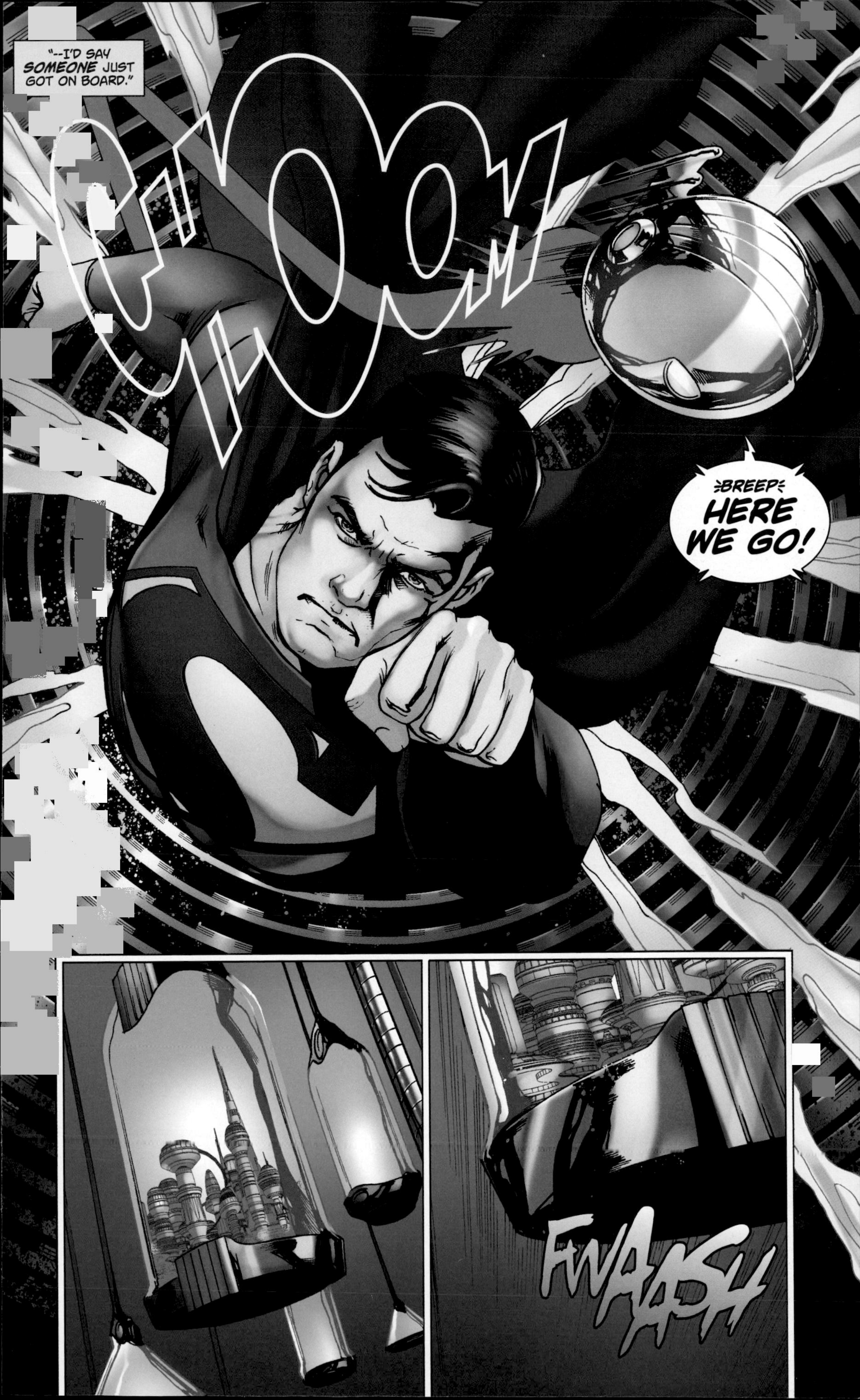
"--I'D SAY SOMEONE JUST GOT ON BOARD."
CHOOM
BREEP HERE WE GO!
FWASH

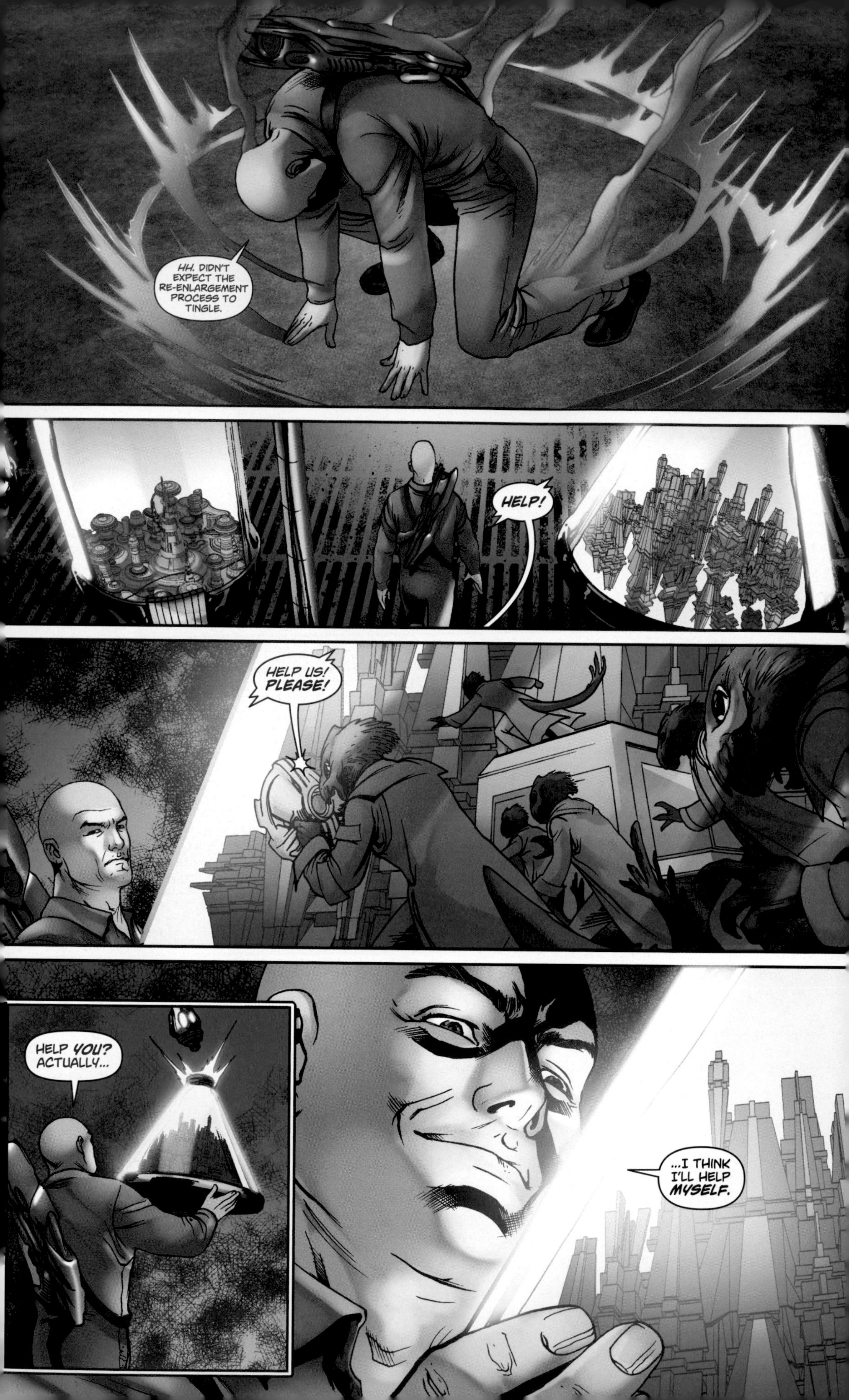
HH. DIDN'T EXPECT THE RE-ENLARGEMENT PROCESS TO TINGLE.
HELP!
HELP US! PLEASE!
HELP YOU? ACTUALLY...
...I THINK I'LL HELP MYSELF.

cover by AARON LOPRESTI & PETE PANTAZIS

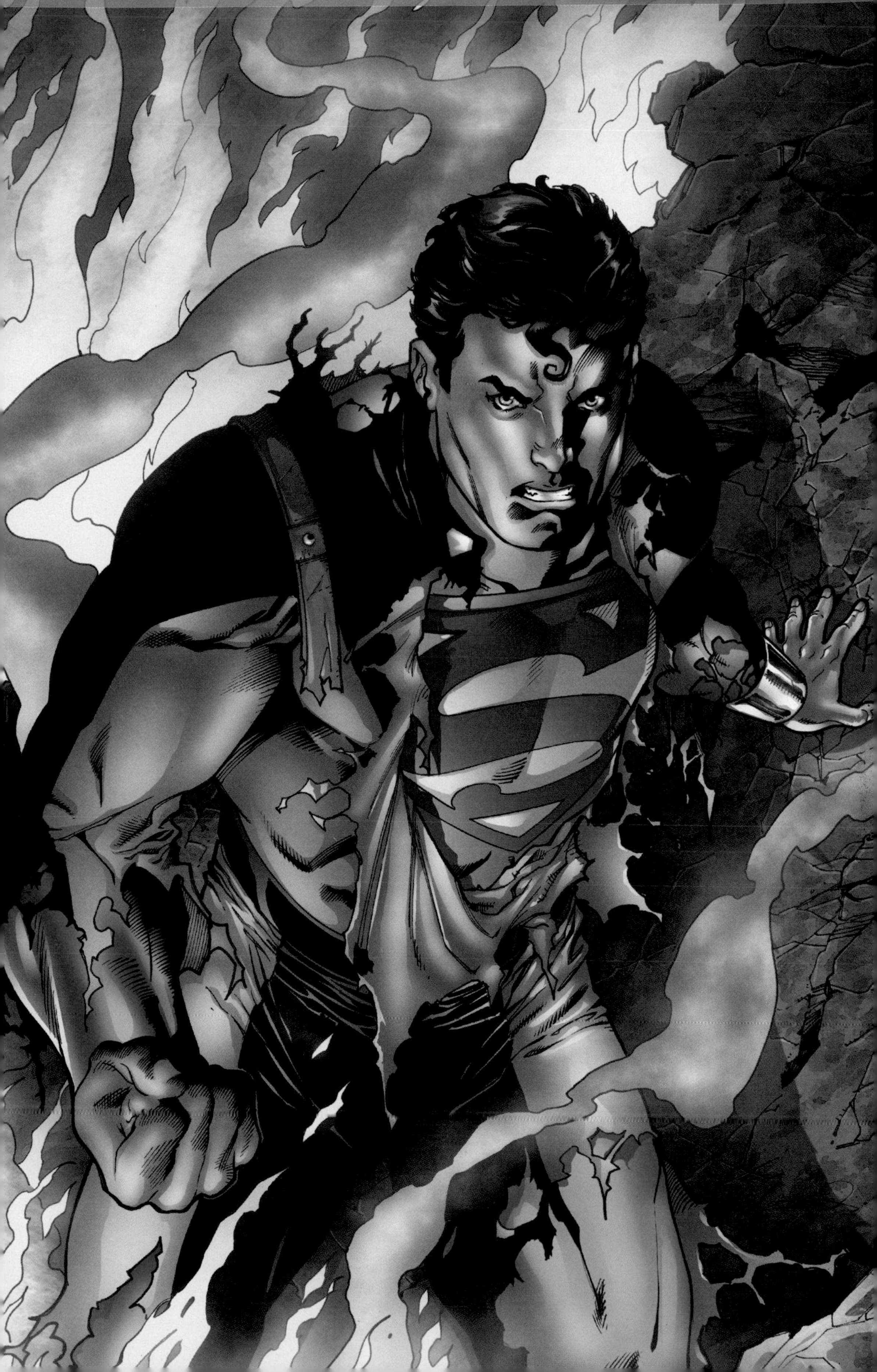

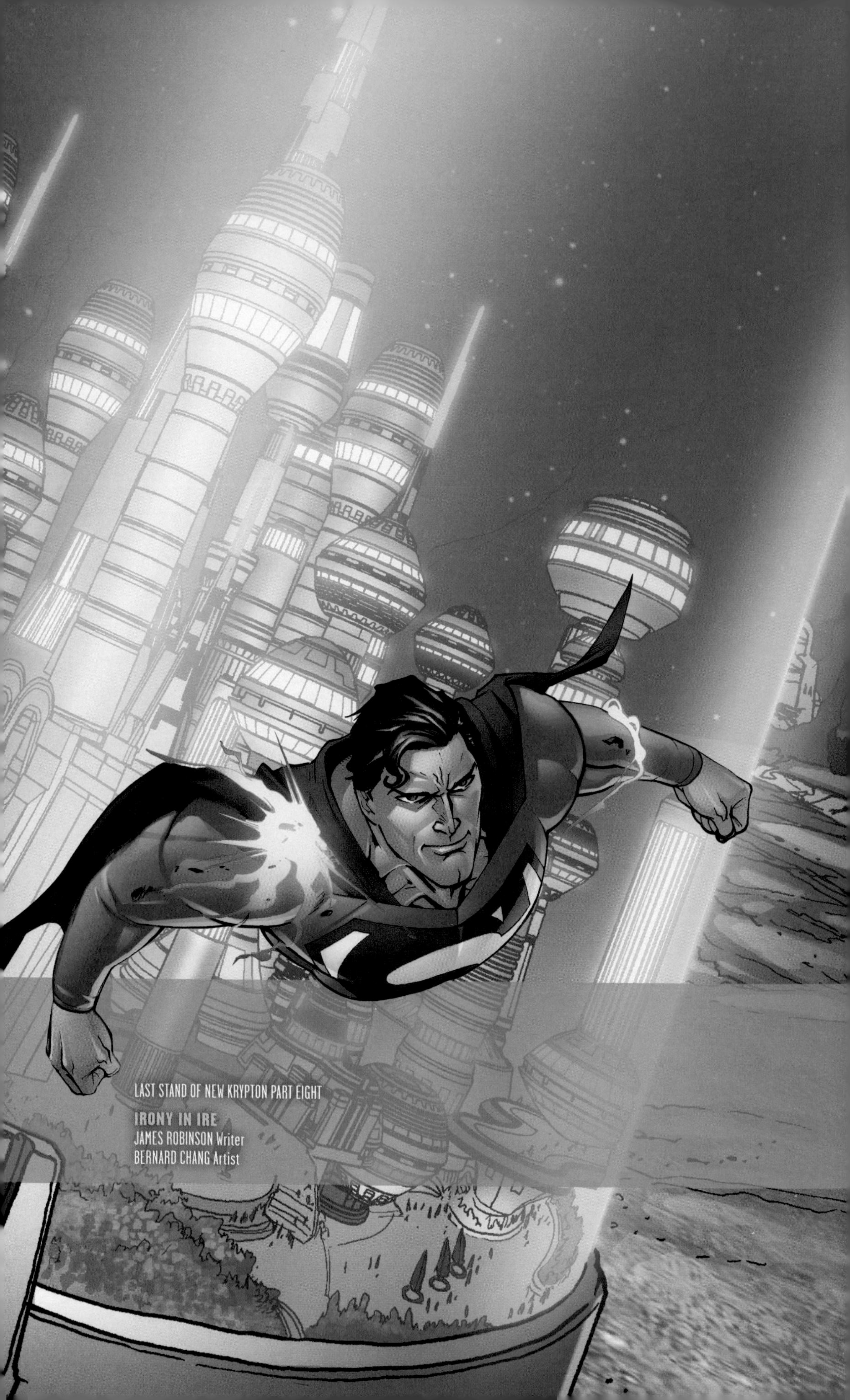
LAST STAND OF NEW KRYPTON PART EIGHT
IRONY IN IRE
JAMES ROBINSON Writer
BERNARD CHANG Artist

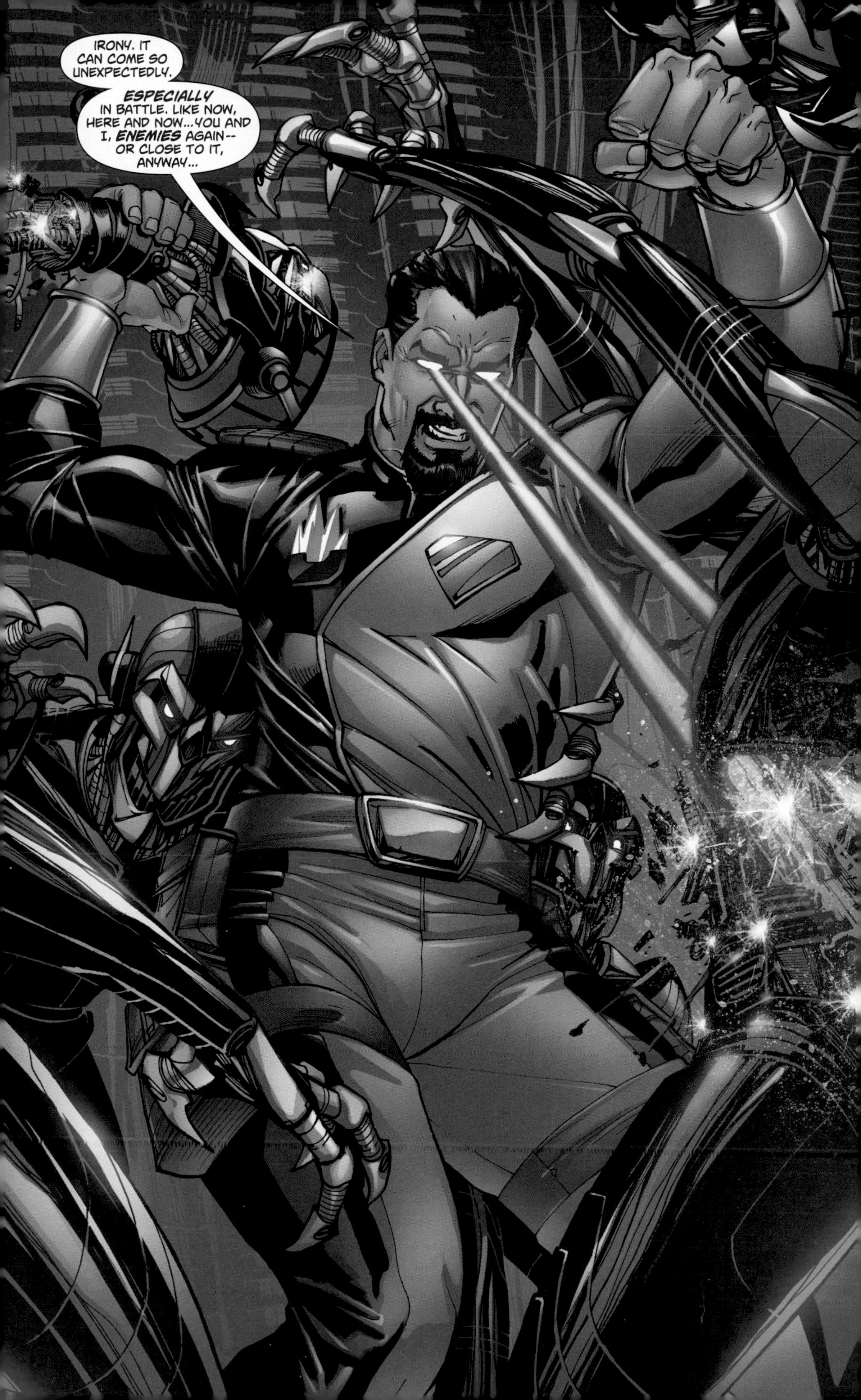
IRONY. IT CAN COME SO UNEXPECTEDLY.
ESPECIALLY IN BATTLE. LIKE NOW, HERE AND NOW...YOU AND I, ENEMIES AGAIN-- OR CLOSE TO IT, ANYWAY...

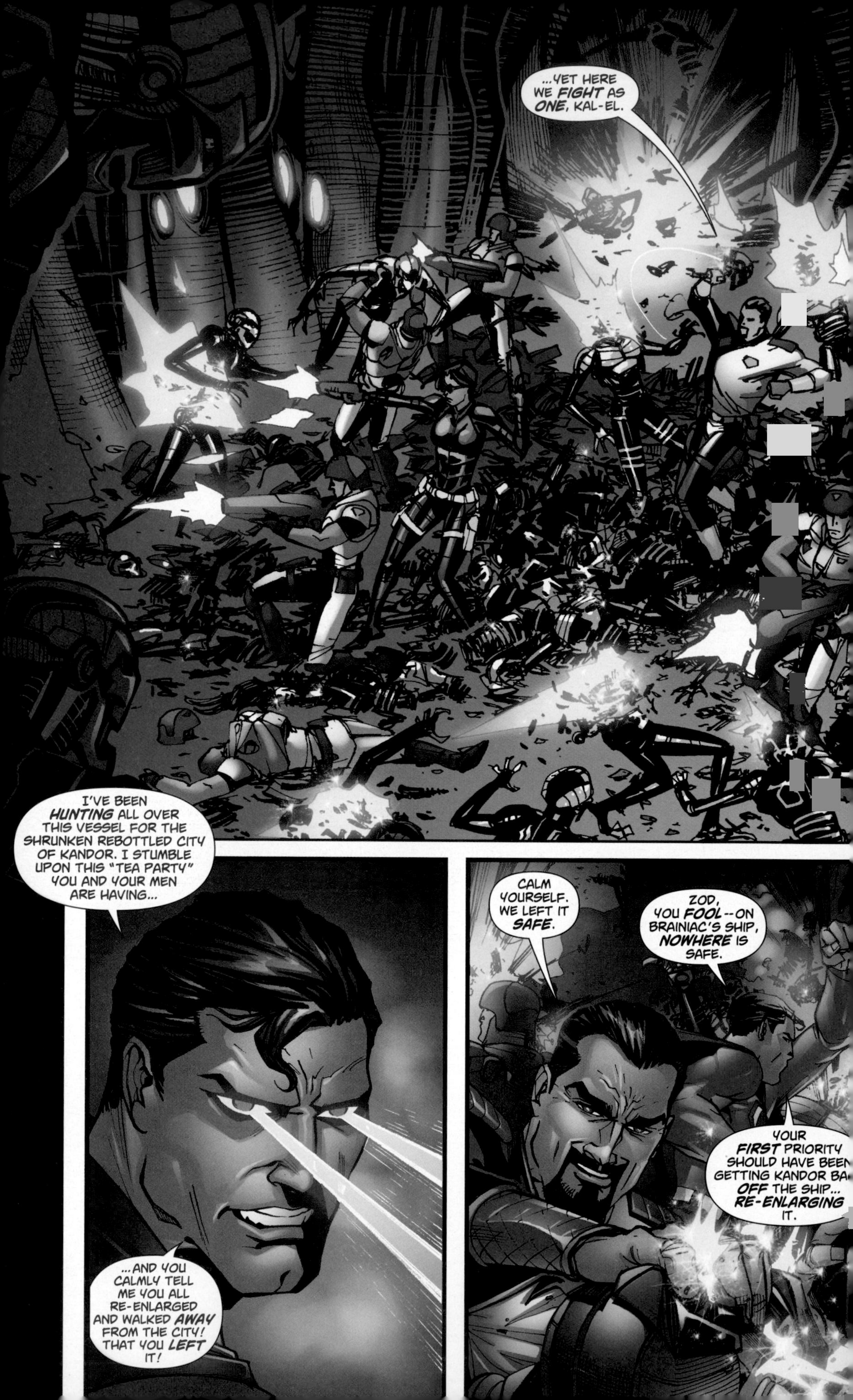
...YET HERE WE FIGHT AS ONE, KAL-EL.
I'VE BEEN HUNTING ALL OVER THIS VESSEL FOR THE SHRUNKEN REBOTTLED CITY OF KANDOR. I STUMBLE UPON THIS "TEA PARTY" YOU AND YOUR MEN ARE HAVING...
...AND YOU CALMLY TELL ME YOU ALL RE-ENLARGED AND WALKED AWAY FROM THE CITY! THAT YOU LEFT IT!
CALM YOURSELF. WE LEFT IT SAFE.
ZOD, YOU FOOL--ON BRAINIAC'S SHIP, NOWHERE IS SAFE.
YOUR FIRST PRIORITY SHOULD HAVE BEEN GETTING KANDOR BA OFF THE SHIP... RE-ENLARGING IT.

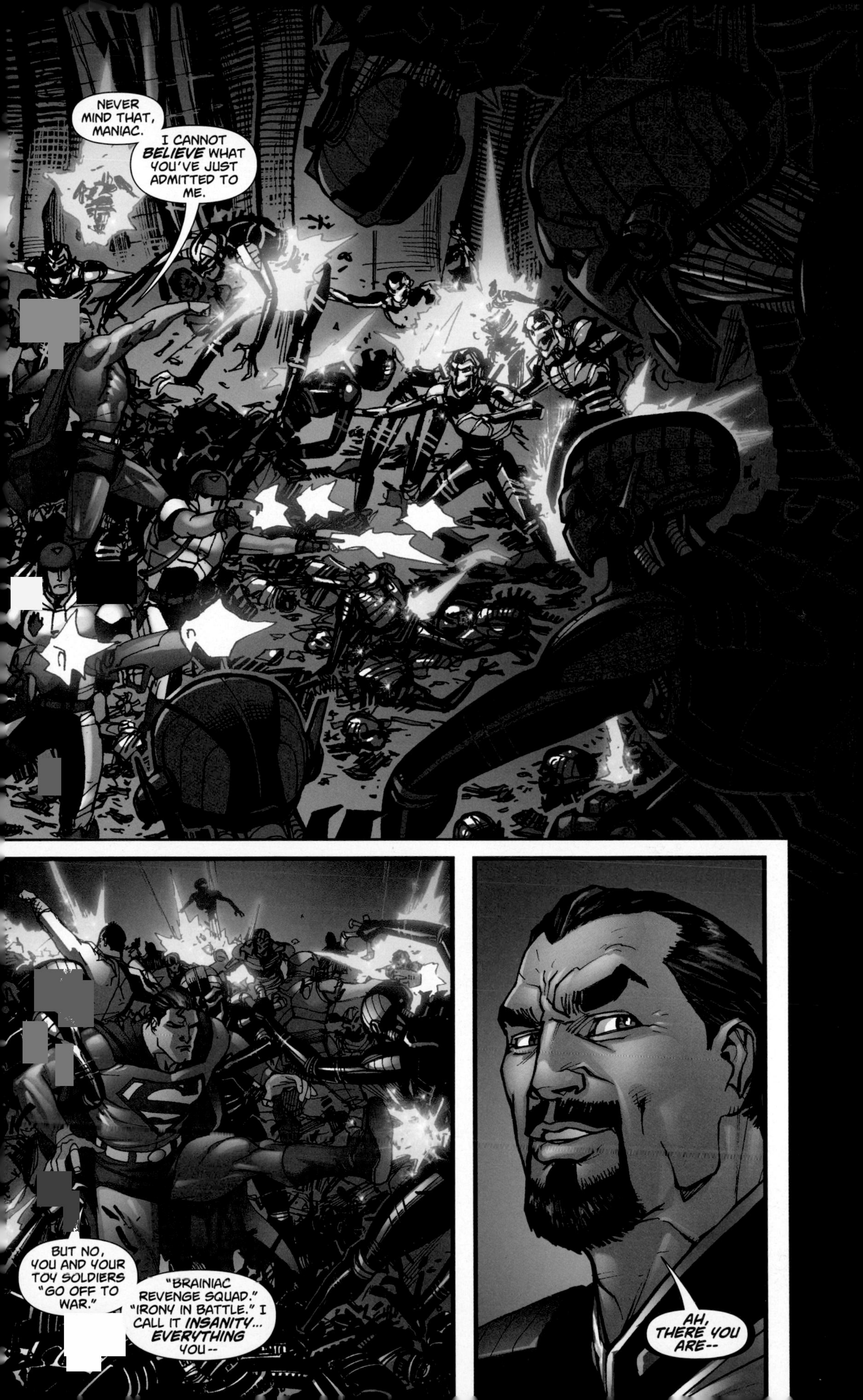
NEVER MIND THAT, MANIAC.
I CANNOT BELIEVE WHAT YOU'VE JUST ADMITTED TO ME.
BUT NO, YOU AND YOUR TOY SOLDIERS "GO OFF TO WAR."
"BRAINIAC REVENGE SQUAD." "IRONY IN BATTLE." I CALL IT INSANITY... EVERYTHING YOU --
AH, THERE YOU ARE--

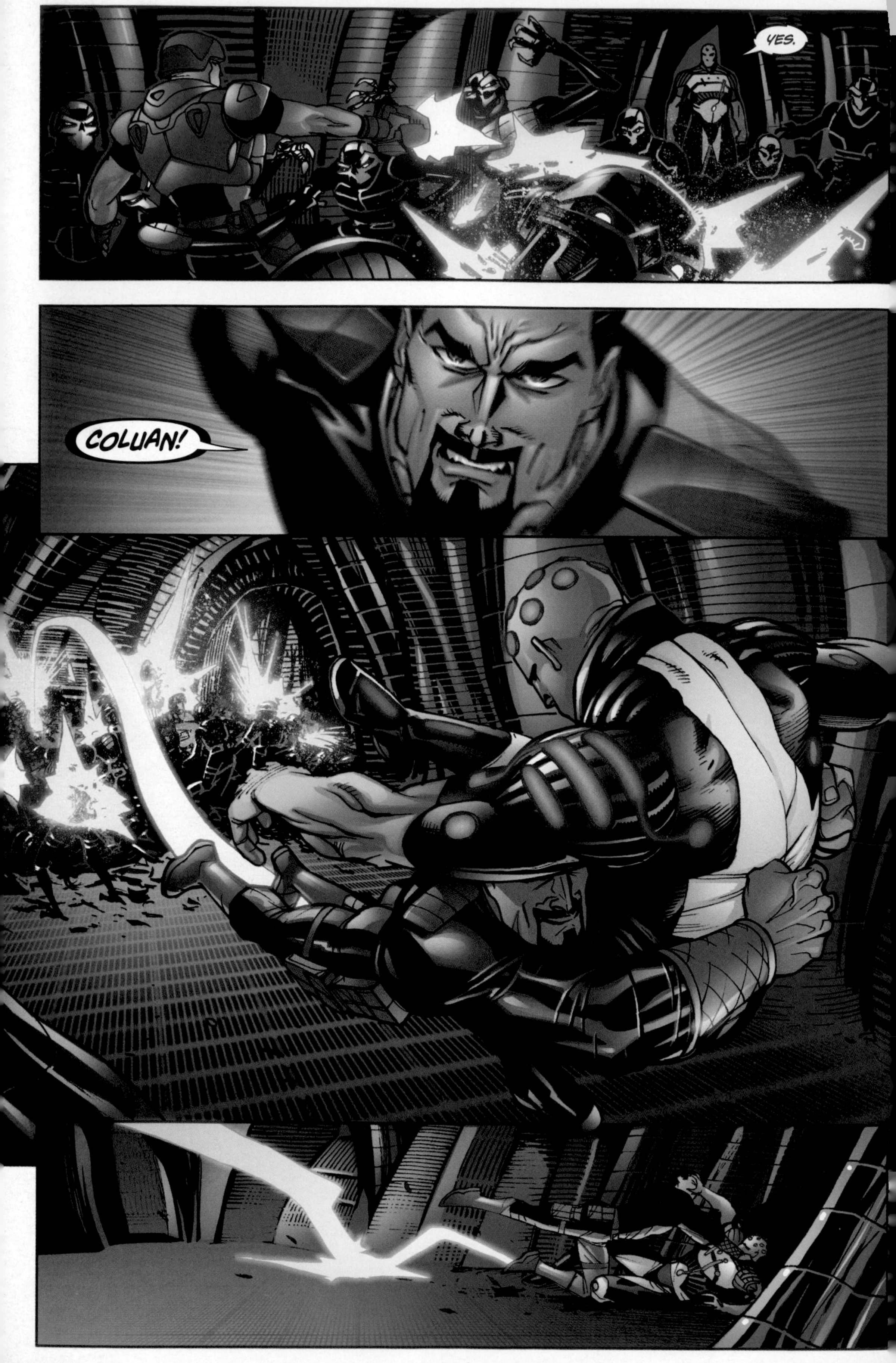
YES.
COLUAN!

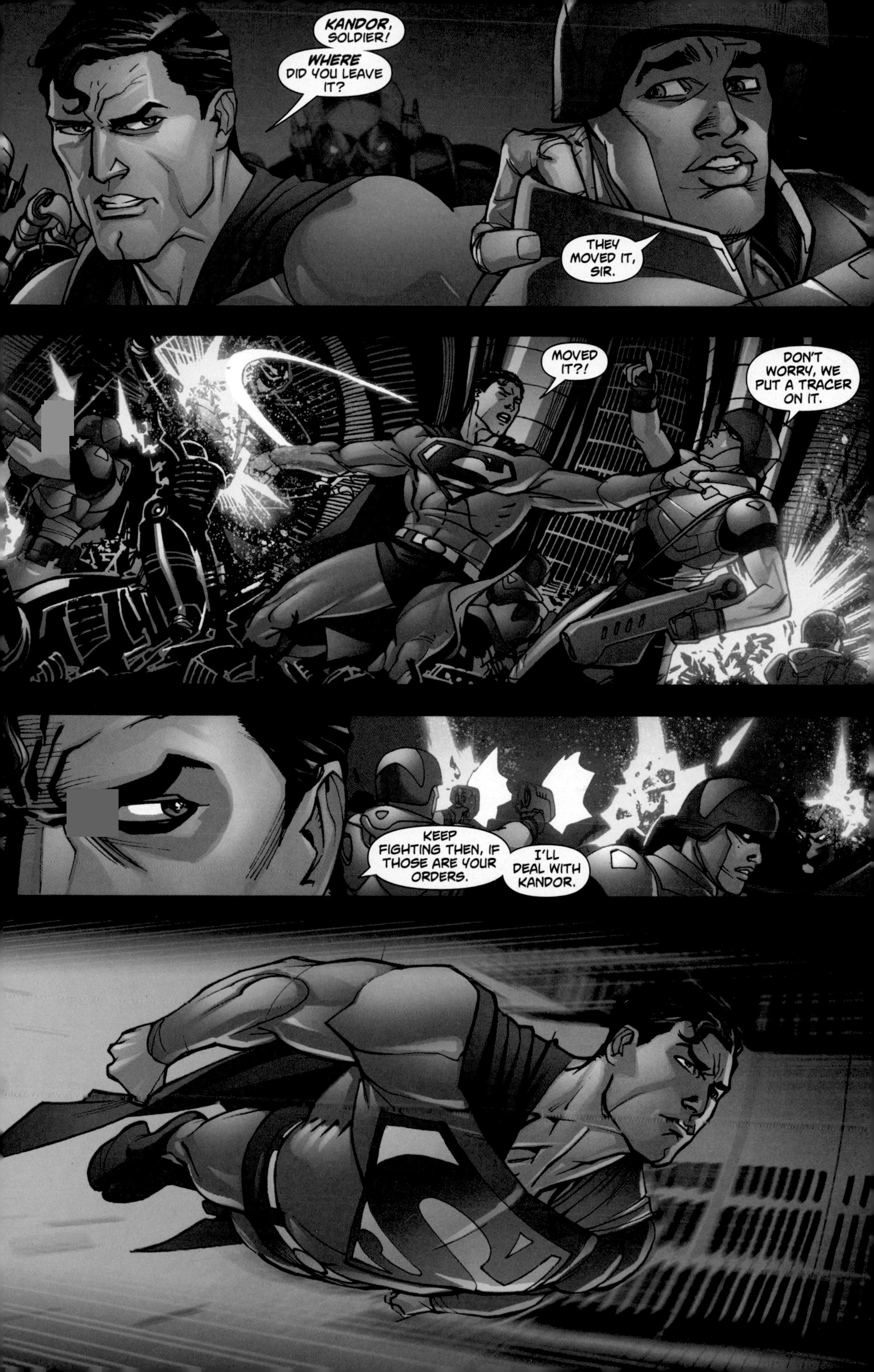

KANDOR, SOLDIER!
WHERE DID YOU LEAVE IT?
THEY MOVED IT, SIR.
MOVED IT?!
DON'T WORRY, WE PUT A TRACER ON IT.
KEEP FIGHTING THEN, IF THOSE ARE YOUR ORDERS.
I'LL DEAL WITH KANDOR.

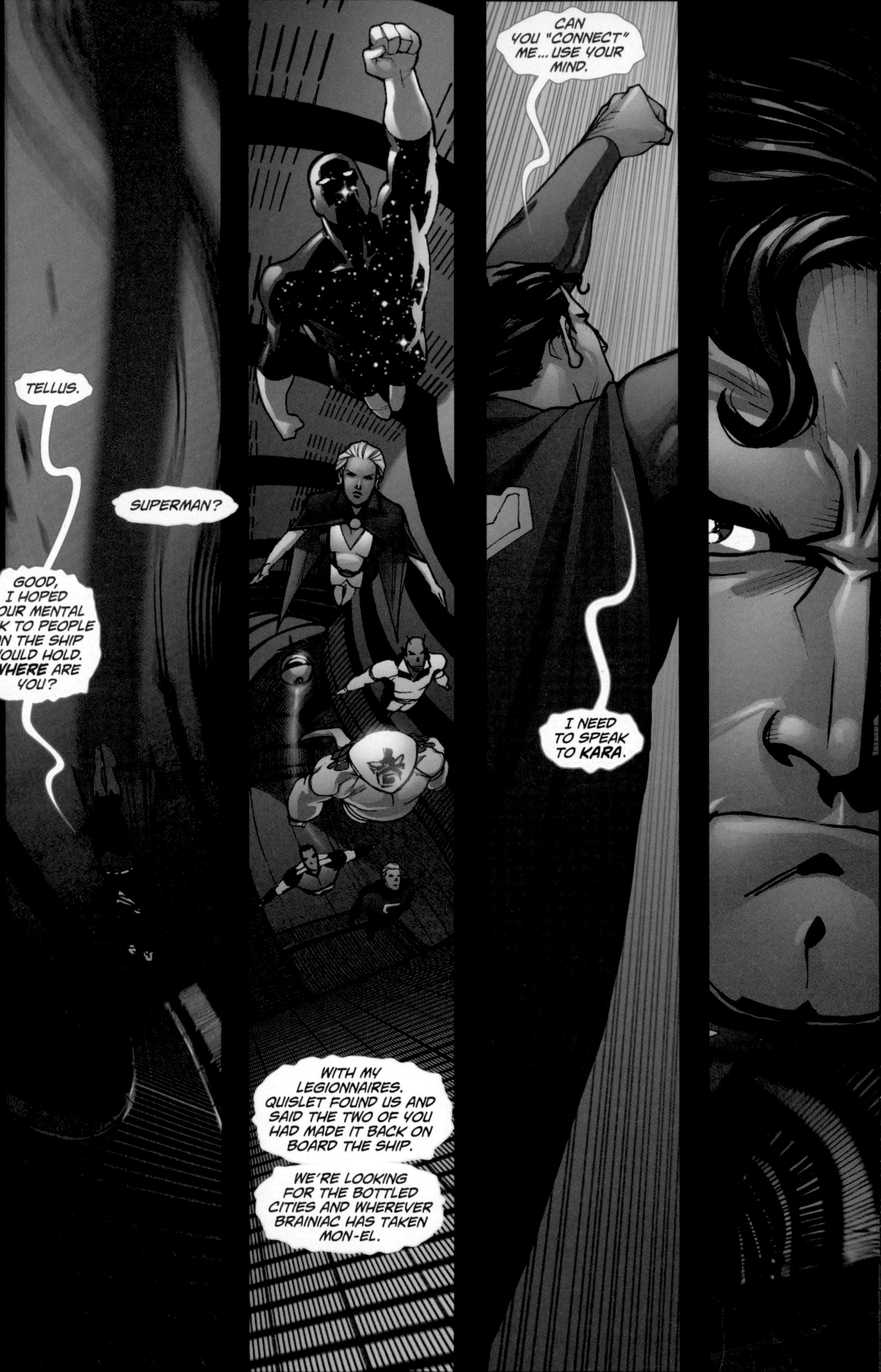
TELLUS.
SUPERMAN?
GOOD, I HOPED YOUR MENTAL LINK TO PEOPLE ON THE SHIP WOULD HOLD. **WHERE** ARE YOU?
WITH MY LEGIONNAIRES. QUISLET FOUND US AND SAID THE TWO OF YOU HAD MADE IT BACK ON BOARD THE SHIP.
WE'RE LOOKING FOR THE BOTTLED CITIES AND WHEREVER BRAINIAC HAS TAKEN MON-EL.
CAN YOU "CONNECT" ME... USE YOUR MIND.
I NEED TO SPEAK TO **KARA**.

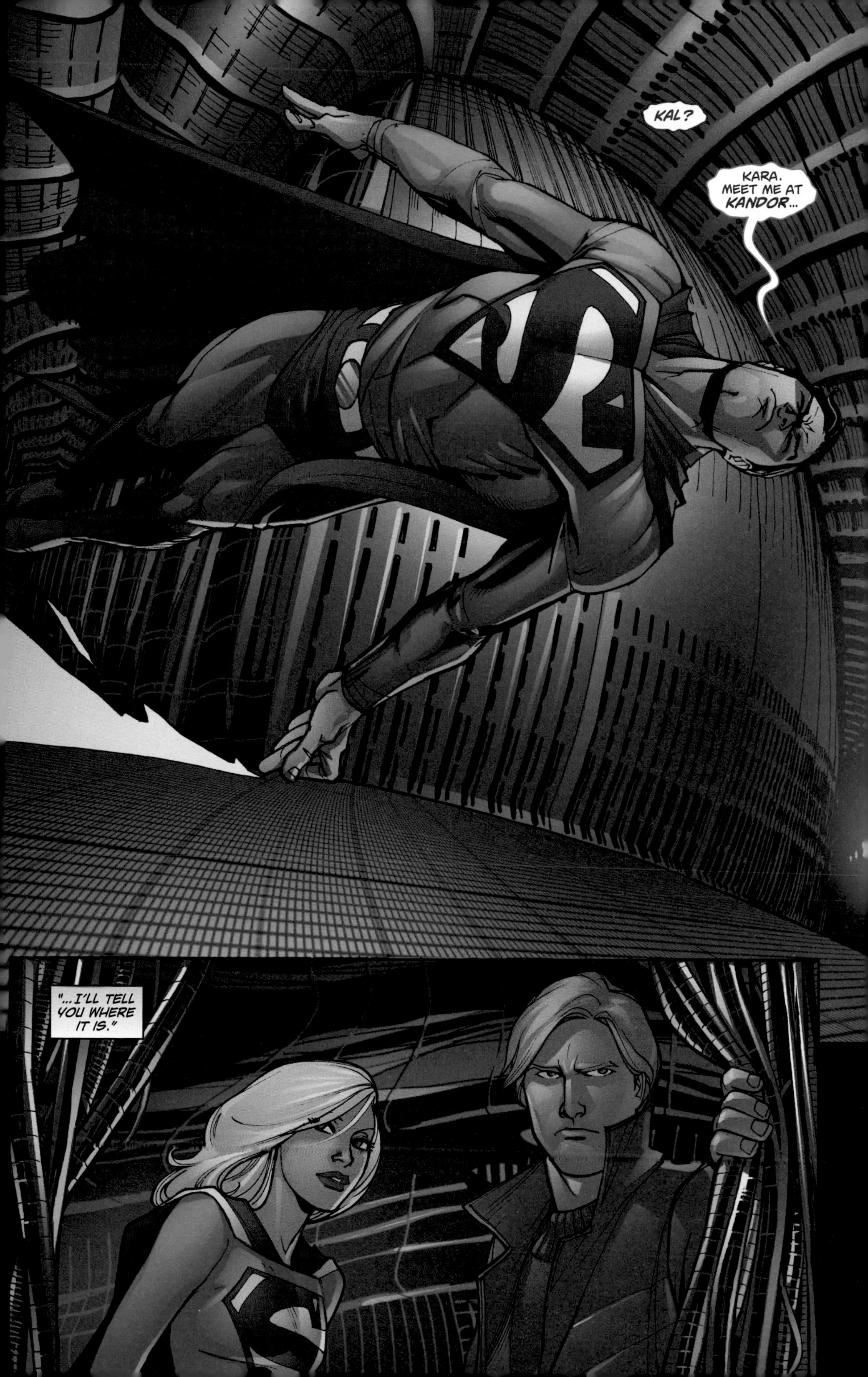
KAL?
KARA. MEET ME AT KANDOR...
"...I'LL TELL YOU WHERE IT IS."

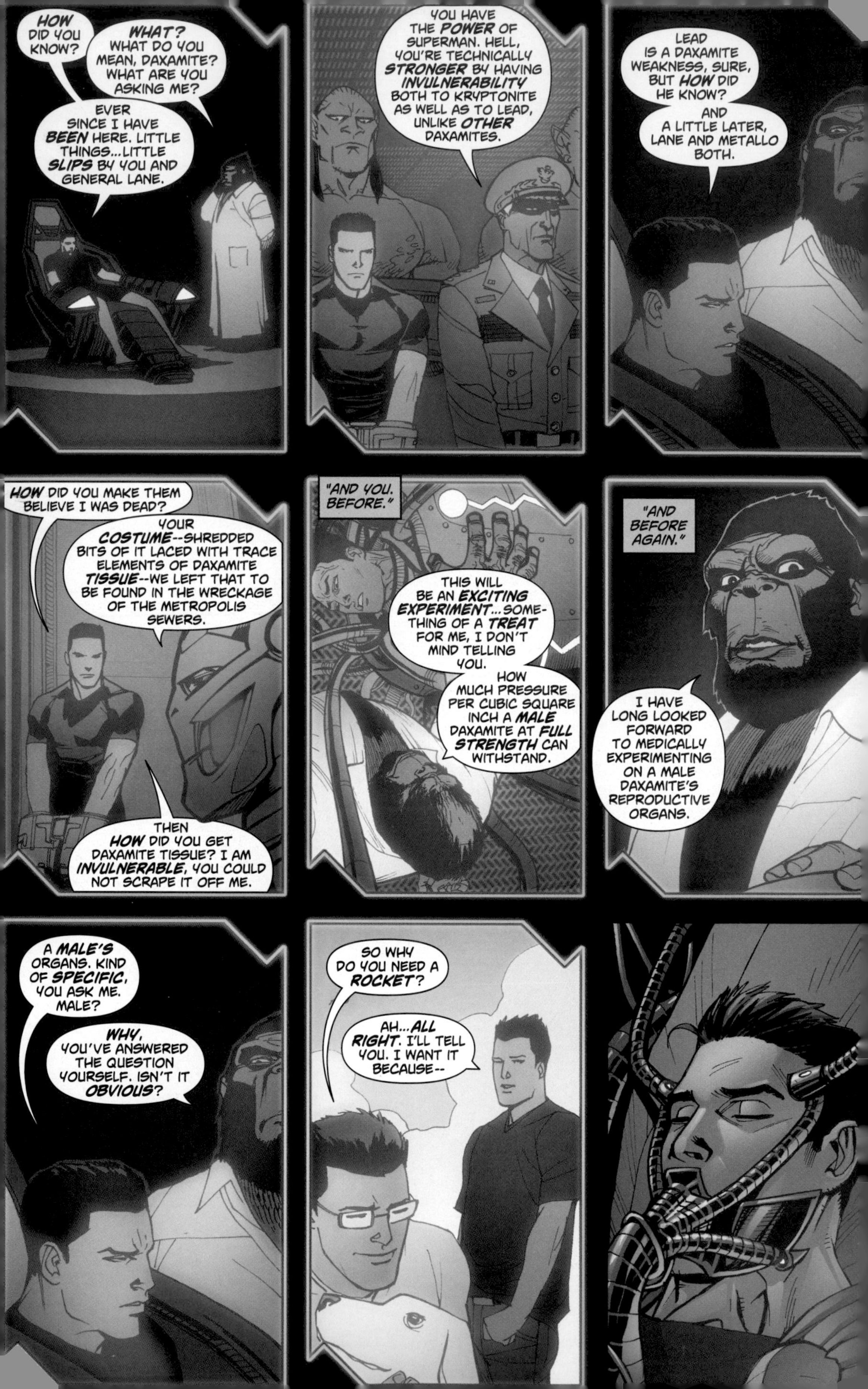
HOW DID YOU KNOW?
WHAT? WHAT DO YOU MEAN, DAXAMITE? WHAT ARE YOU ASKING ME?
EVER SINCE I HAVE BEEN HERE. LITTLE THINGS...LITTLE SLIPS BY YOU AND GENERAL LANE.
YOU HAVE THE POWER OF SUPERMAN. HELL, YOU'RE TECHNICALLY STRONGER BY HAVING INVULNERABILITY BOTH TO KRYPTONITE AS WELL AS TO LEAD, UNLIKE OTHER DAXAMITES.
LEAD IS A DAXAMITE WEAKNESS, SURE, BUT HOW DID HE KNOW?
AND A LITTLE LATER, LANE AND METALLO BOTH.
HOW DID YOU MAKE THEM BELIEVE I WAS DEAD?
YOUR COSTUME--SHREDDED BITS OF IT LACED WITH TRACE ELEMENTS OF DAXAMITE TISSUE--WE LEFT THAT TO BE FOUND IN THE WRECKAGE OF THE METROPOLIS SEWERS.
THEN HOW DID YOU GET DAXAMITE TISSUE? I AM INVULNERABLE, YOU COULD NOT SCRAPE IT OFF ME.
"AND YOU. BEFORE."
THIS WILL BE AN EXCITING EXPERIMENT...SOMETHING OF A TREAT FOR ME, I DON'T MIND TELLING YOU.
HOW MUCH PRESSURE PER CUBIC SQUARE INCH A MALE DAXAMITE AT FULL STRENGTH CAN WITHSTAND.
"AND BEFORE AGAIN."
I HAVE LONG LOOKED FORWARD TO MEDICALLY EXPERIMENTING ON A MALE DAXAMITE'S REPRODUCTIVE ORGANS.
A MALE'S ORGANS. KIND OF SPECIFIC, YOU ASK ME. MALE?
WHY, YOU'VE ANSWERED THE QUESTION YOURSELF. ISN'T IT OBVIOUS?
SO WHY DO YOU NEED A ROCKET?
AH...ALL RIGHT. I'LL TELL YOU. I WANT IT BECAUSE--

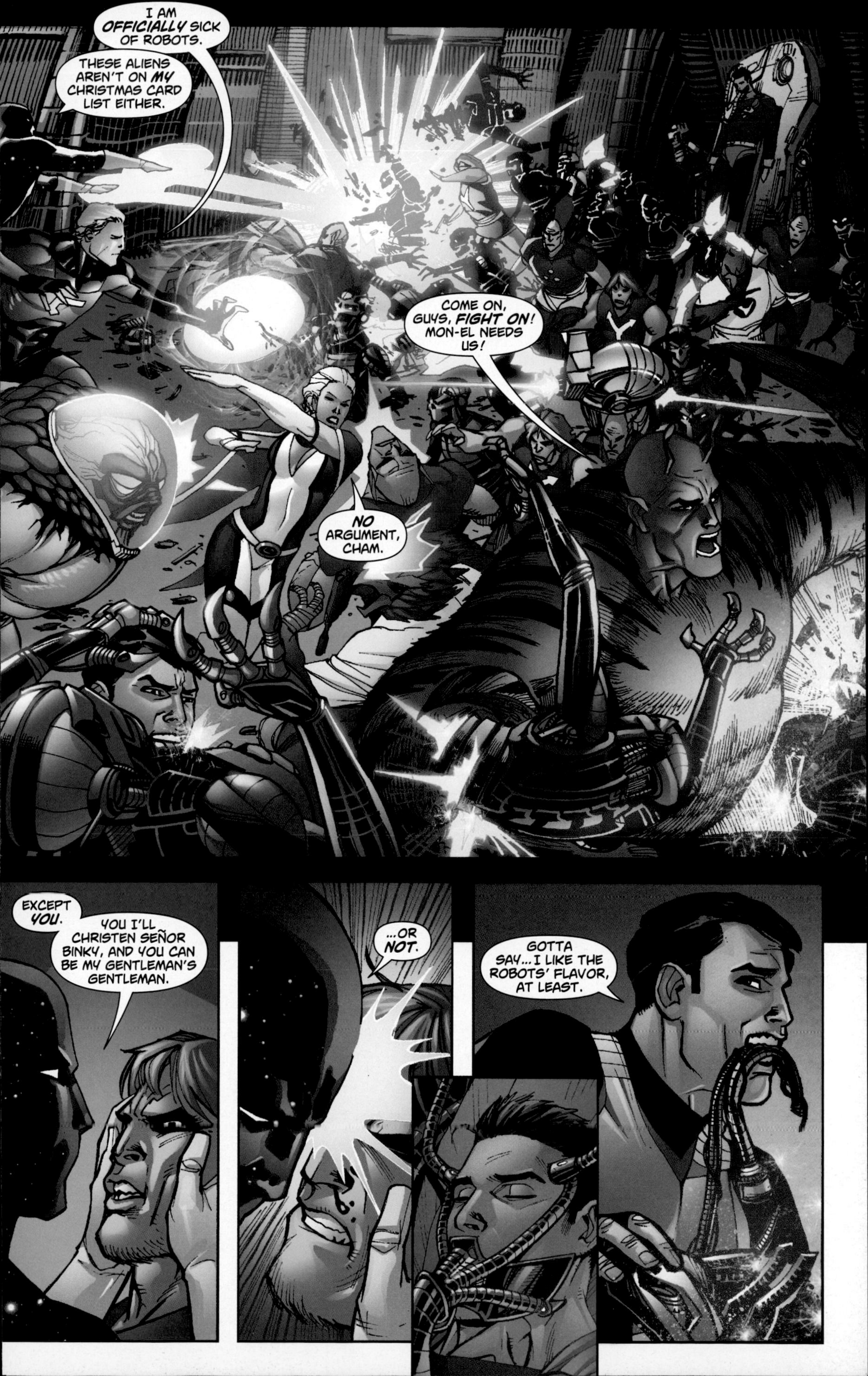
I AM OFFICIALLY SICK OF ROBOTS.
THESE ALIENS AREN'T ON MY CHRISTMAS CARD LIST EITHER.
COME ON, GUYS, FIGHT ON! MON-EL NEEDS US!
NO ARGUMENT, CHAM.
EXCEPT YOU.
YOU I'LL CHRISTEN SEÑOR BINKY, AND YOU CAN BE MY GENTLEMAN'S GENTLEMAN.
...OR NOT.
GOTTA SAY... I LIKE THE ROBOTS' FLAVOR, AT LEAST.

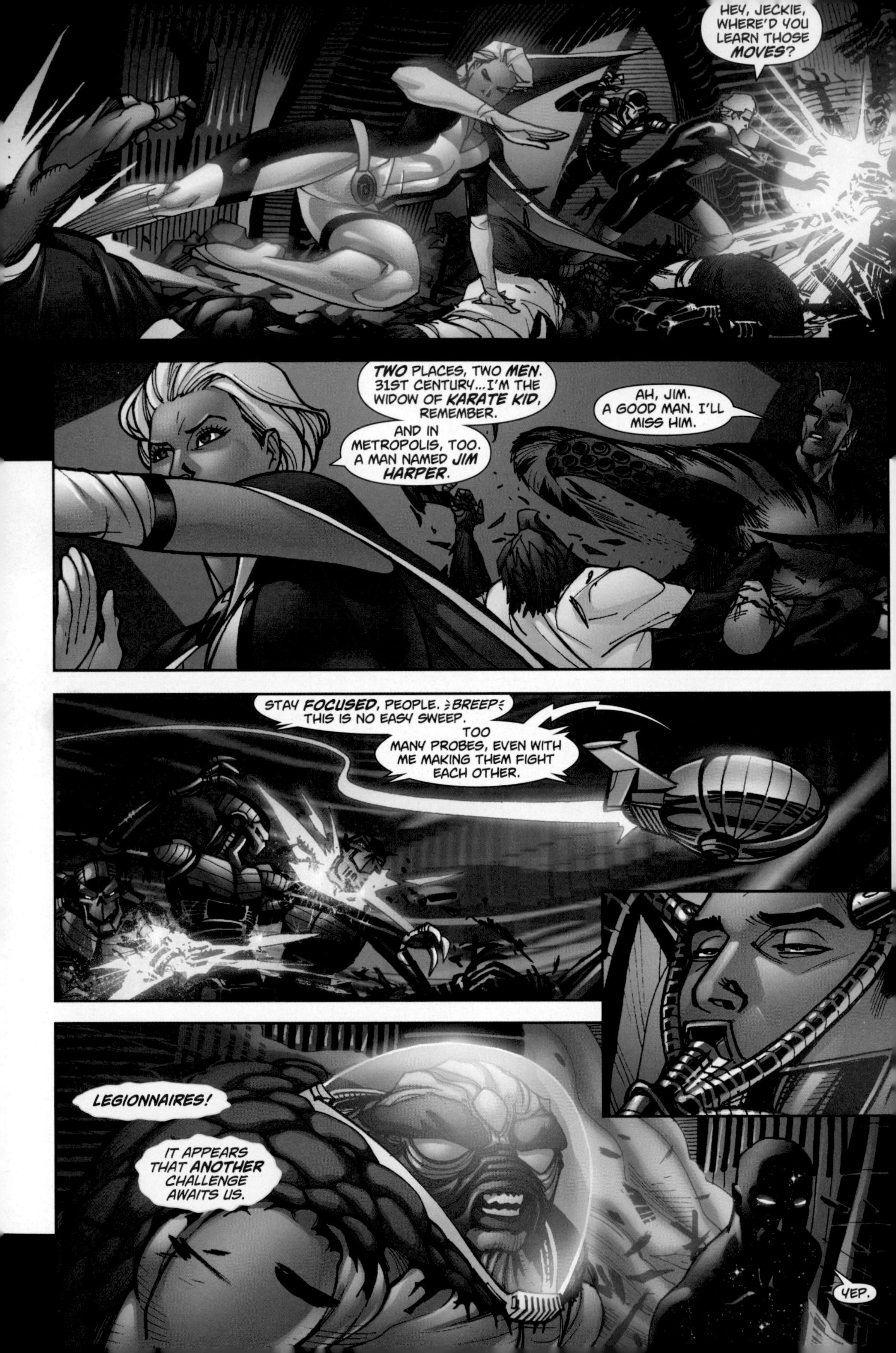
HEY, JECKIE, WHERE'D YOU LEARN THOSE MOVES?
TWO PLACES, TWO MEN. 31ST CENTURY...I'M THE WIDOW OF KARATE KID, REMEMBER.
AND IN METROPOLIS, TOO. A MAN NAMED JIM HARPER.
AH, JIM. A GOOD MAN. I'LL MISS HIM.
STAY FOCUSED, PEOPLE. BREEP THIS IS NO EASY SWEEP.
TOO MANY PROBES, EVEN WITH ME MAKING THEM FIGHT EACH OTHER.
LEGIONNAIRES!
IT APPEARS THAT ANOTHER CHALLENGE AWAITS US.
YEP.

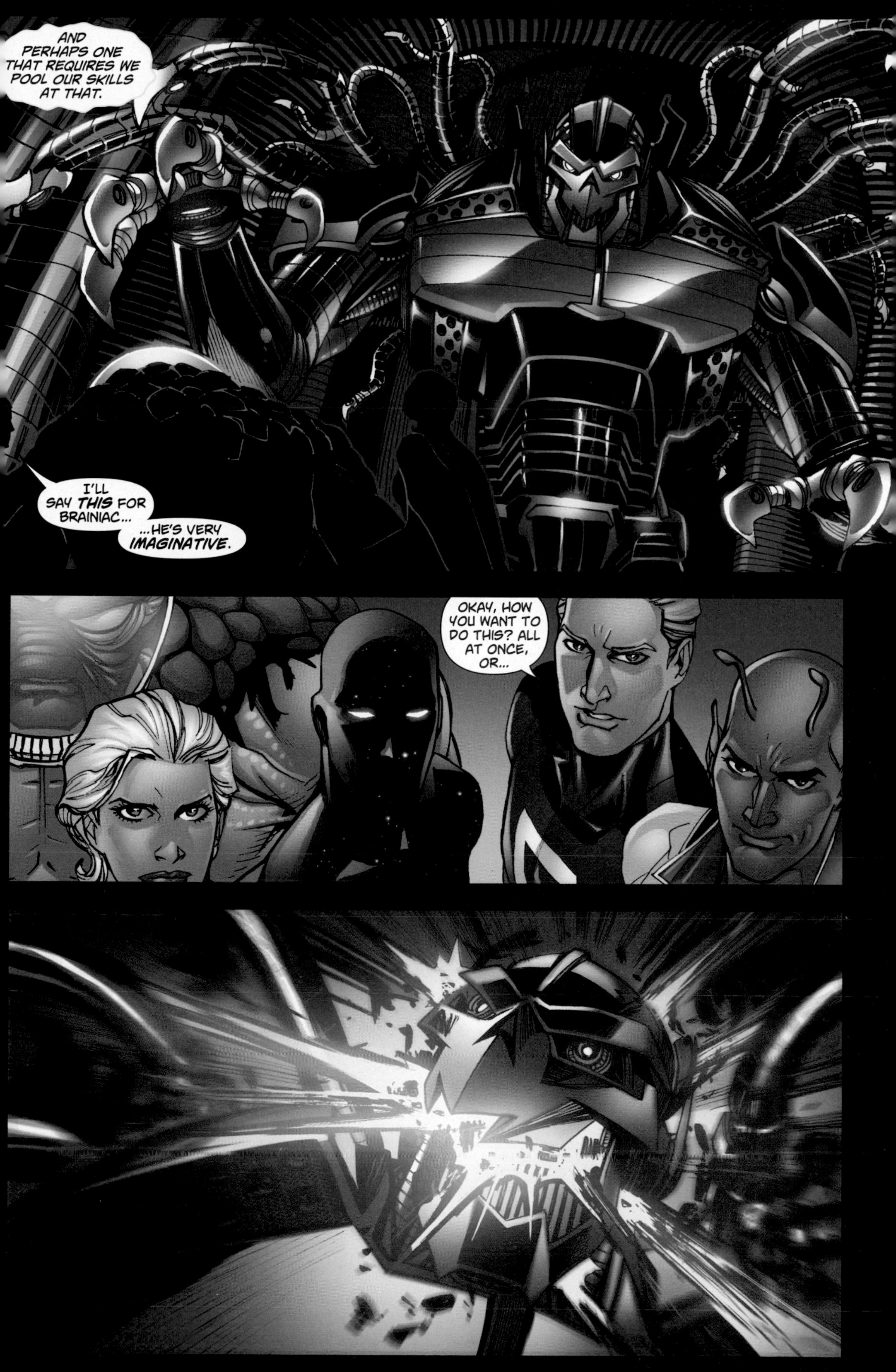
AND PERHAPS ONE THAT REQUIRES WE POOL OUR SKILLS AT THAT.
I'LL SAY **THIS** FOR BRAINIAC...
...HE'S VERY ***IMAGINATIVE***.
OKAY, HOW YOU WANT TO DO THIS? ALL AT ONCE, OR...

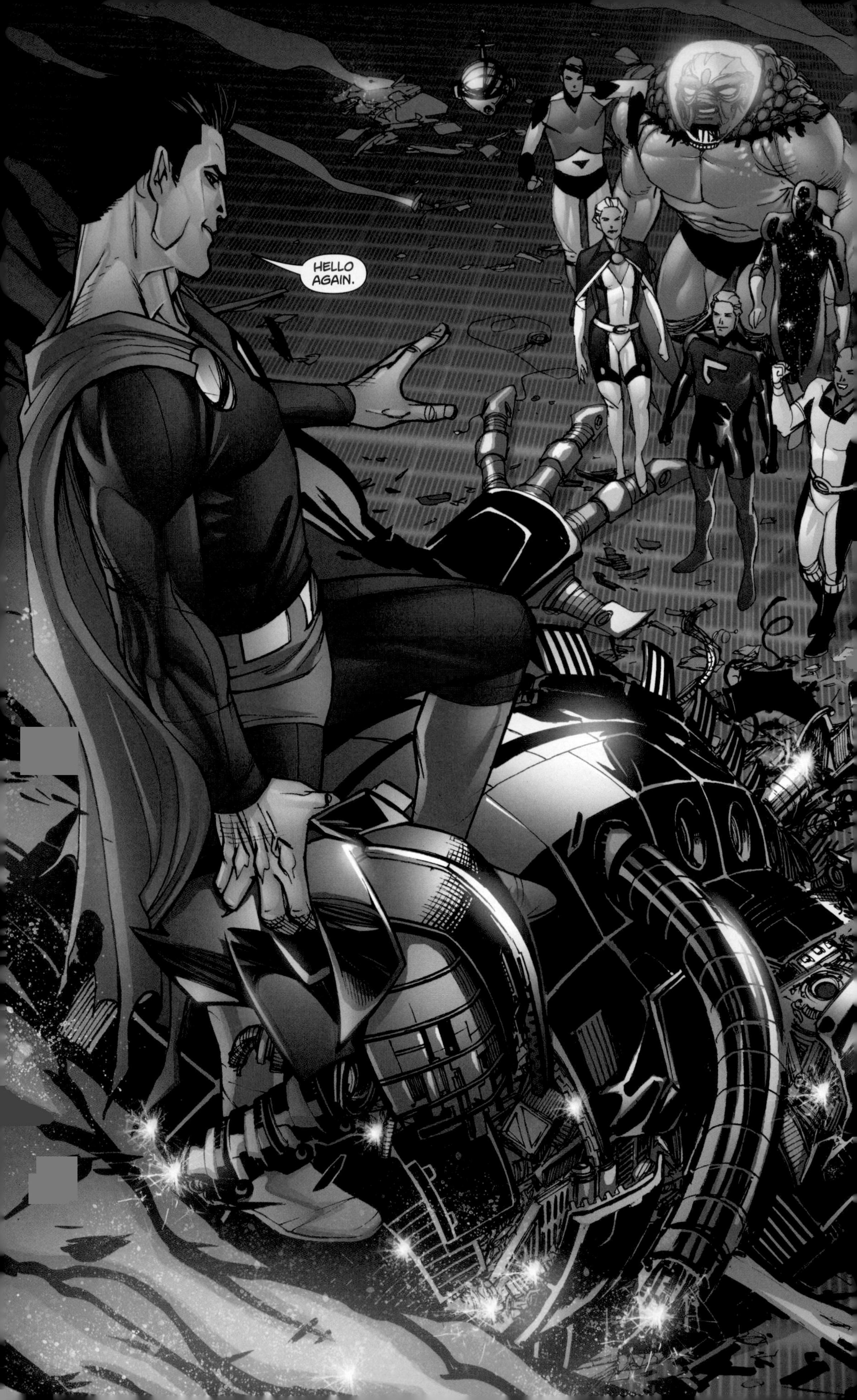
HELLO AGAIN.

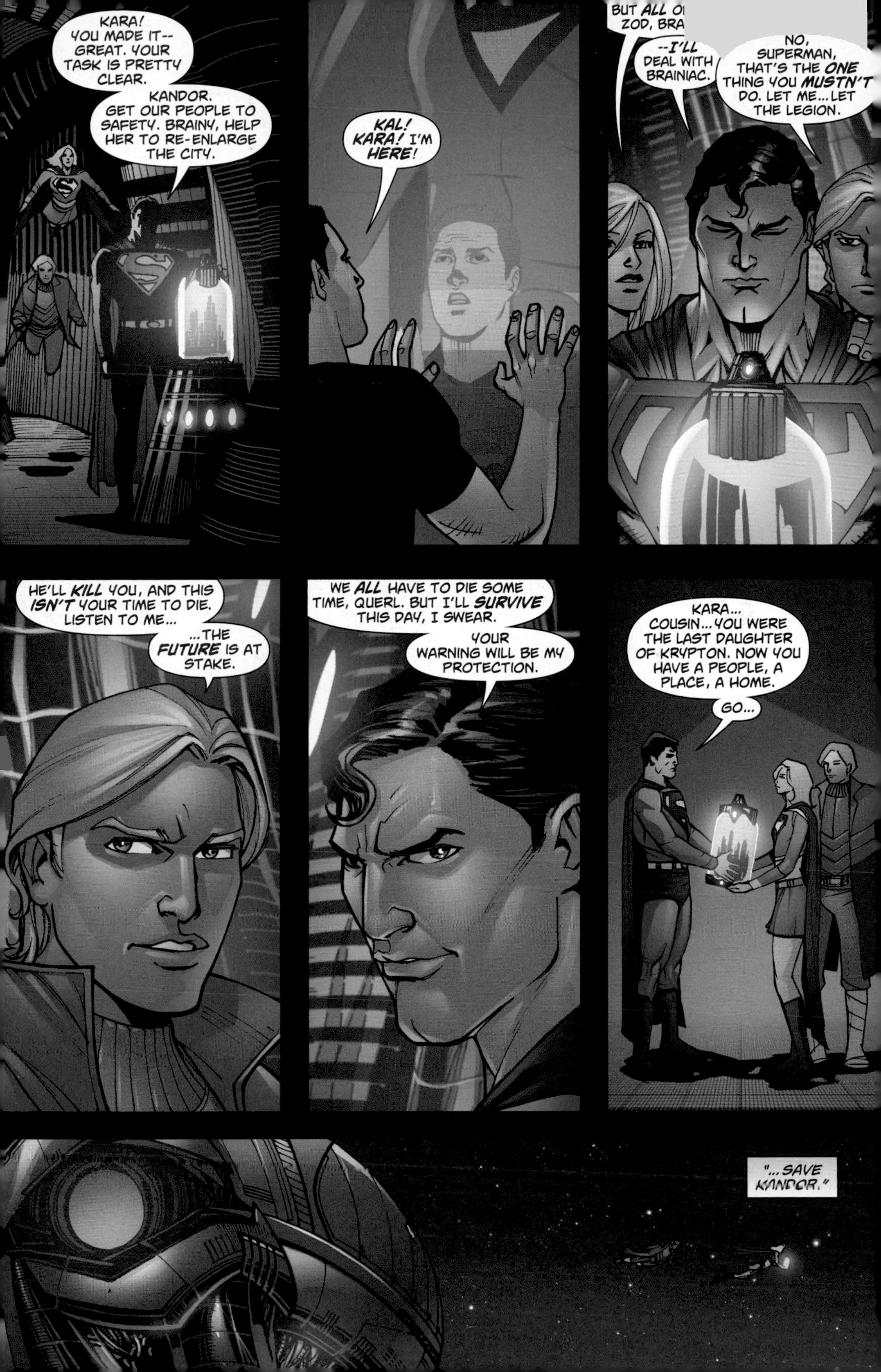
KARA! YOU MADE IT-- GREAT. YOUR TASK IS PRETTY CLEAR.
KANDOR. GET OUR PEOPLE TO SAFETY. BRAINY, HELP HER TO RE-ENLARGE THE CITY.
KAL! KARA! I'M HERE!
BUT ALL OF ZOD, BRA
--I'LL DEAL WITH BRAINIAC.
NO, SUPERMAN, THAT'S THE ONE THING YOU MUSTN'T DO. LET ME...LET THE LEGION.
HE'LL KILL YOU, AND THIS ISN'T YOUR TIME TO DIE. LISTEN TO ME...
...THE FUTURE IS AT STAKE.
WE ALL HAVE TO DIE SOME TIME, QUERL. BUT I'LL SURVIVE THIS DAY, I SWEAR.
YOUR WARNING WILL BE MY PROTECTION.
KARA... COUSIN...YOU WERE THE LAST DAUGHTER OF KRYPTON. NOW YOU HAVE A PEOPLE, A PLACE, A HOME.
GO...
"...SAVE KANDOR."

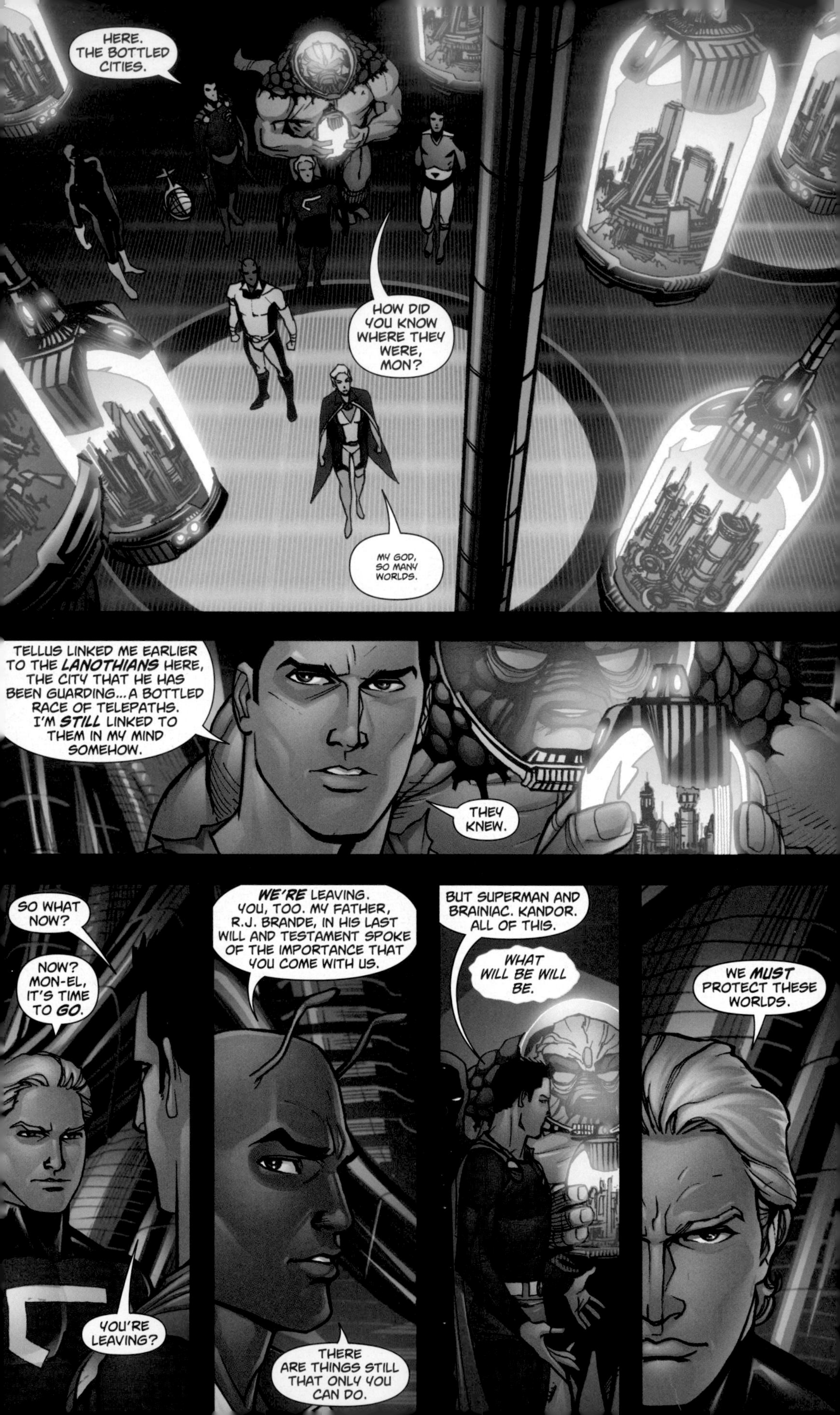
HERE. THE BOTTLED CITIES.
HOW DID YOU KNOW WHERE THEY WERE, MON?
MY GOD, SO MANY WORLDS.
TELLUS LINKED ME EARLIER TO THE LANOTHIANS HERE, THE CITY THAT HE HAS BEEN GUARDING... A BOTTLED RACE OF TELEPATHS. I'M STILL LINKED TO THEM IN MY MIND SOMEHOW.
THEY KNEW.
SO WHAT NOW?
NOW? MON-EL, IT'S TIME TO GO.
YOU'RE LEAVING?
WE'RE LEAVING. YOU, TOO. MY FATHER, R.J. BRANDE, IN HIS LAST WILL AND TESTAMENT SPOKE OF THE IMPORTANCE THAT YOU COME WITH US.
THERE ARE THINGS STILL THAT ONLY YOU CAN DO.
BUT SUPERMAN AND BRAINIAC. KANDOR. ALL OF THIS.
WHAT WILL BE WILL BE.
WE MUST PROTECT THESE WORLDS.

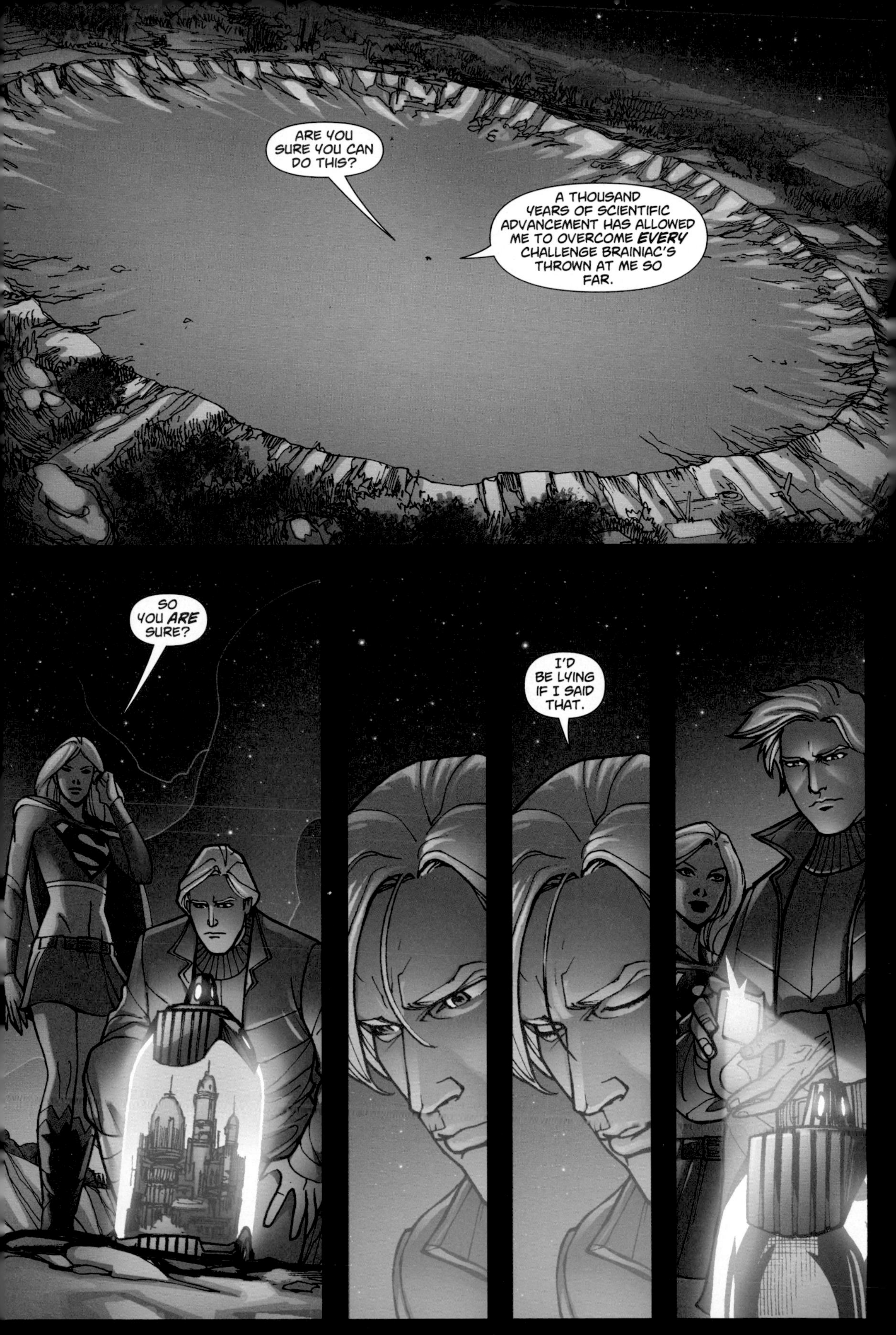
ARE YOU SURE YOU CAN DO THIS?
A THOUSAND YEARS OF SCIENTIFIC ADVANCEMENT HAS ALLOWED ME TO OVERCOME EVERY CHALLENGE BRAINIAC'S THROWN AT ME SO FAR.
SO YOU ARE SURE?
I'D BE LYING IF I SAID THAT.

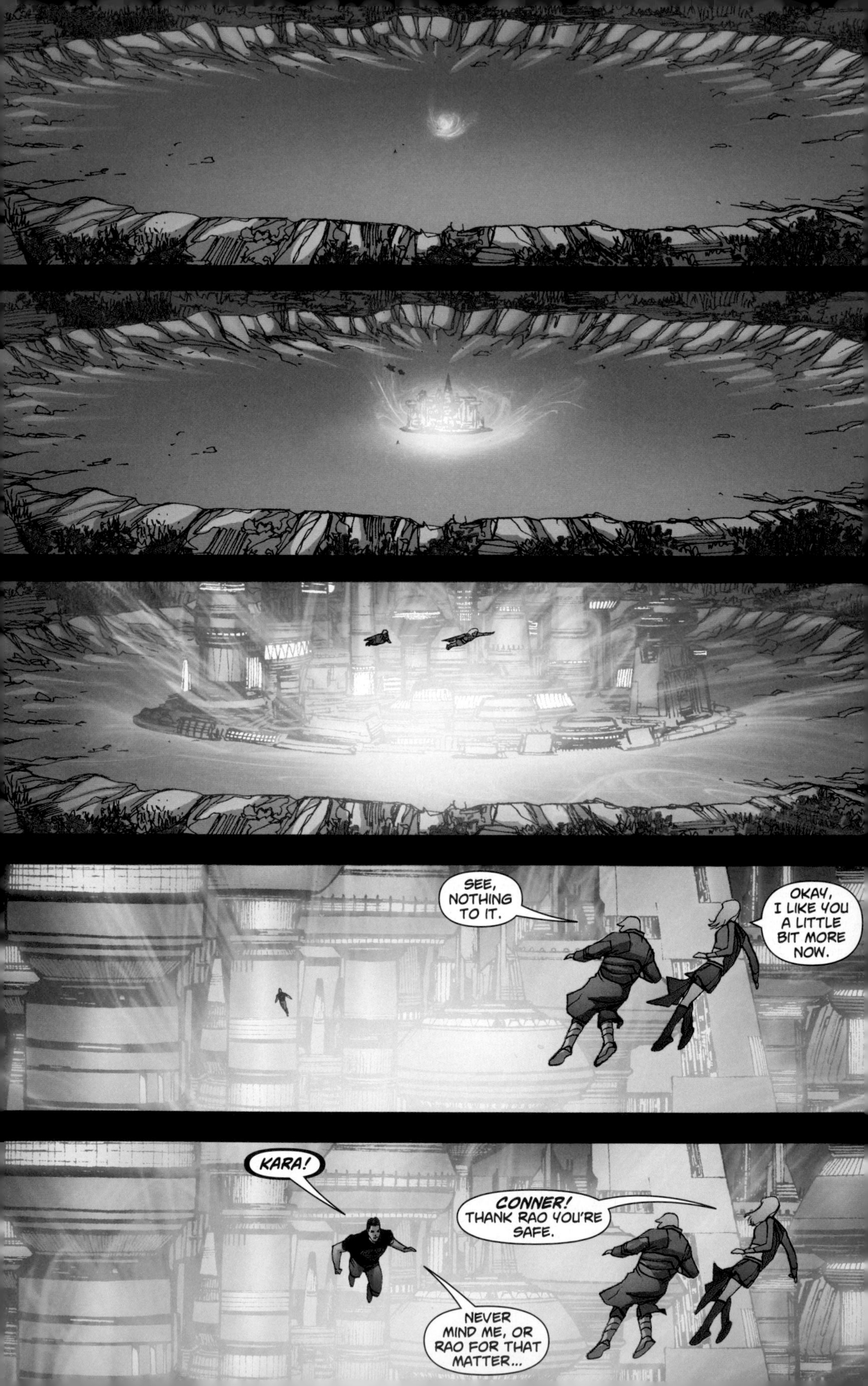
SEE, NOTHING TO IT.
OKAY, I LIKE YOU A LITTLE BIT MORE NOW.
KARA!
CONNER! THANK RAO YOU'RE SAFE.
NEVER MIND ME, OR RAO FOR THAT MATTER...

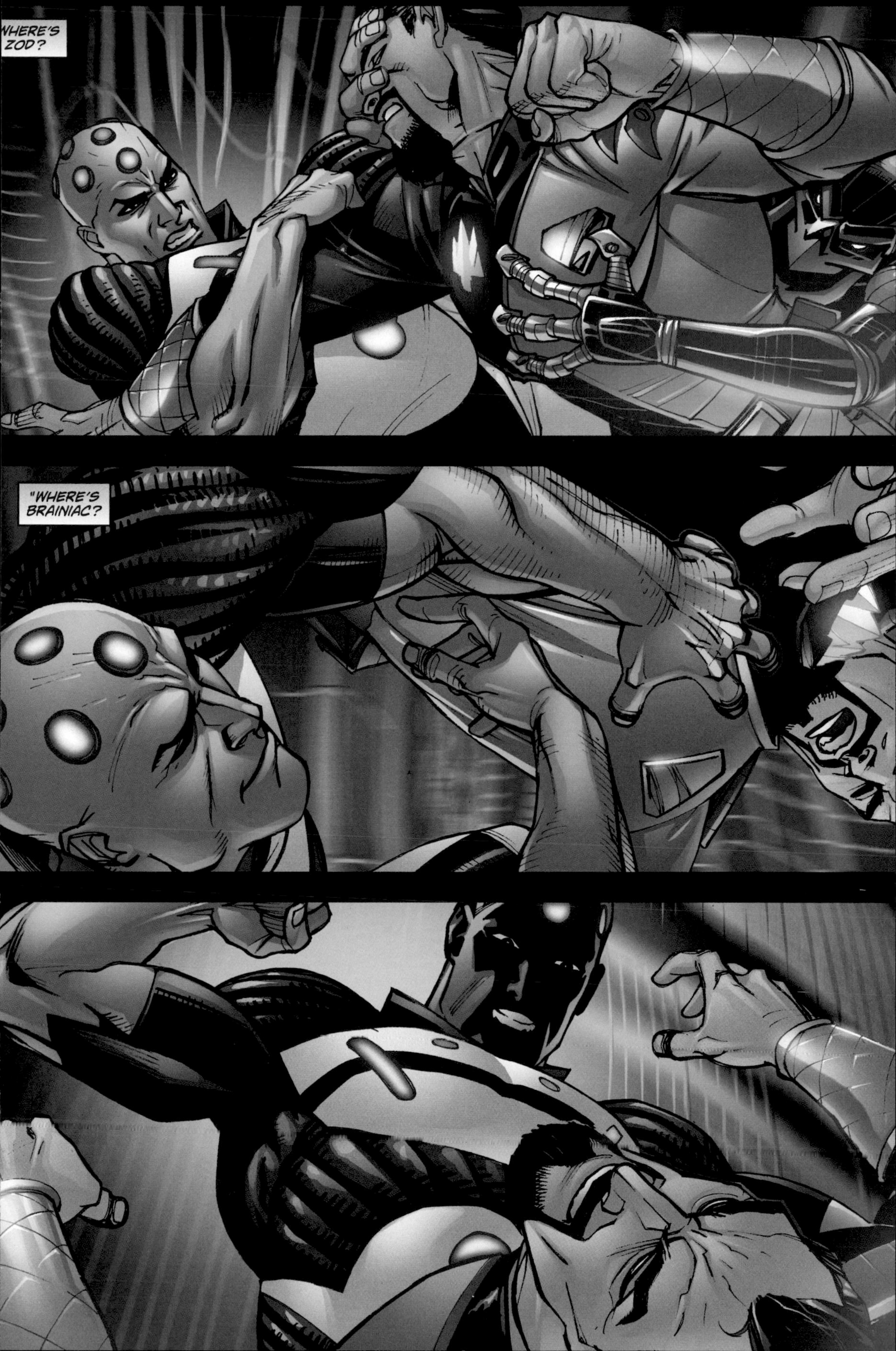
WHERE'S ZOD?
"WHERE'S BRAINIAC?

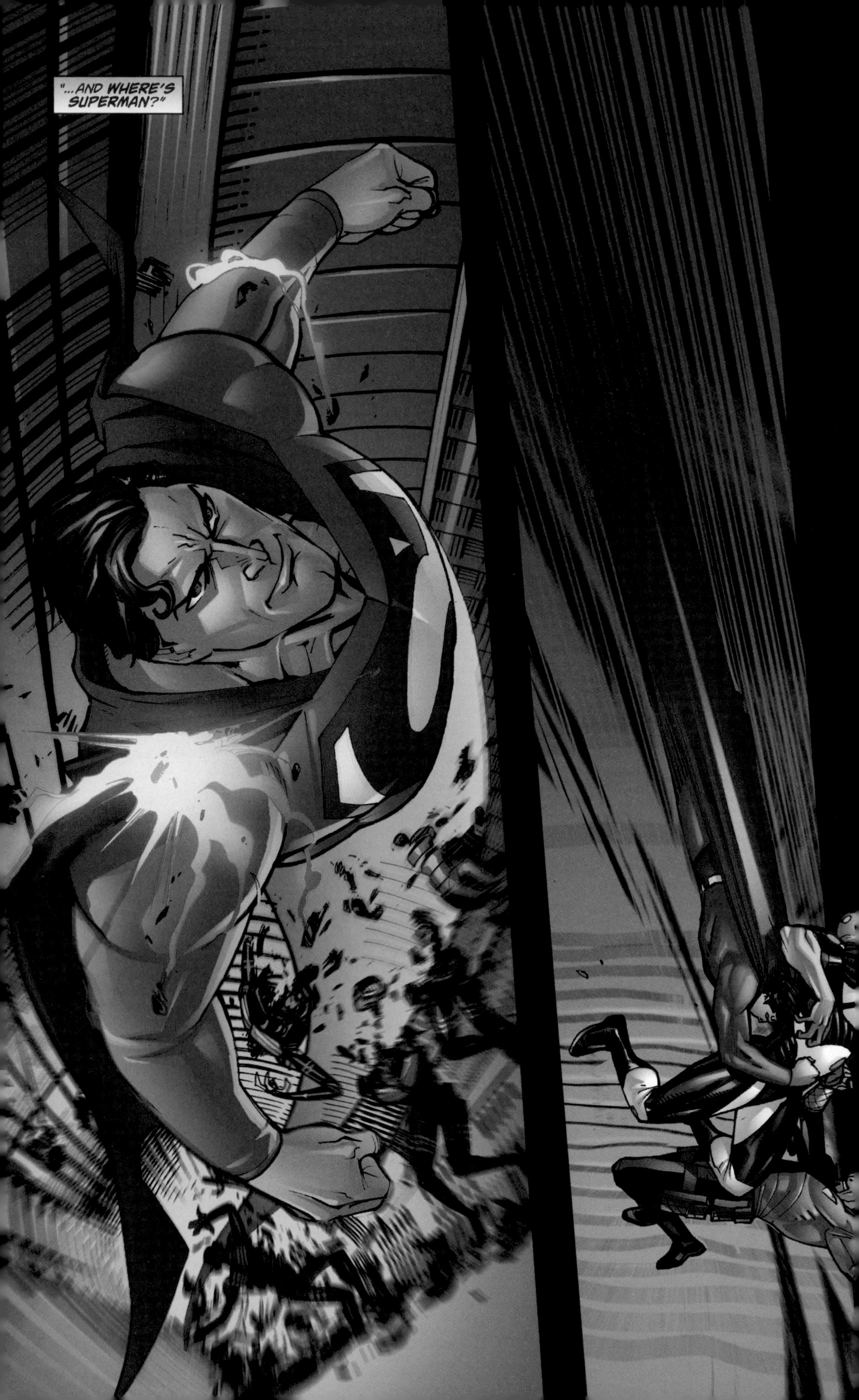
"...AND WHERE'S SUPERMAN?"

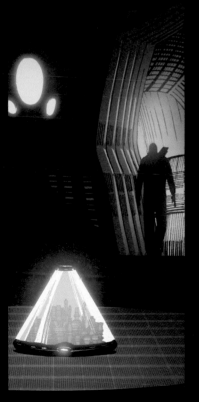

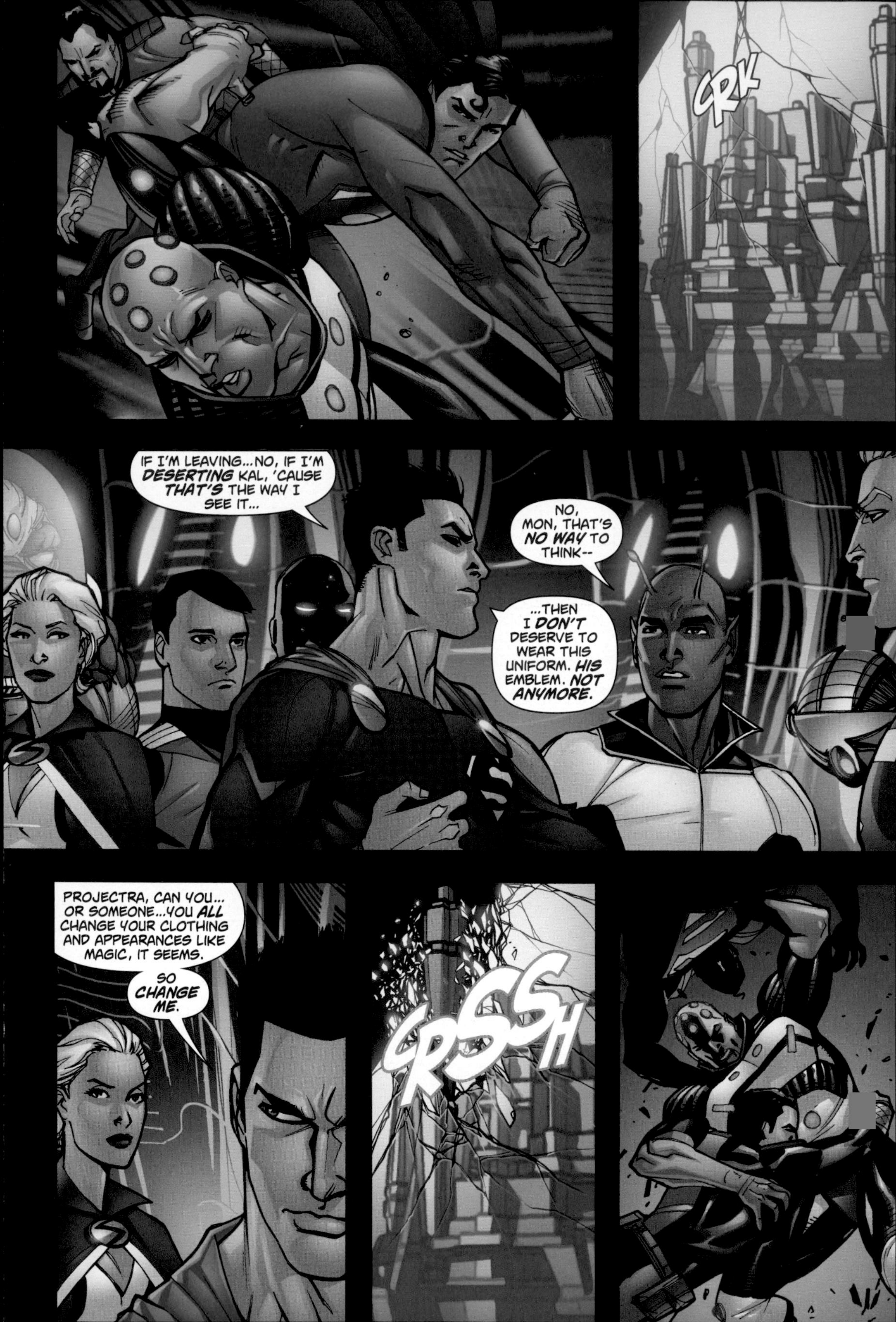
CRK
IF I'M LEAVING...NO, IF I'M DESERTING KAL, 'CAUSE THAT'S THE WAY I SEE IT...
NO, MON, THAT'S NO WAY TO THINK--
...THEN I DON'T DESERVE TO WEAR THIS UNIFORM. HIS EMBLEM. NOT ANYMORE.
PROJECTRA, CAN YOU... OR SOMEONE...YOU ALL CHANGE YOUR CLOTHING AND APPEARANCES LIKE MAGIC, IT SEEMS.
SO CHANGE ME.
CRSSSH

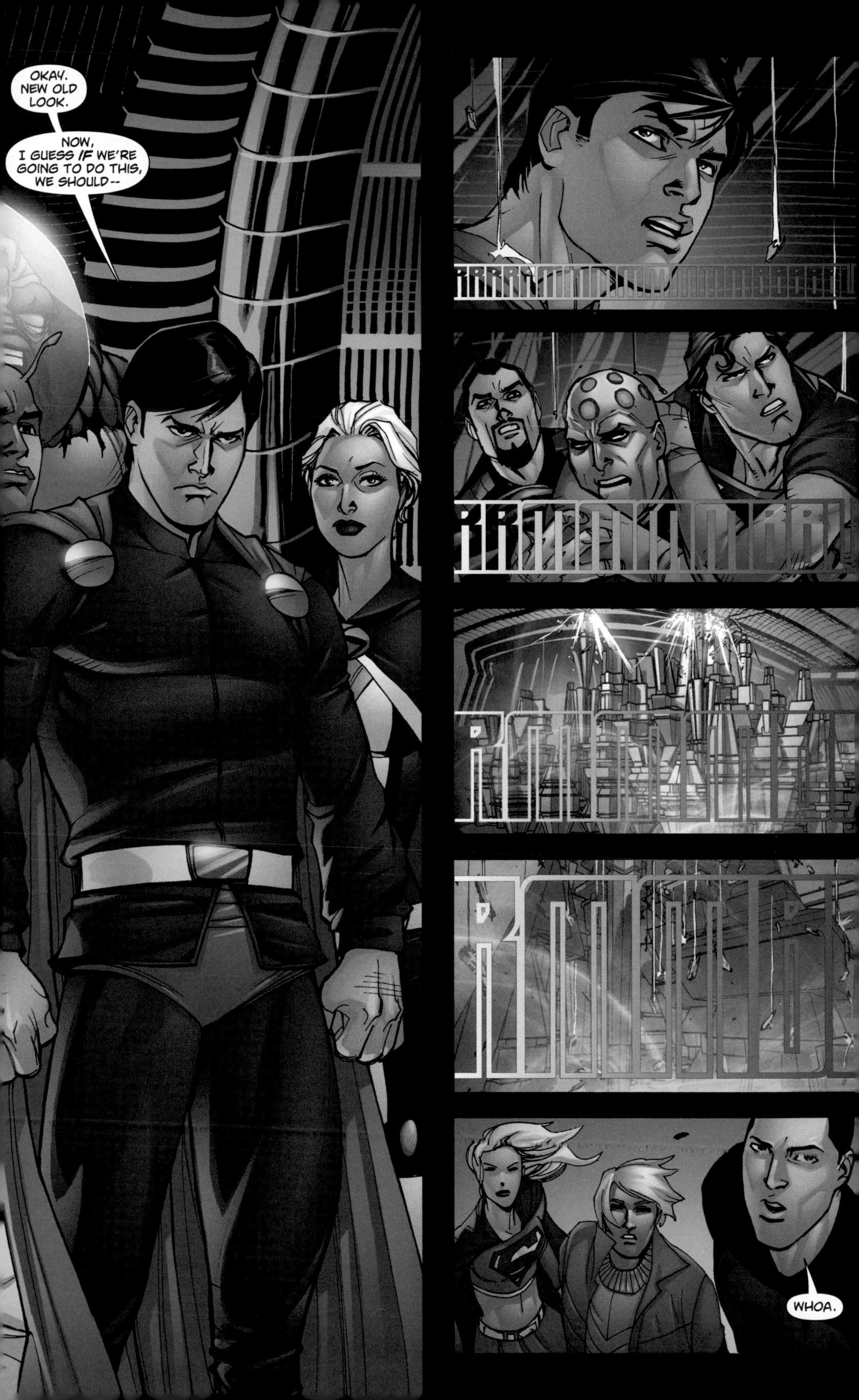
OKAY. NEW OLD LOOK.
NOW, I GUESS IF WE'RE GOING TO DO THIS, WE SHOULD--
WHOA.

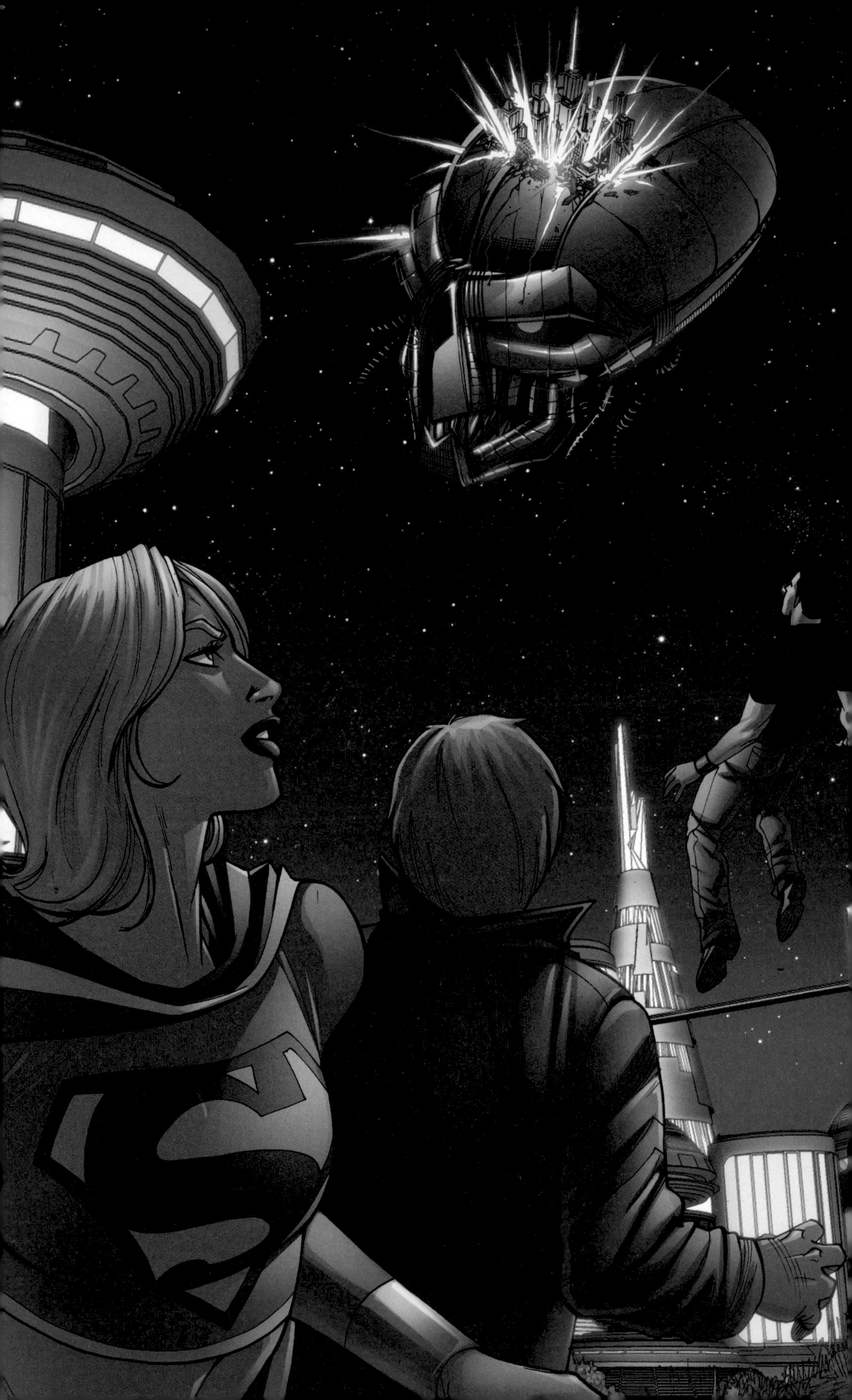

cover by **RYAN SOOK**

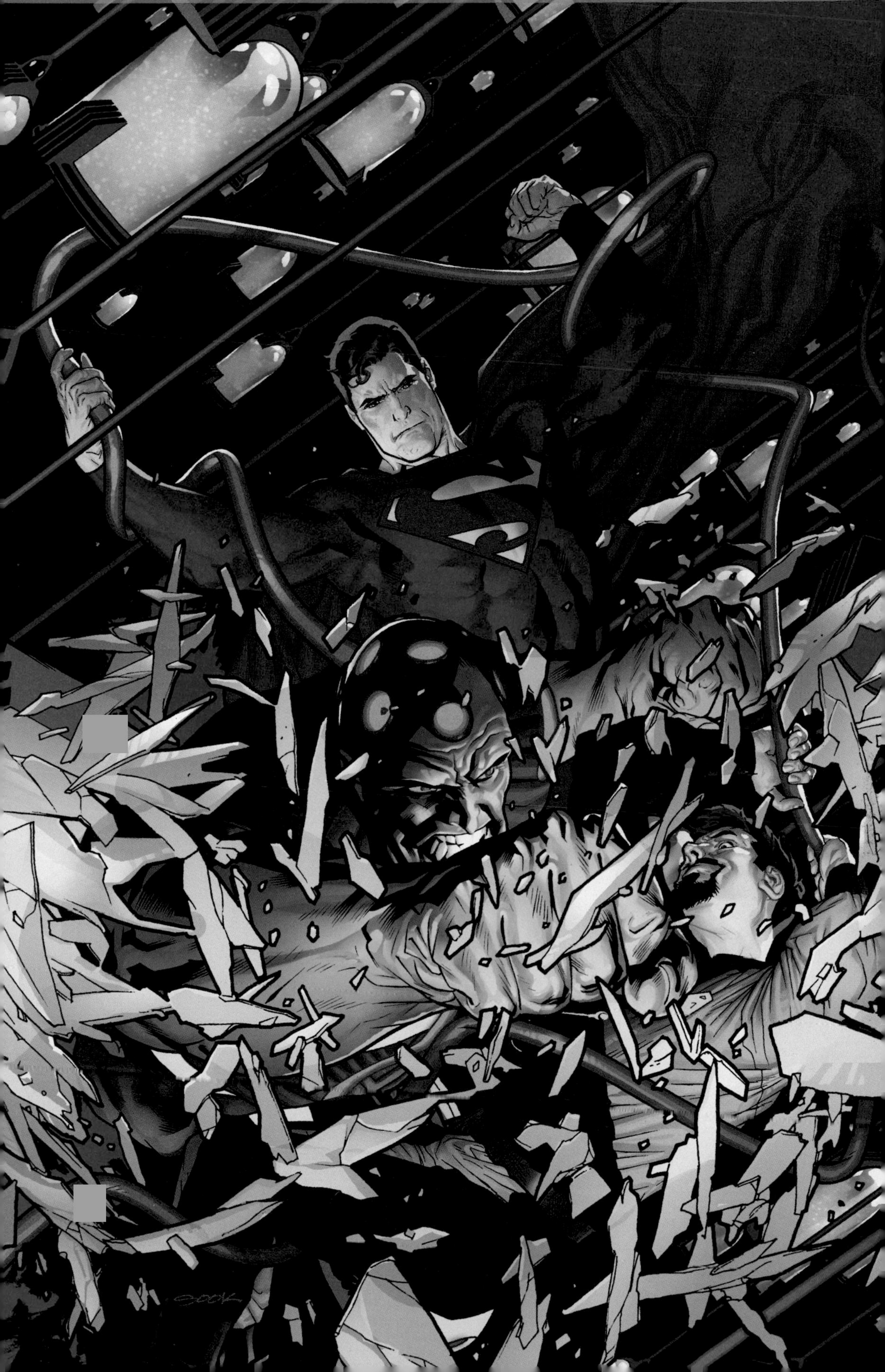

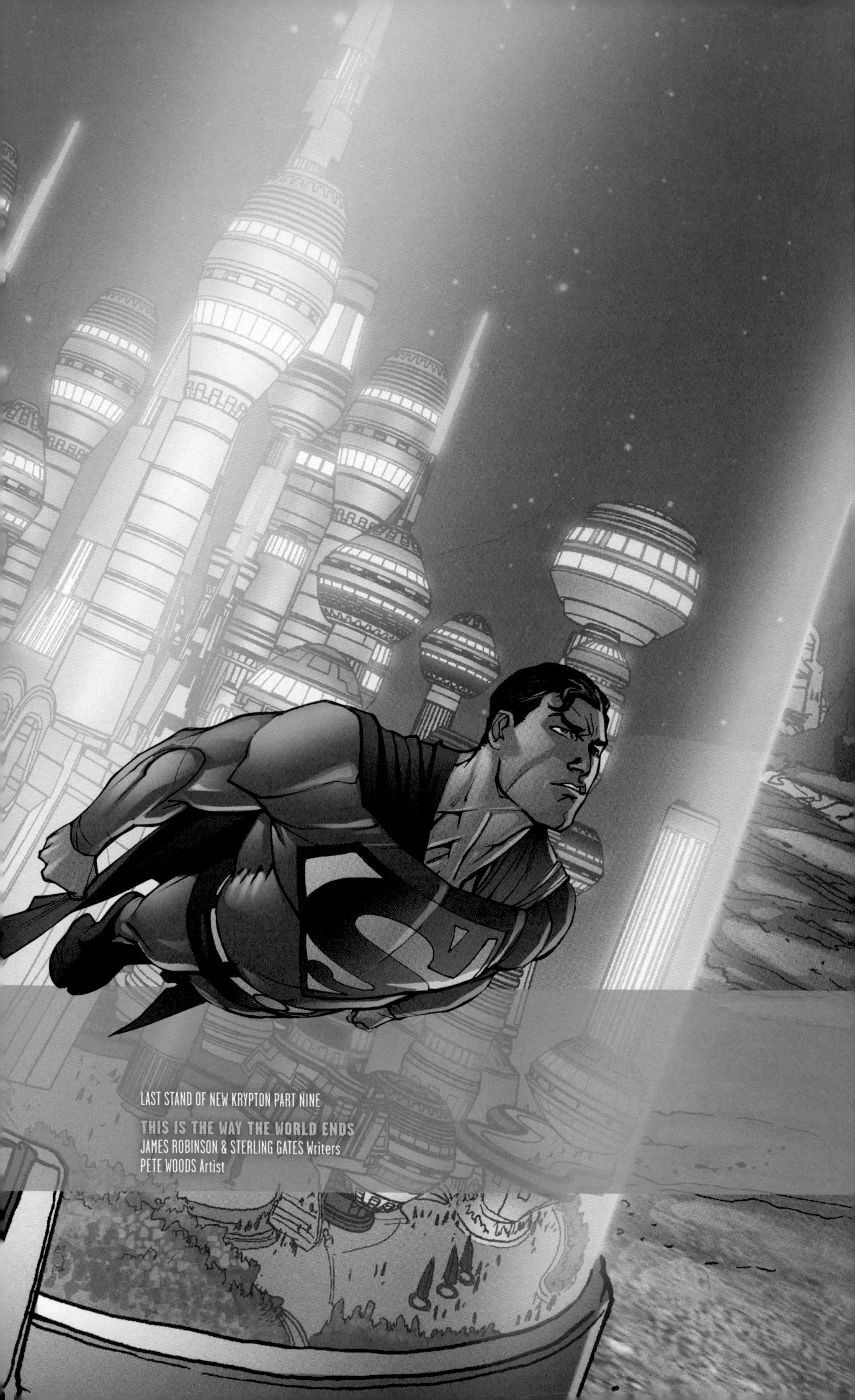

LAST STAND OF NEW KRYPTON PART NINE
THIS IS THE WAY THE WORLD ENDS
JAMES ROBINSON & STERLING GATES Writers
PETE WOODS Artist

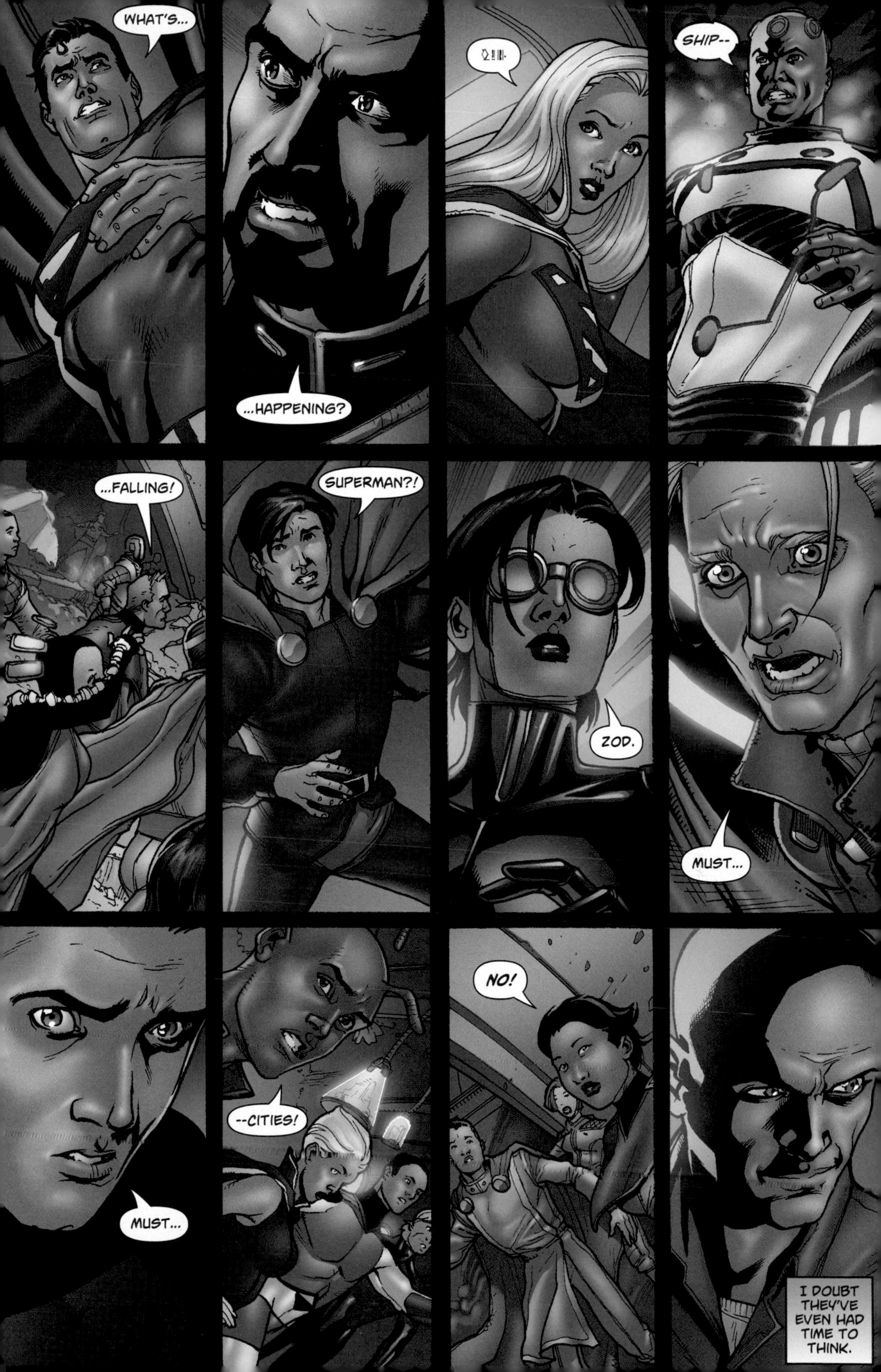
WHAT'S...
...HAPPENING?
SHIP--
...FALLING!
SUPERMAN?!
ZOD.
MUST...
MUST...
--CITIES!
NO!
I DOUBT THEY'VE EVEN HAD TIME TO THINK.

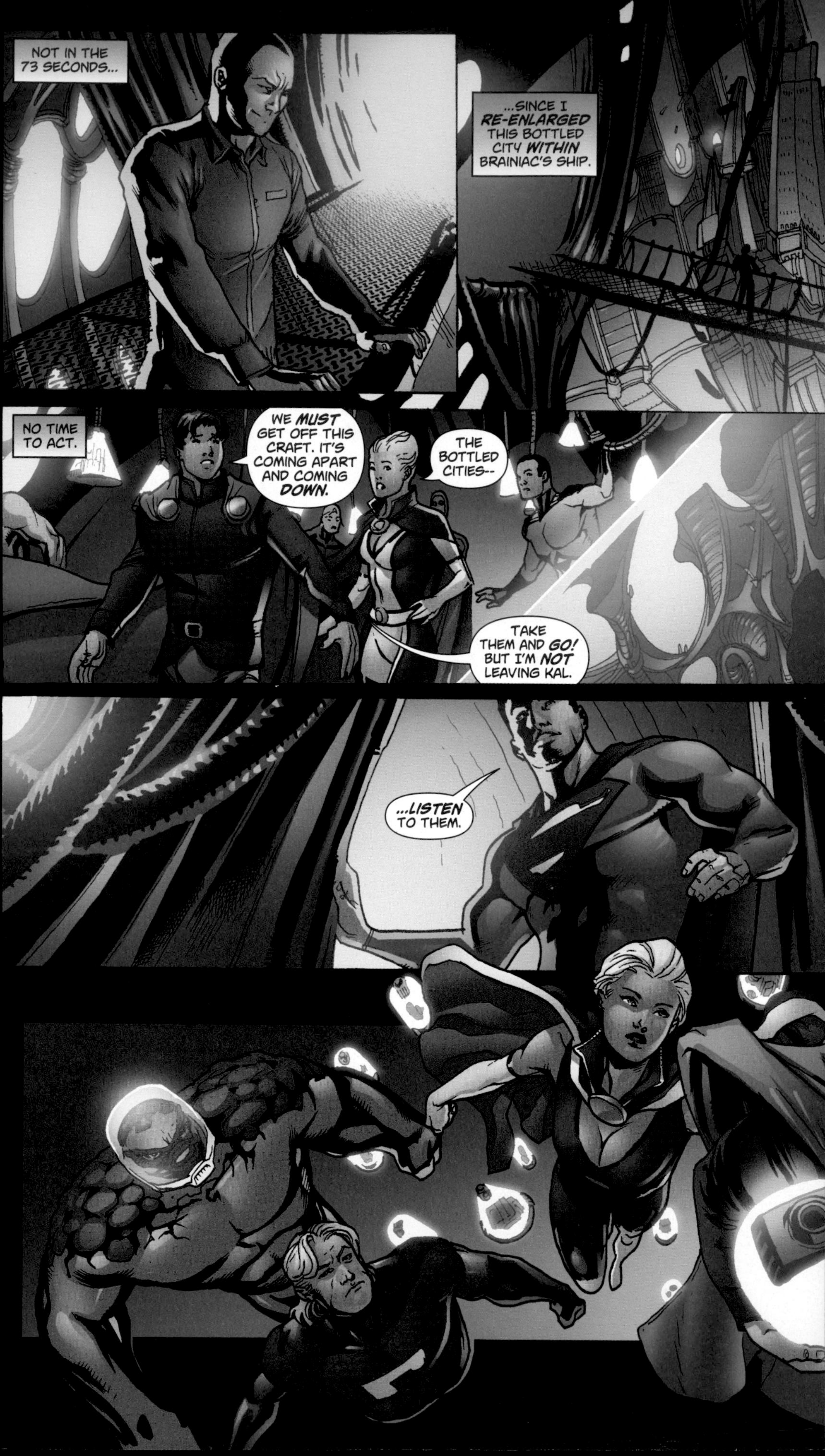
NOT IN THE 73 SECONDS...
...SINCE I RE-ENLARGED THIS BOTTLED CITY WITHIN BRAINIAC'S SHIP.
NO TIME TO ACT.
WE MUST GET OFF THIS CRAFT. IT'S COMING APART AND COMING DOWN.
THE BOTTLED CITIES--
TAKE THEM AND GO! BUT I'M NOT LEAVING KAL.
...LISTEN TO THEM.

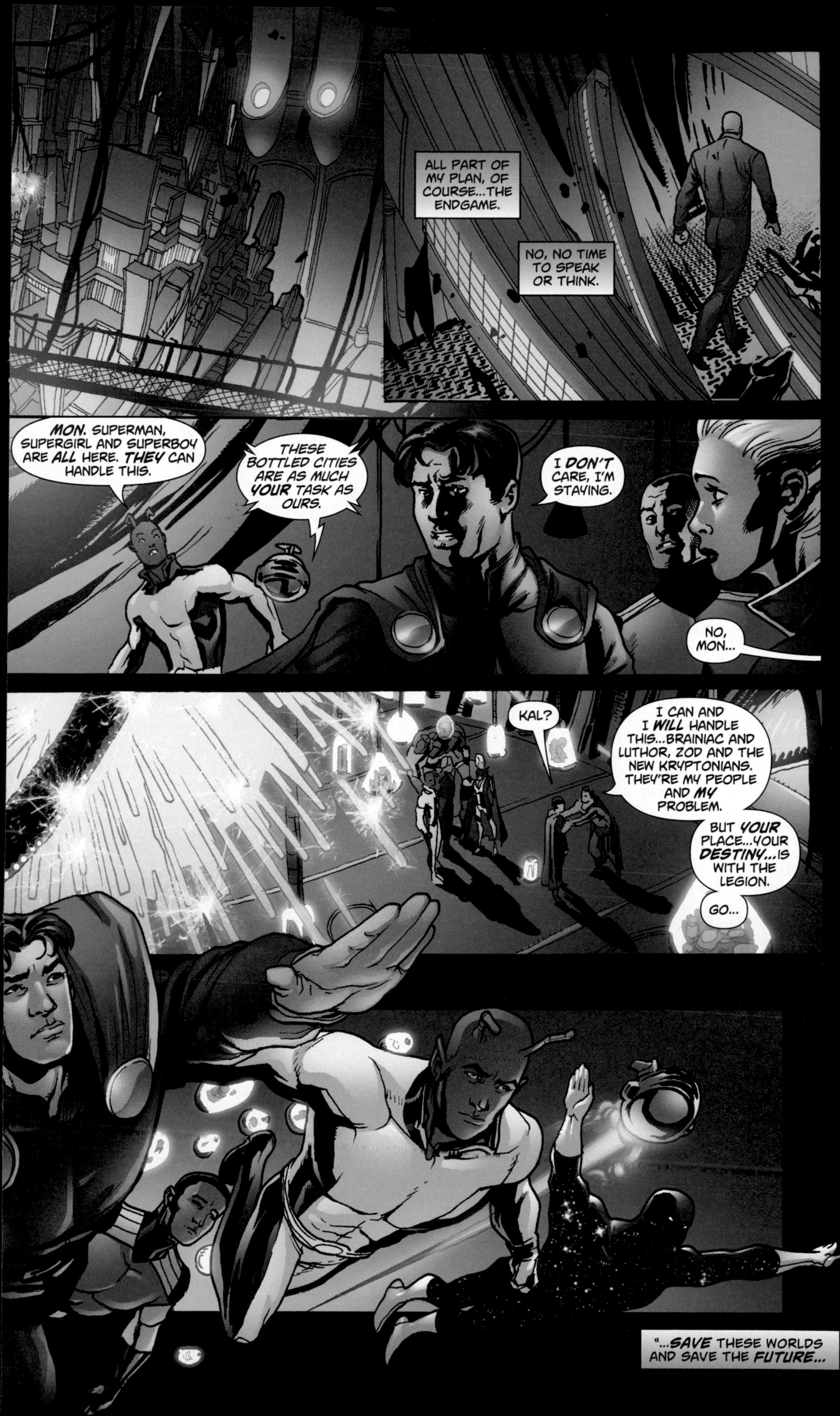
ALL PART OF MY PLAN, OF COURSE...THE ENDGAME.
NO, NO TIME TO SPEAK OR THINK.
MON. SUPERMAN, SUPERGIRL AND SUPERBOY ARE ALL HERE. THEY CAN HANDLE THIS.
THESE BOTTLED CITIES ARE AS MUCH YOUR TASK AS OURS.
I DON'T CARE, I'M STAYING.
NO, MON...
KAL?
I CAN AND I WILL HANDLE THIS...BRAINIAC AND LUTHOR, ZOD AND THE NEW KRYPTONIANS. THEY'RE MY PEOPLE AND MY PROBLEM.
BUT YOUR PLACE...YOUR DESTINY...IS WITH THE LEGION.
GO...
"...SAVE THESE WORLDS AND SAVE THE FUTURE...

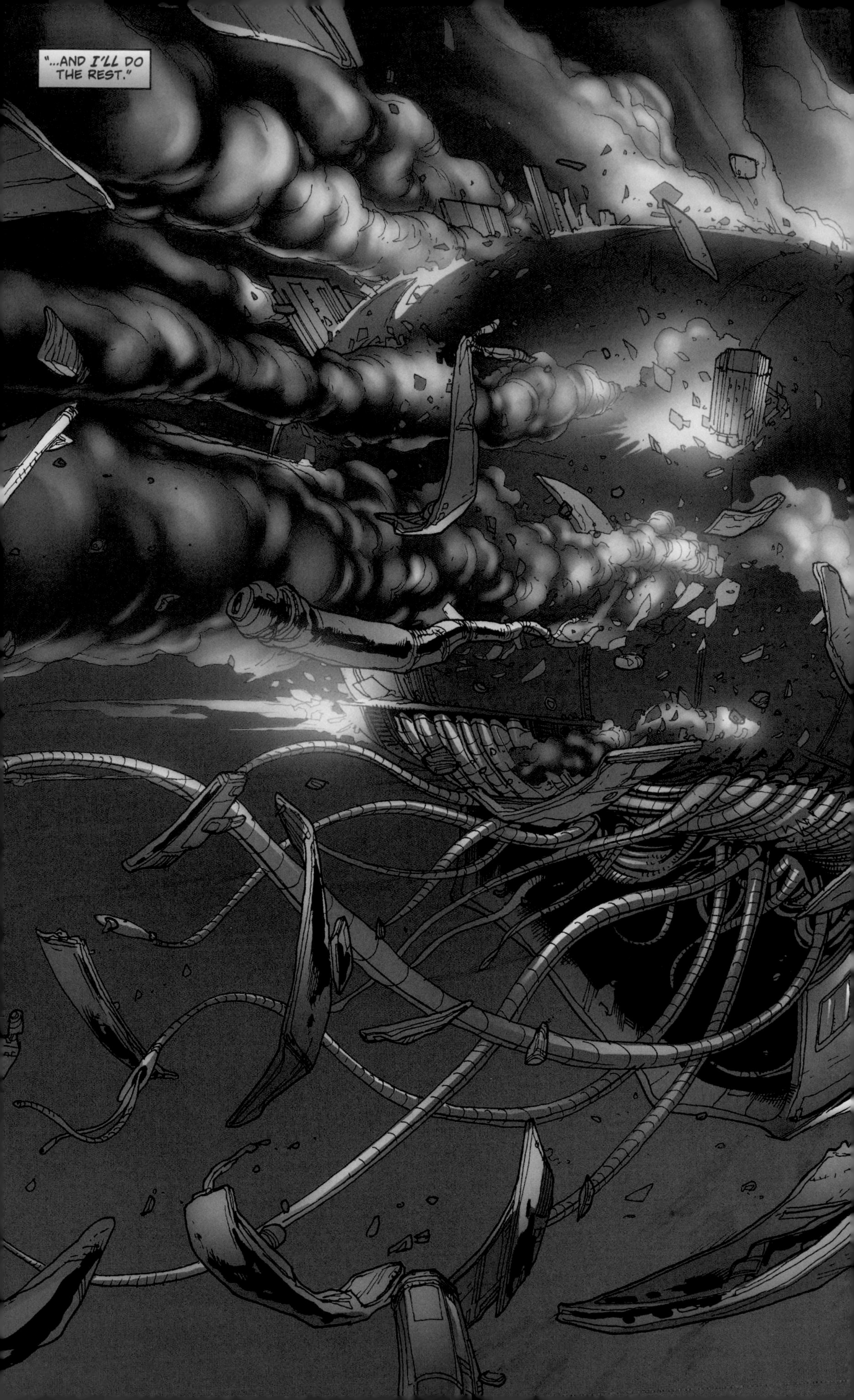
"...AND I'LL DO THE REST."

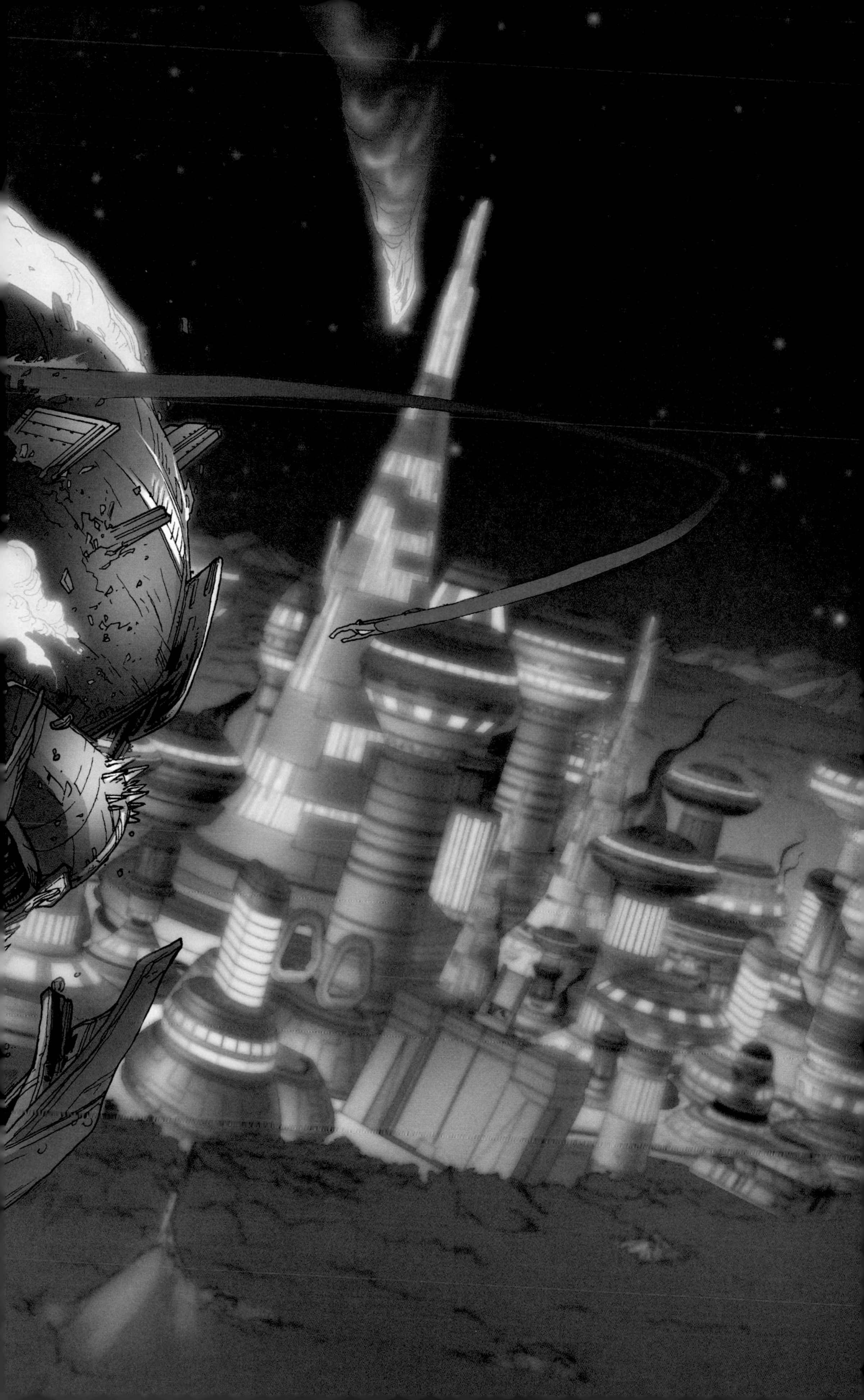

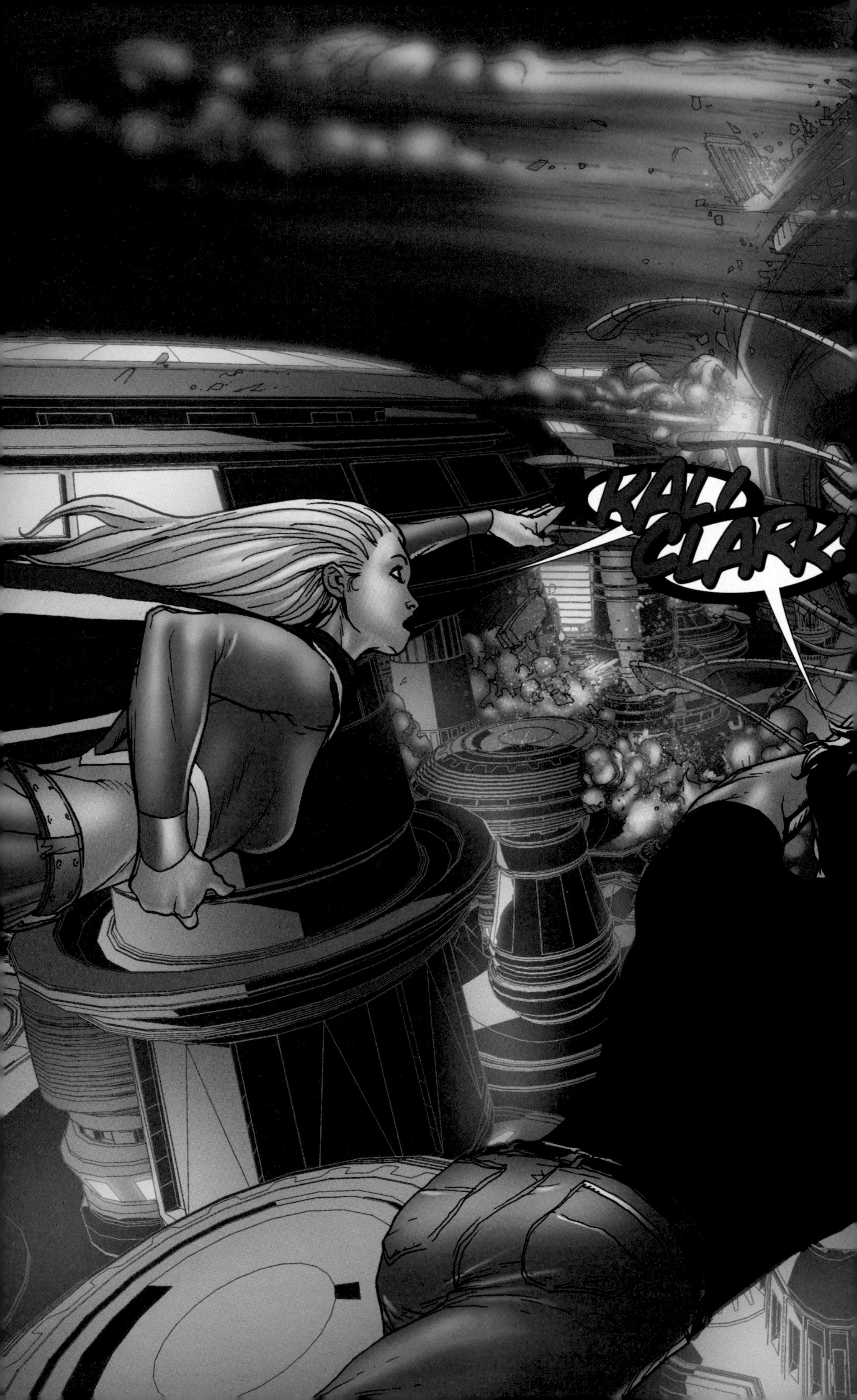
KAL! CLARK!

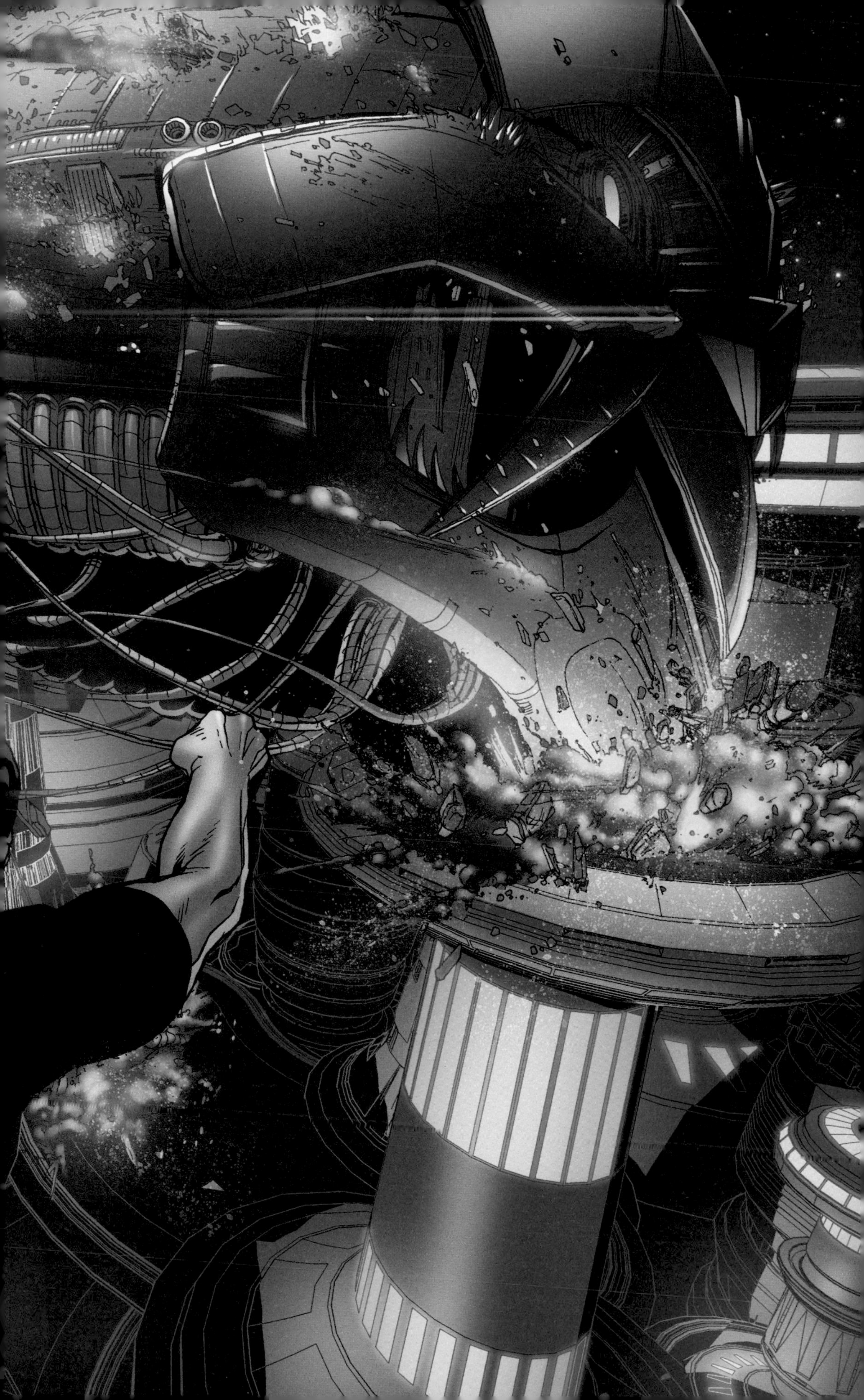

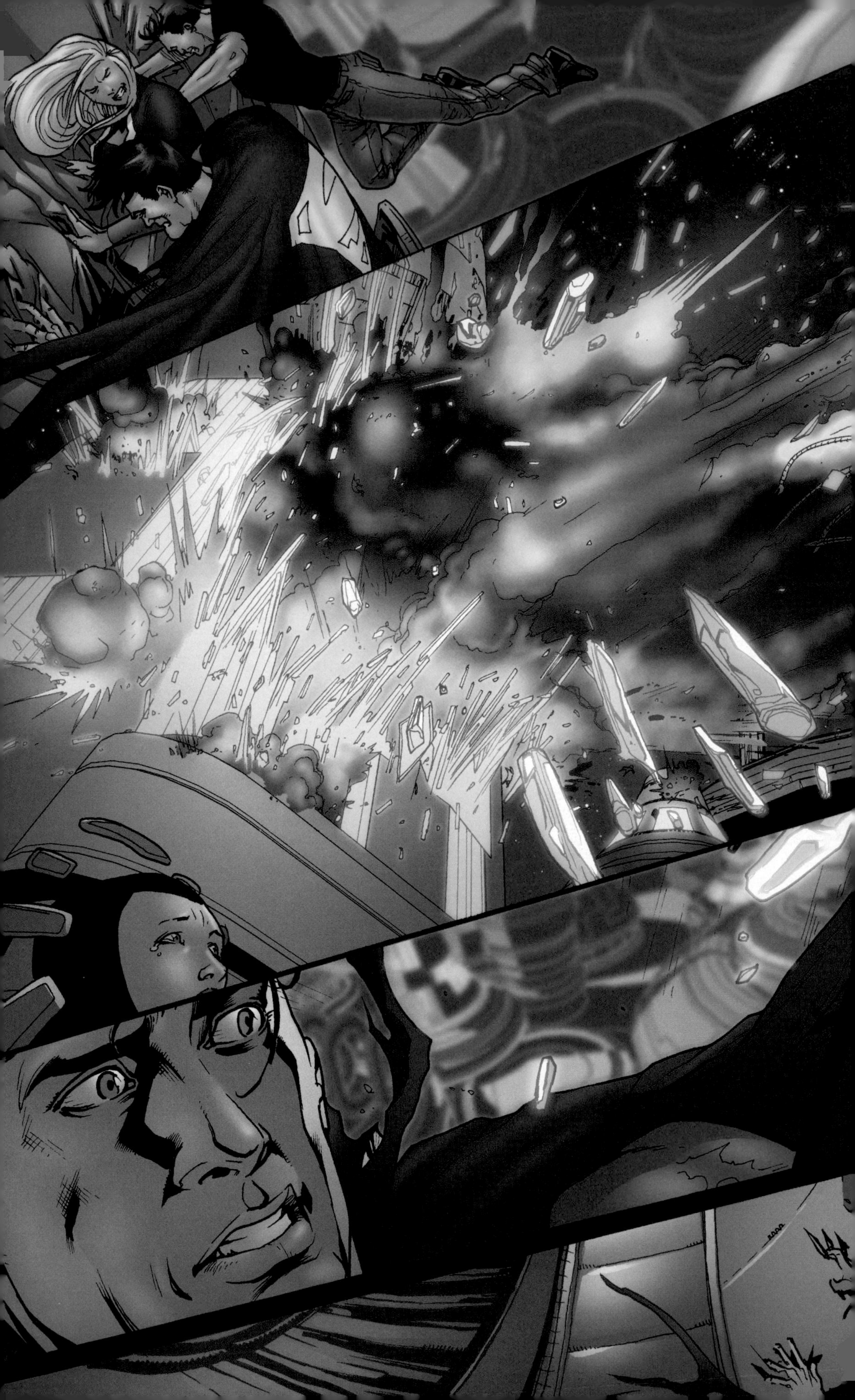

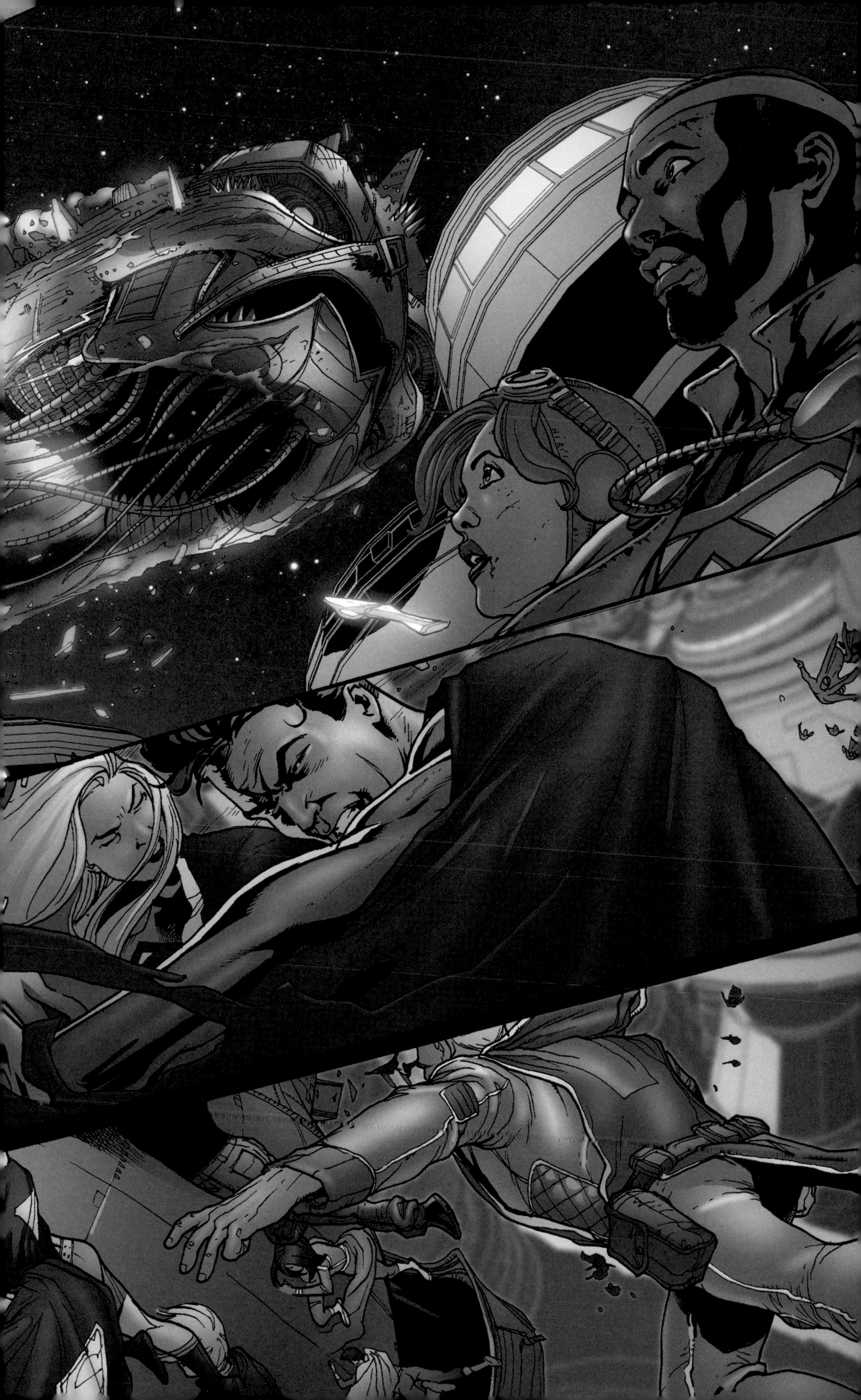

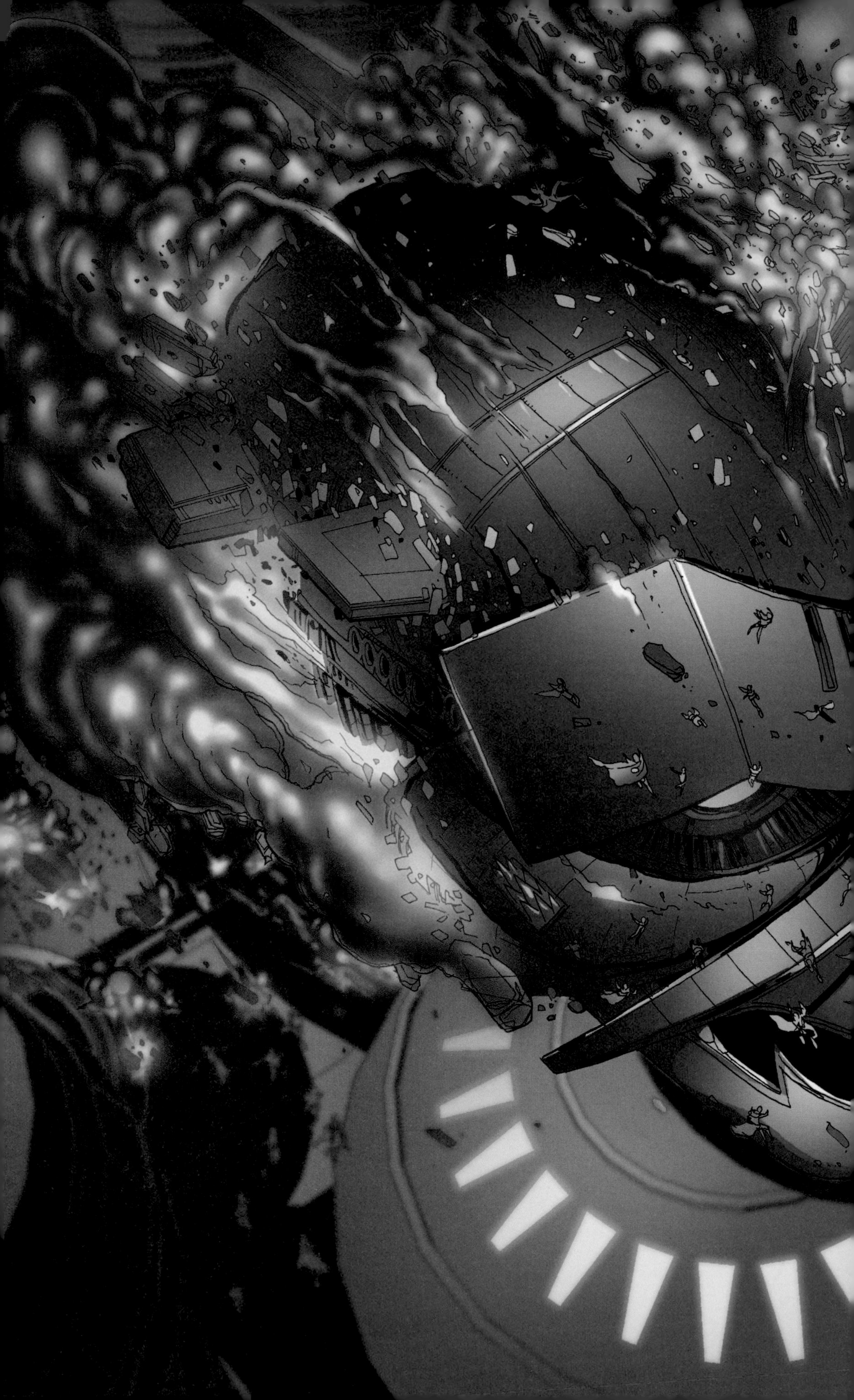

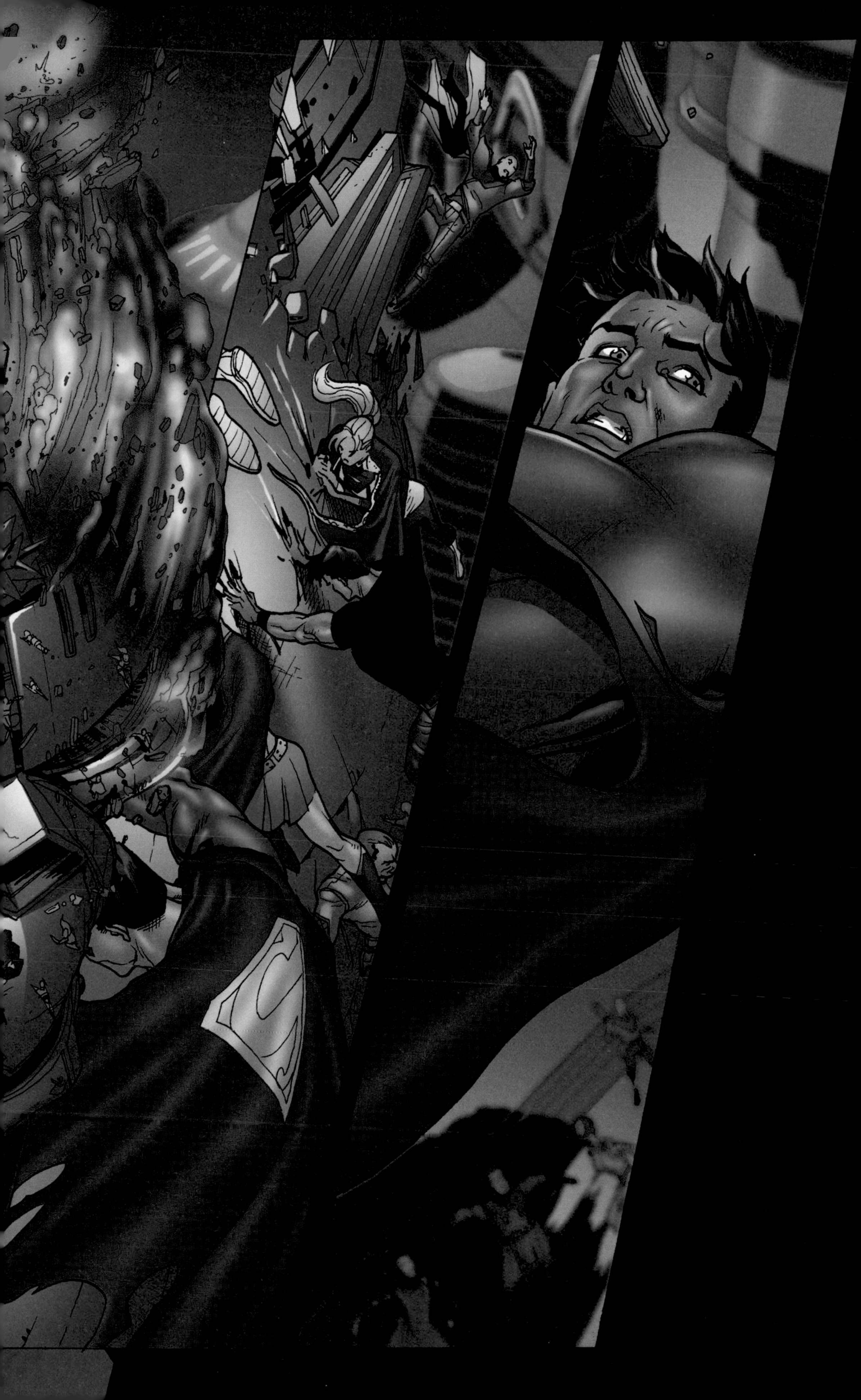

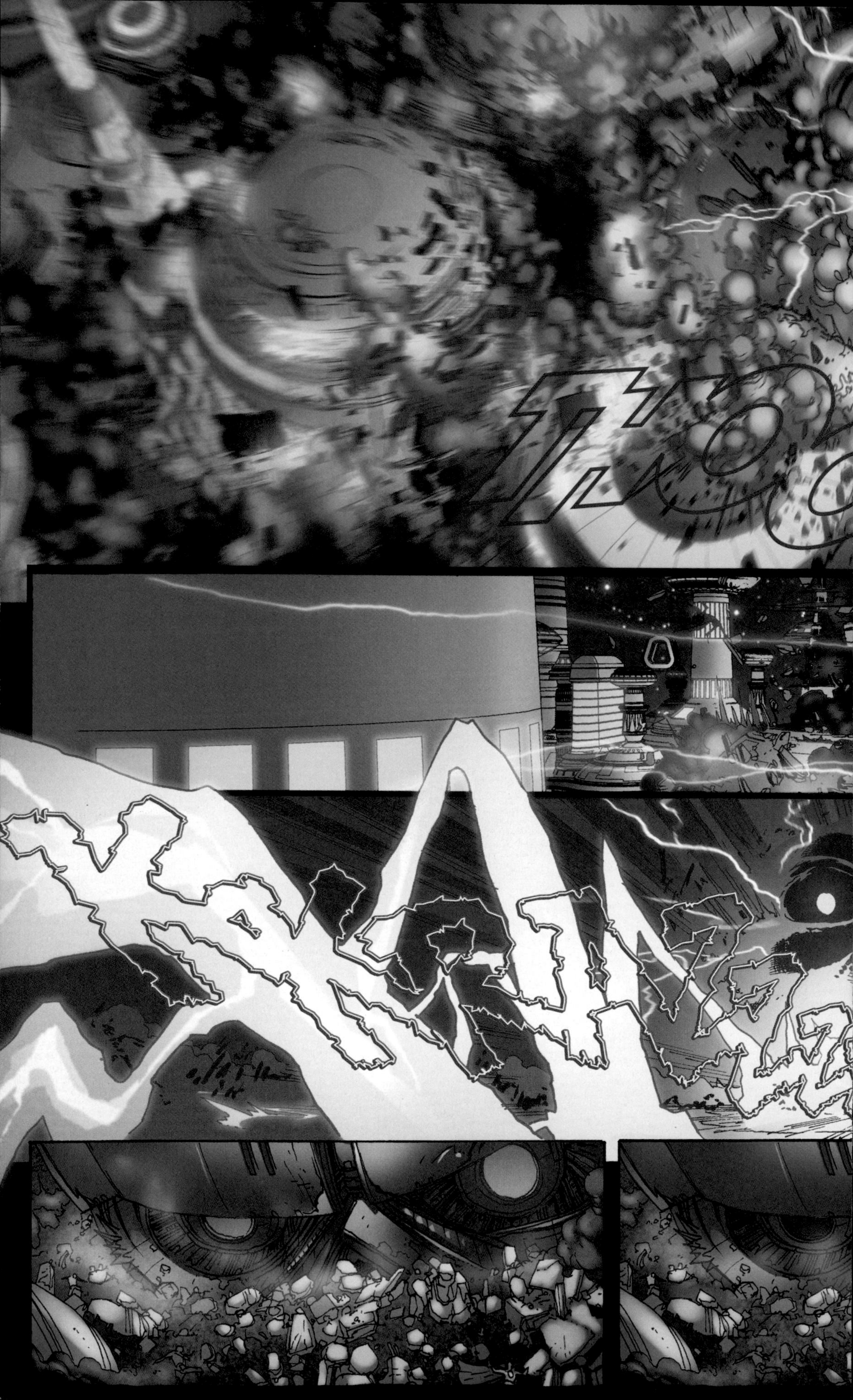

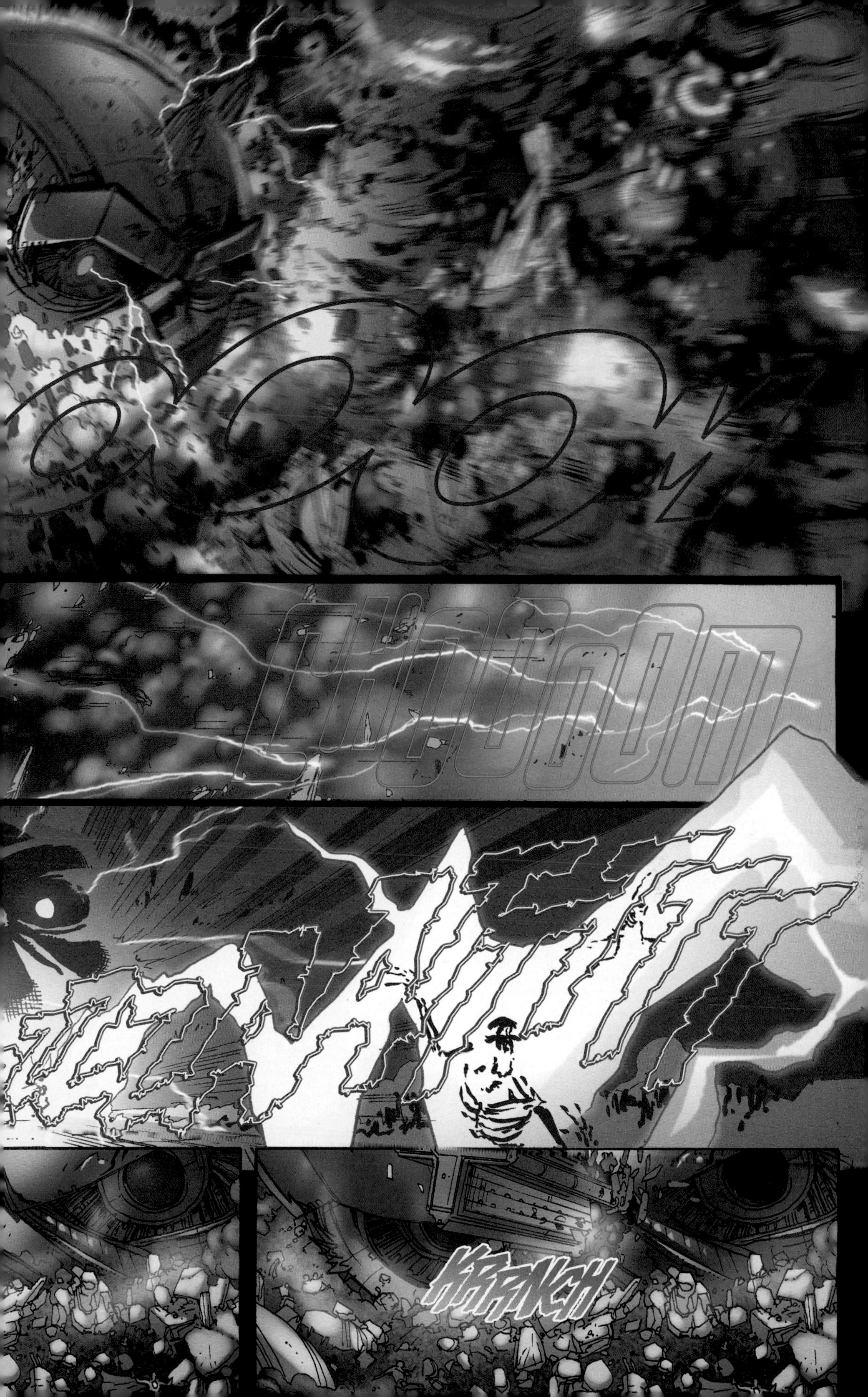
CHOOOOM
KRRANCH

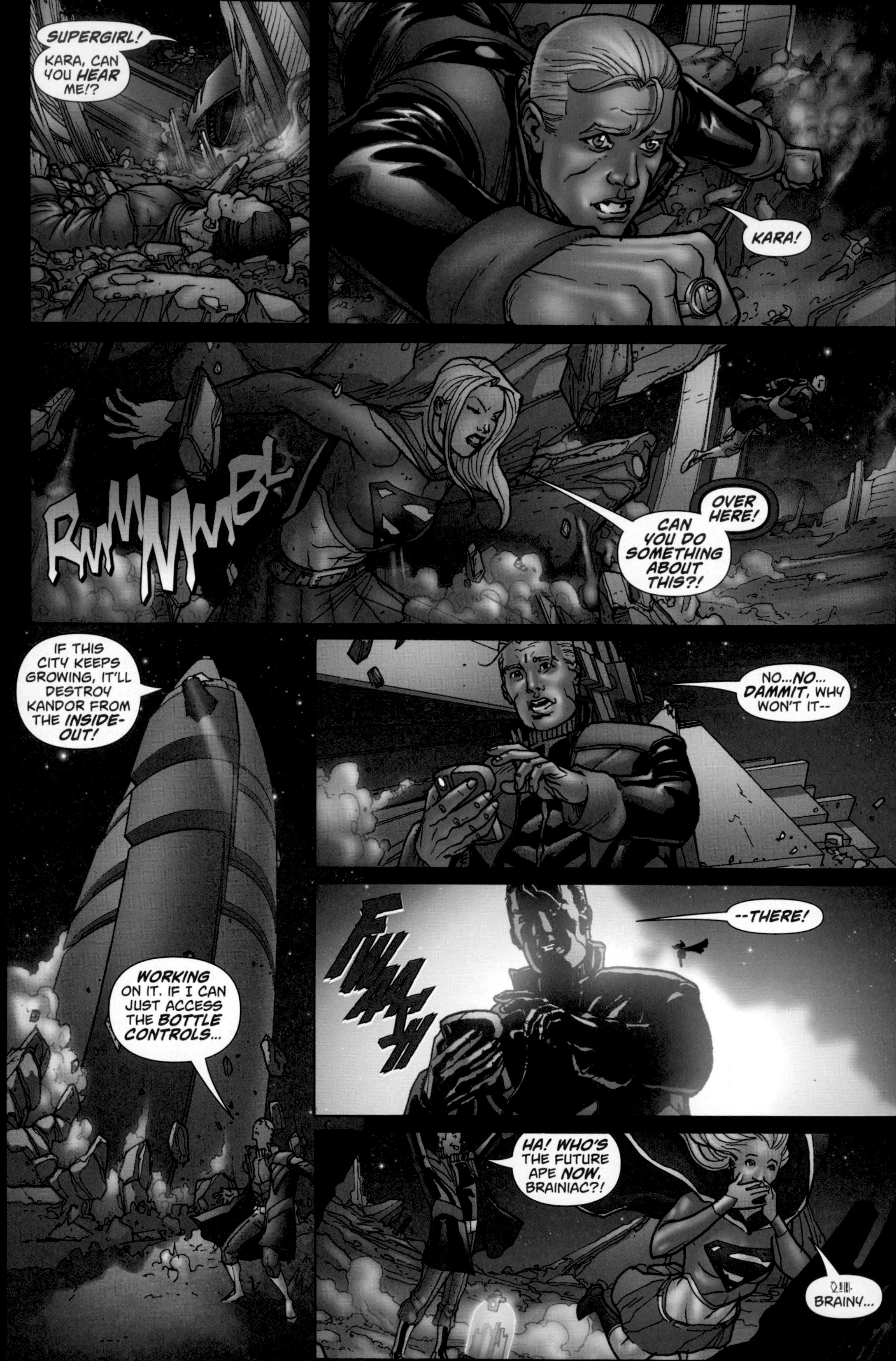
SUPERGIRL!
KARA, CAN YOU HEAR ME!?
KARA!
OVER HERE!
CAN YOU DO SOMETHING ABOUT THIS?!
IF THIS CITY KEEPS GROWING, IT'LL DESTROY KANDOR FROM THE INSIDE-OUT!
WORKING ON IT. IF I CAN JUST ACCESS THE BOTTLE CONTROLS...
NO...NO... DAMMIT, WHY WON'T IT--
--THERE!
HA! WHO'S THE FUTURE APE NOW, BRAINIAC?!
BRAINY...

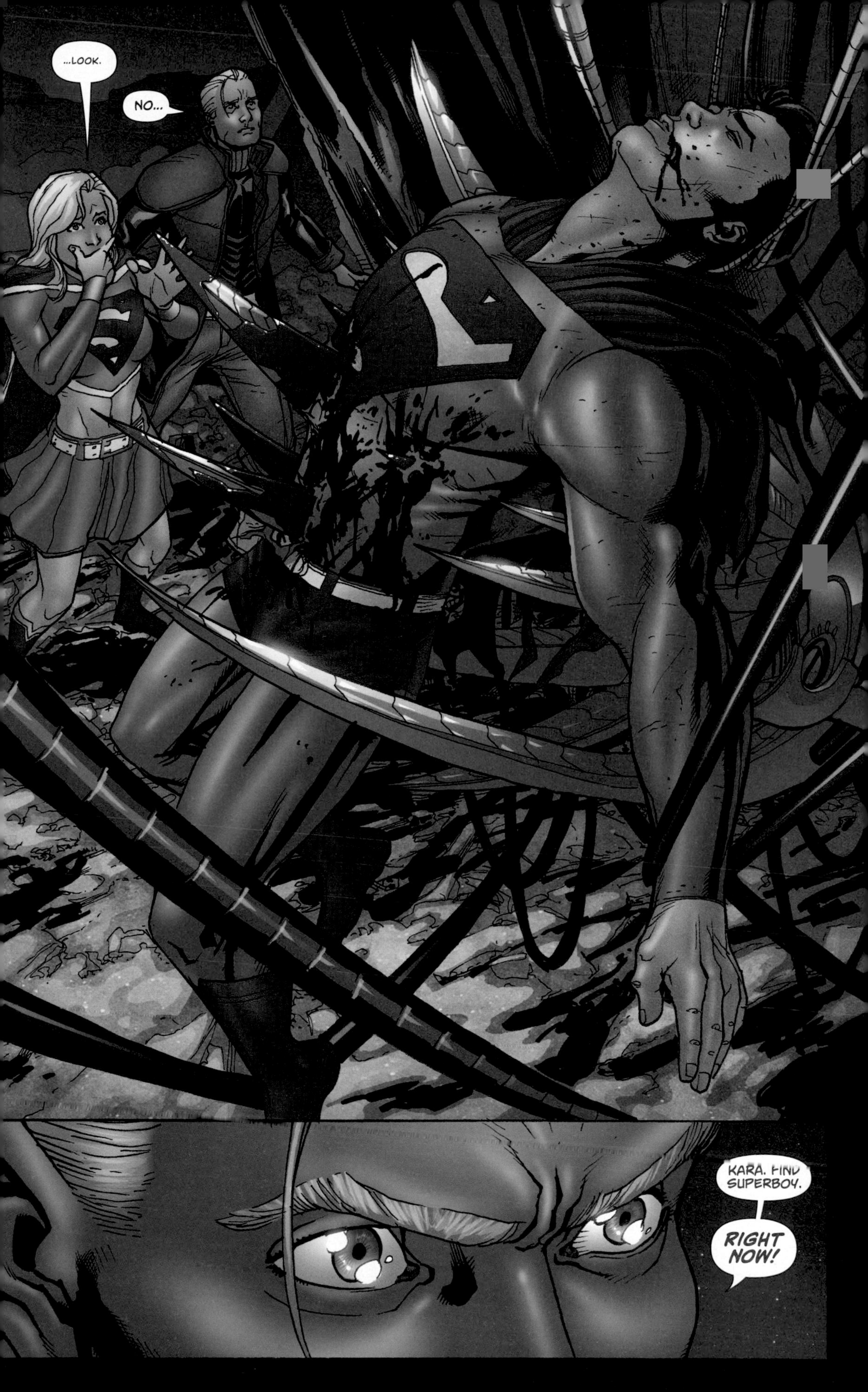
...LOOK.
NO...
KARA. FIND SUPERBOY.
RIGHT NOW!

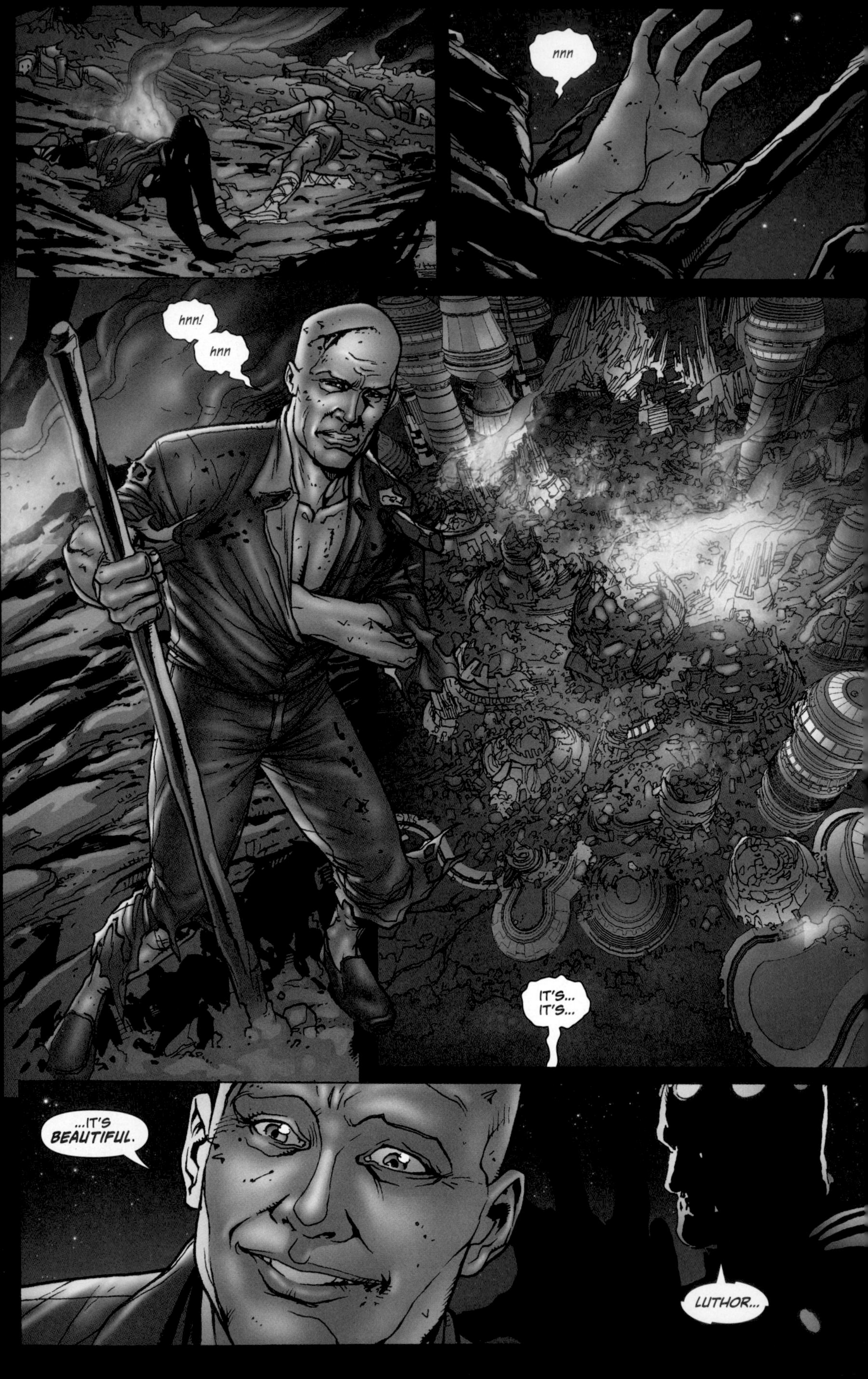
nnn
hnn!
hnn
IT'S... IT'S...
...IT'S BEAUTIFUL.
LUTHOR...

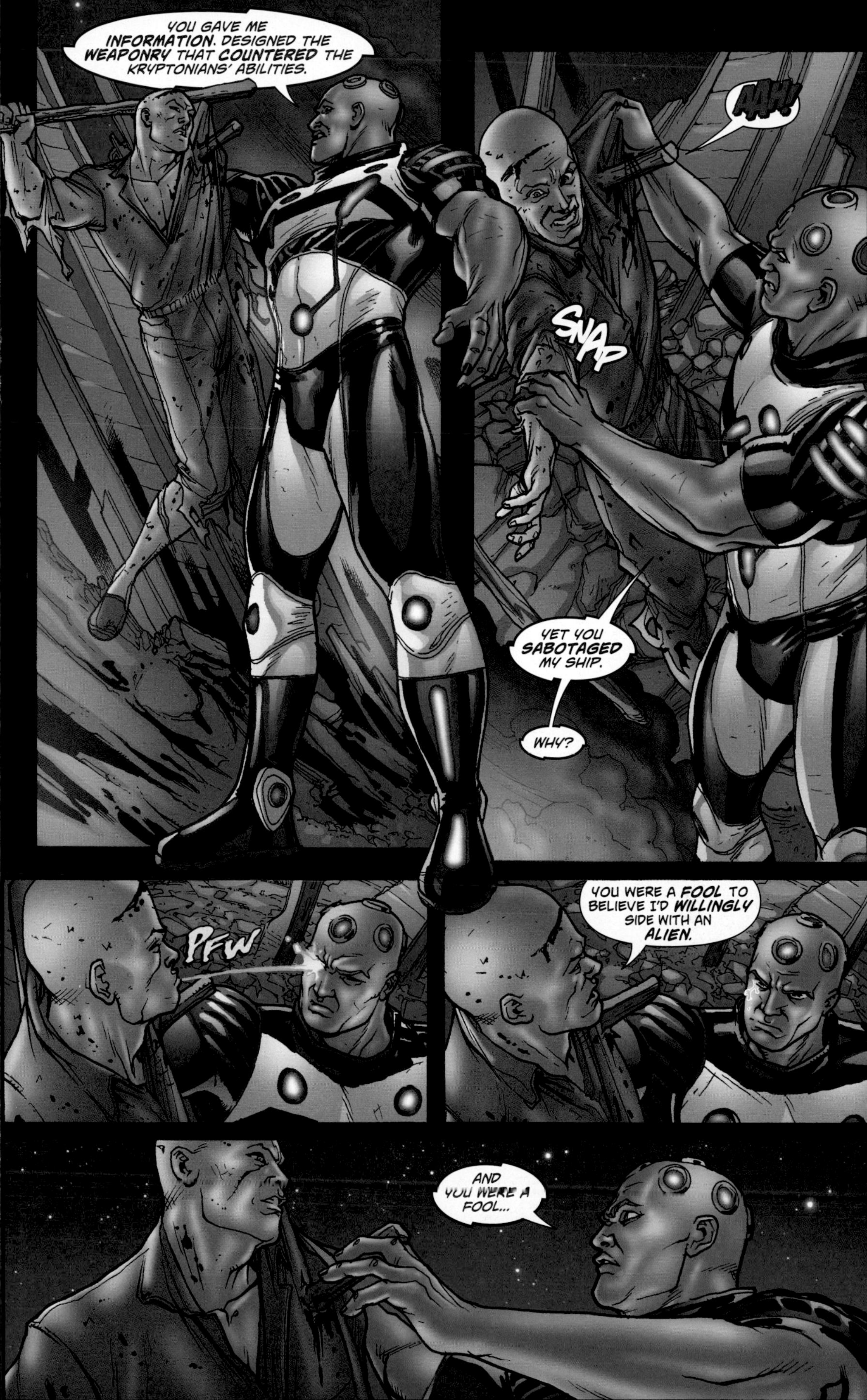

YOU GAVE ME INFORMATION. DESIGNED THE WEAPONRY THAT COUNTERED THE KRYPTONIANS' ABILITIES.
AAH!
SNAP
YET YOU SABOTAGED MY SHIP.
WHY?
PFW
YOU WERE A FOOL TO BELIEVE I'D WILLINGLY SIDE WITH AN ALIEN.
AND YOU WERE A FOOL...

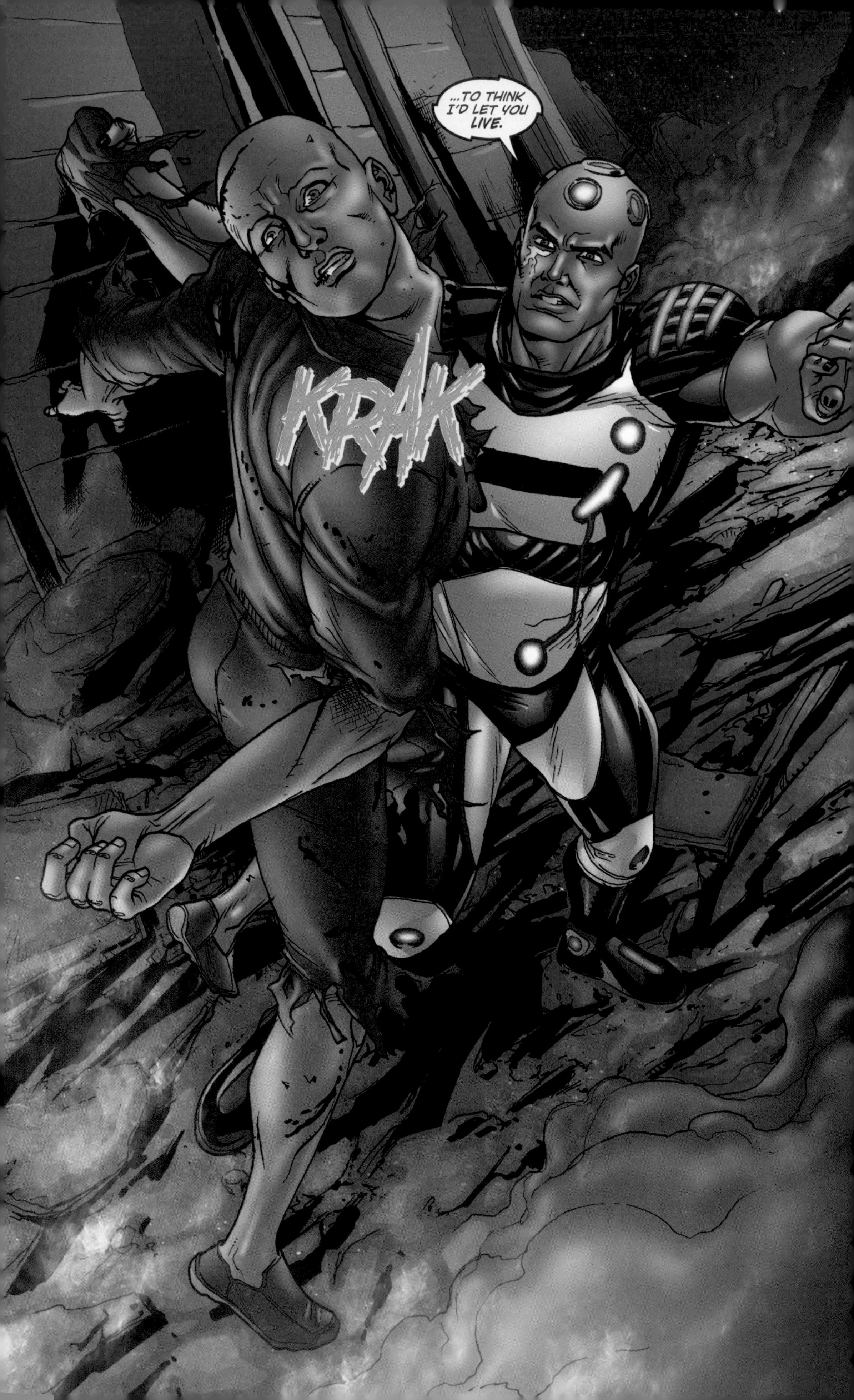
...TO THINK I'D LET YOU LIVE.
KRAK

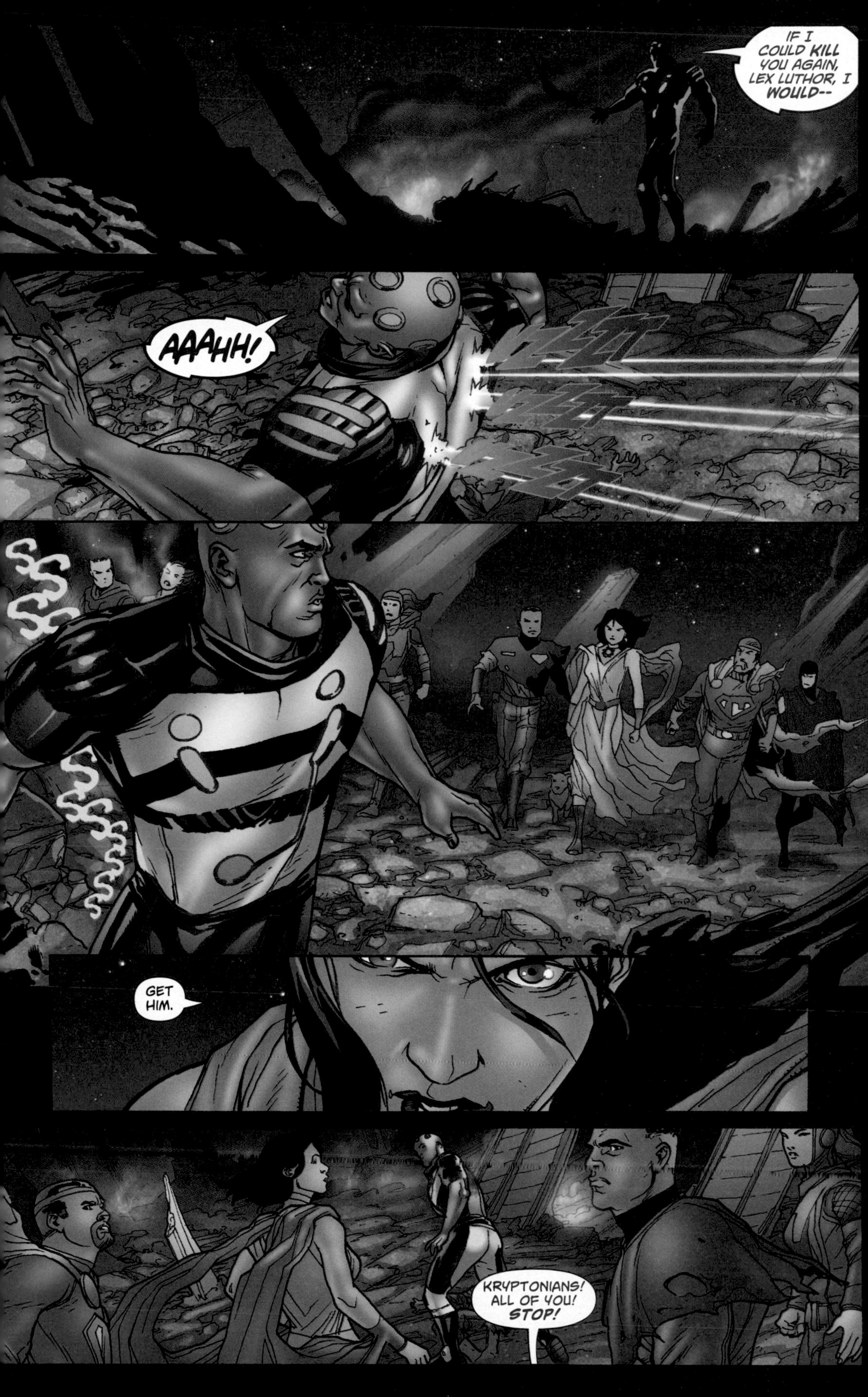
IF I COULD KILL YOU AGAIN, LEX LUTHOR, I WOULD--
AAAHH!
GET HIM.
KRYPTONIANS! ALL OF YOU! STOP!

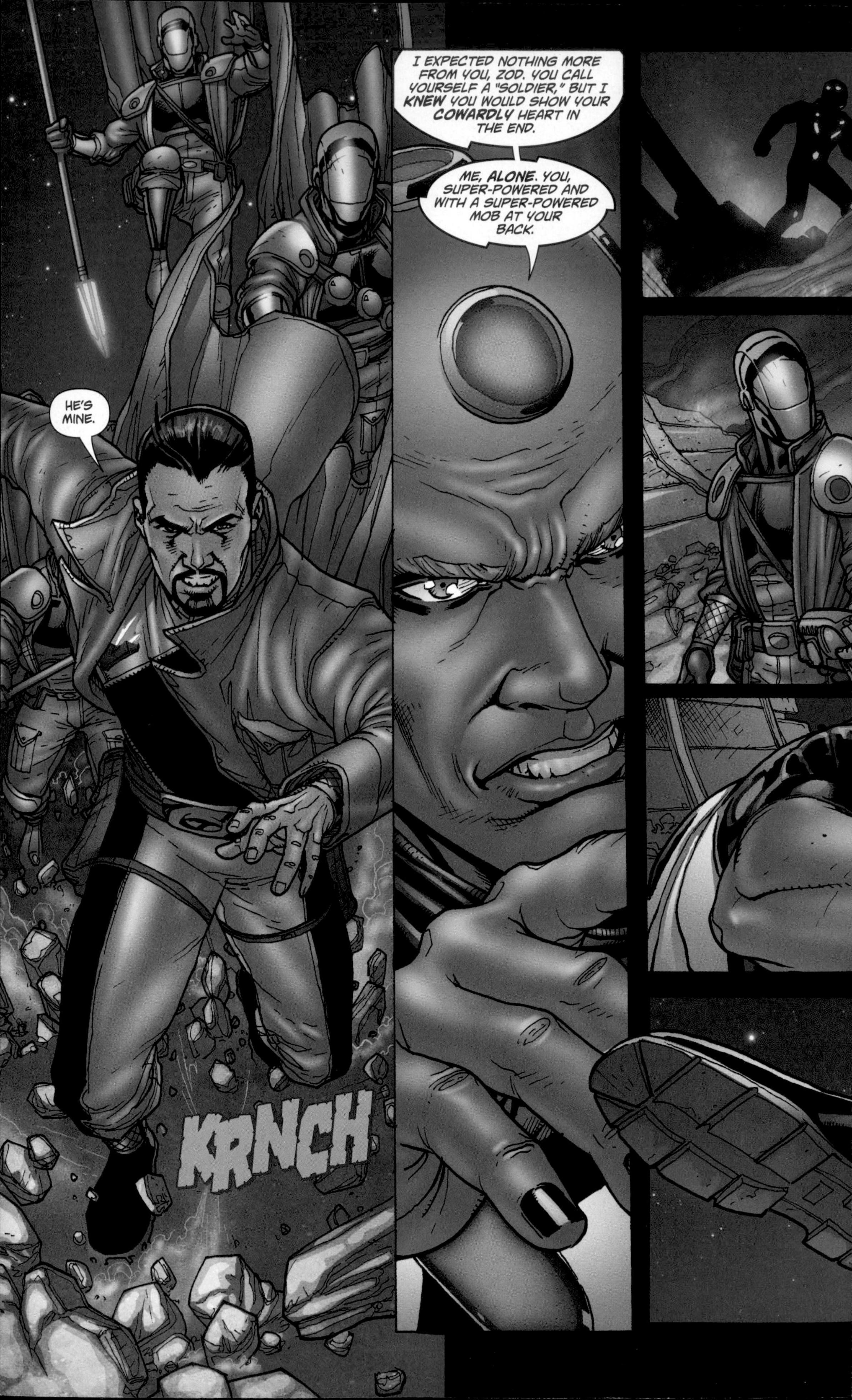
HE'S MINE.
KRNCH
I EXPECTED NOTHING MORE FROM YOU, ZOD. YOU CALL YOURSELF A "SOLDIER," BUT I KNEW YOU WOULD SHOW YOUR COWARDLY HEART IN THE END.
ME, ALONE. YOU, SUPER-POWERED AND WITH A SUPER-POWERED MOB AT YOUR BACK.

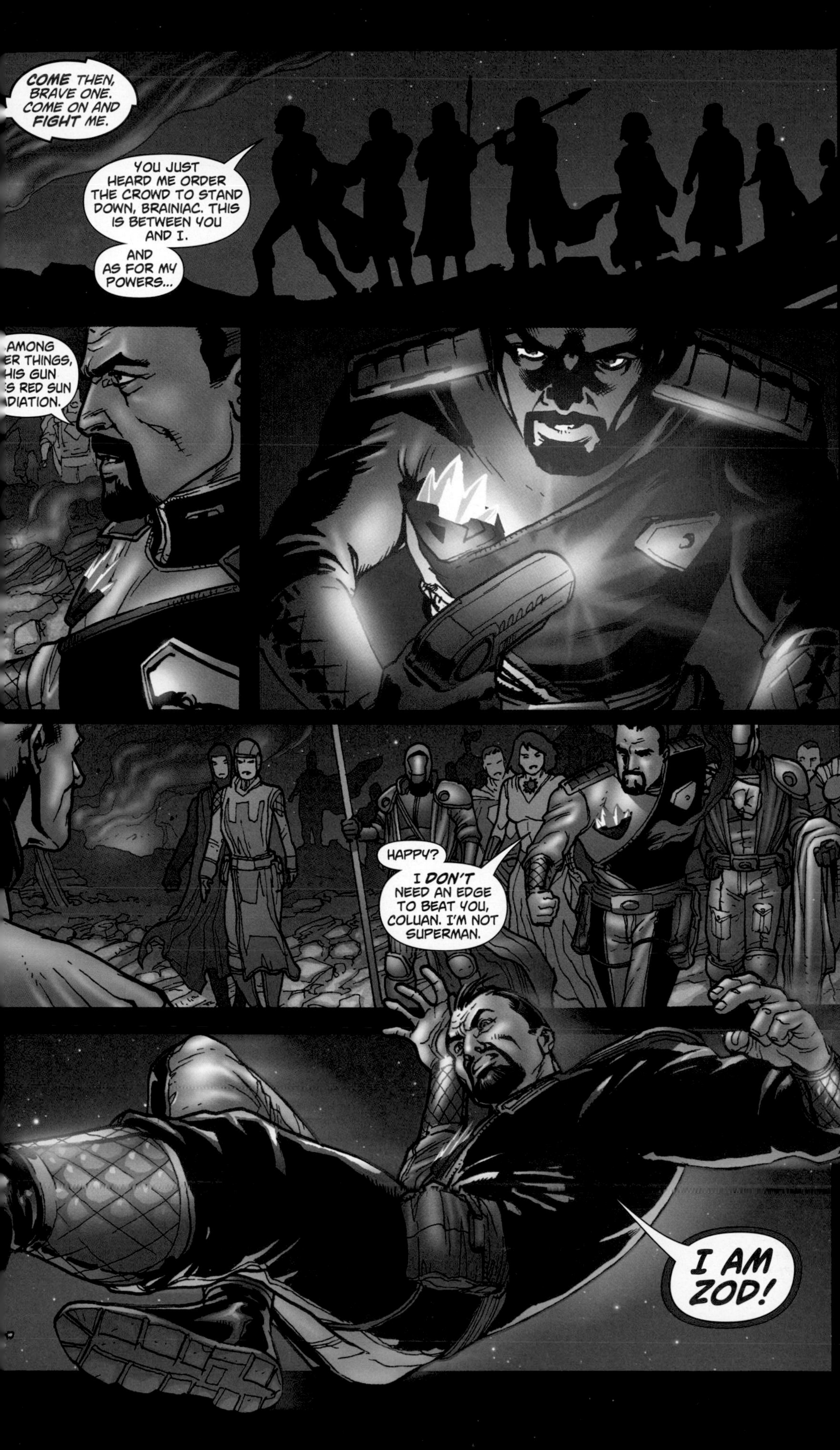
COME THEN, BRAVE ONE. COME ON AND FIGHT ME.
YOU JUST HEARD ME ORDER THE CROWD TO STAND DOWN, BRAINIAC. THIS IS BETWEEN YOU AND I.
AND AS FOR MY POWERS...
AMONG ER THINGS, HIS GUN S RED SUN DIATION.
HAPPY?
I DON'T NEED AN EDGE TO BEAT YOU, COLUAN. I'M NOT SUPERMAN.
I AM ZOD!

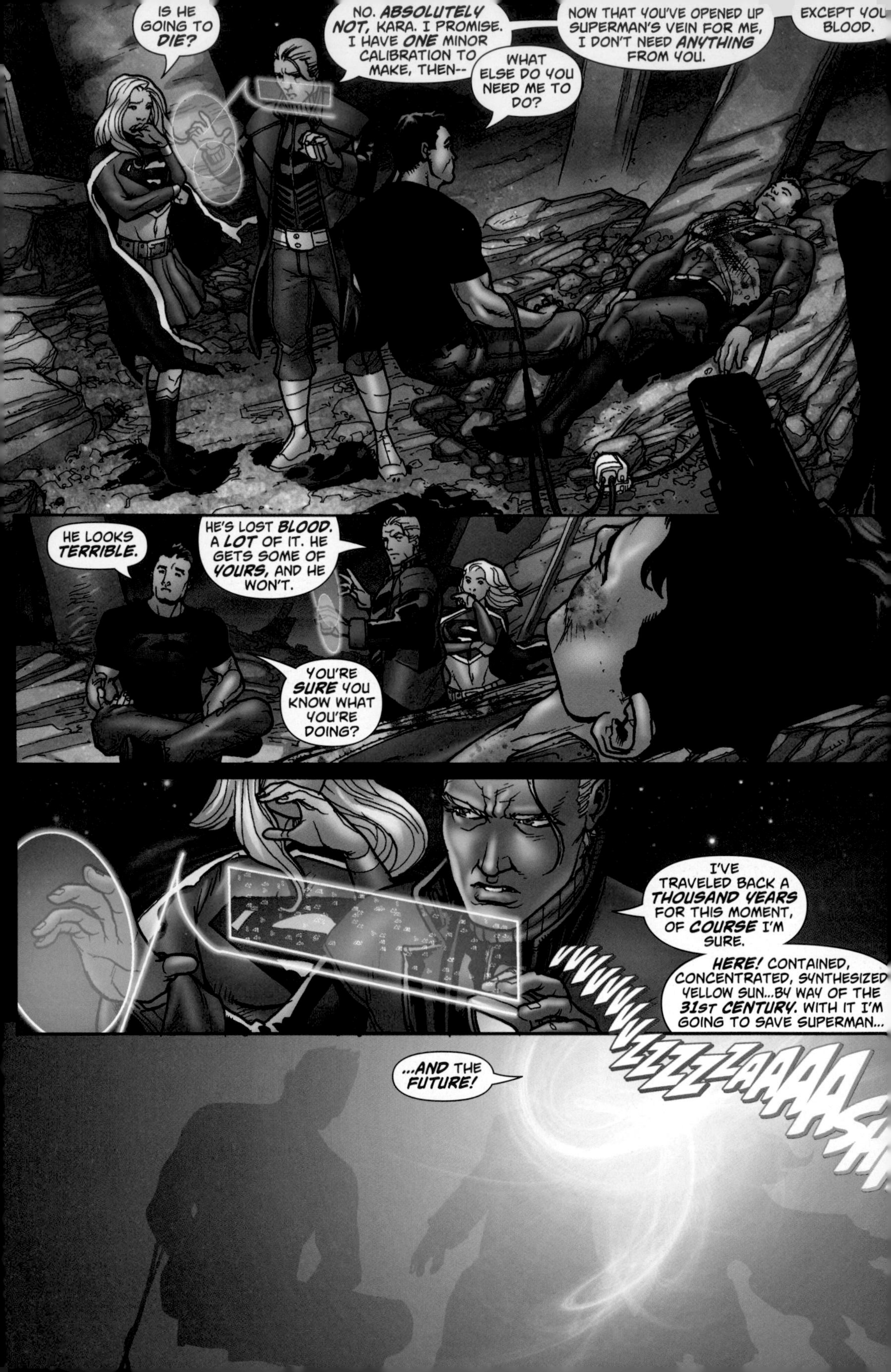
IS HE GOING TO DIE?
NO. ABSOLUTELY NOT, KARA. I PROMISE. I HAVE ONE MINOR CALIBRATION TO MAKE, THEN--
WHAT ELSE DO YOU NEED ME TO DO?
NOW THAT YOU'VE OPENED UP SUPERMAN'S VEIN FOR ME, I DON'T NEED ANYTHING FROM YOU.
EXCEPT YOU BLOOD.
HE LOOKS TERRIBLE.
HE'S LOST BLOOD. A LOT OF IT. HE GETS SOME OF YOURS, AND HE WON'T.
YOU'RE SURE YOU KNOW WHAT YOU'RE DOING?
I'VE TRAVELED BACK A THOUSAND YEARS FOR THIS MOMENT, OF COURSE I'M SURE.
HERE! CONTAINED, CONCENTRATED, SYNTHESIZED YELLOW SUN...BY WAY OF THE 31ST CENTURY. WITH IT I'M GOING TO SAVE SUPERMAN...
VVVVVVVVZZZZZAAAASH
...AND THE FUTURE!

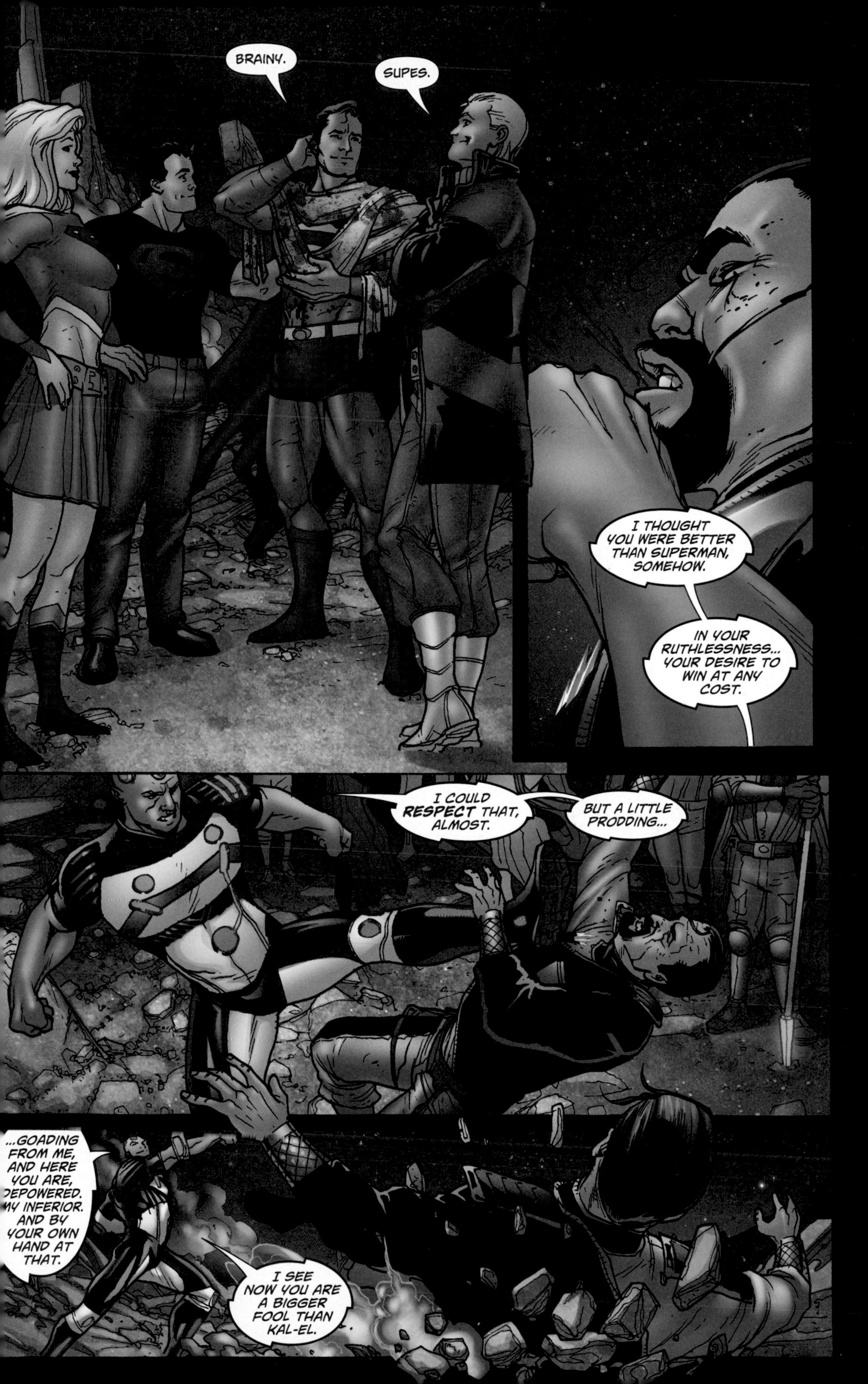
BRAINY.
SUPES.
I THOUGHT YOU WERE BETTER THAN SUPERMAN, SOMEHOW.
IN YOUR RUTHLESSNESS... YOUR DESIRE TO WIN AT ANY COST.
I COULD **RESPECT** THAT, ALMOST.
BUT A LITTLE PRODDING...
...GOADING FROM ME, AND HERE YOU ARE, DEPOWERED. MY INFERIOR. AND BY YOUR OWN HAND AT THAT.
I SEE NOW YOU ARE A BIGGER FOOL THAN KAL-EL.

SAY WHAT YOU WANT, COLUAN, I'M *NOT* LISTENING.

BATTLE *ISN'T* WORD-PLAY.

IT'S *SKILL.*

AFTER YOU TOOK KANDOR THE *FIRST* TIME...

...I SWORE AN *OATH...*

...ONE DAY YOU WOULD KNEEL BEFORE ME...

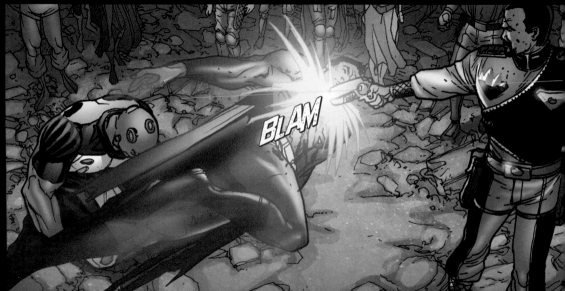

BLAM

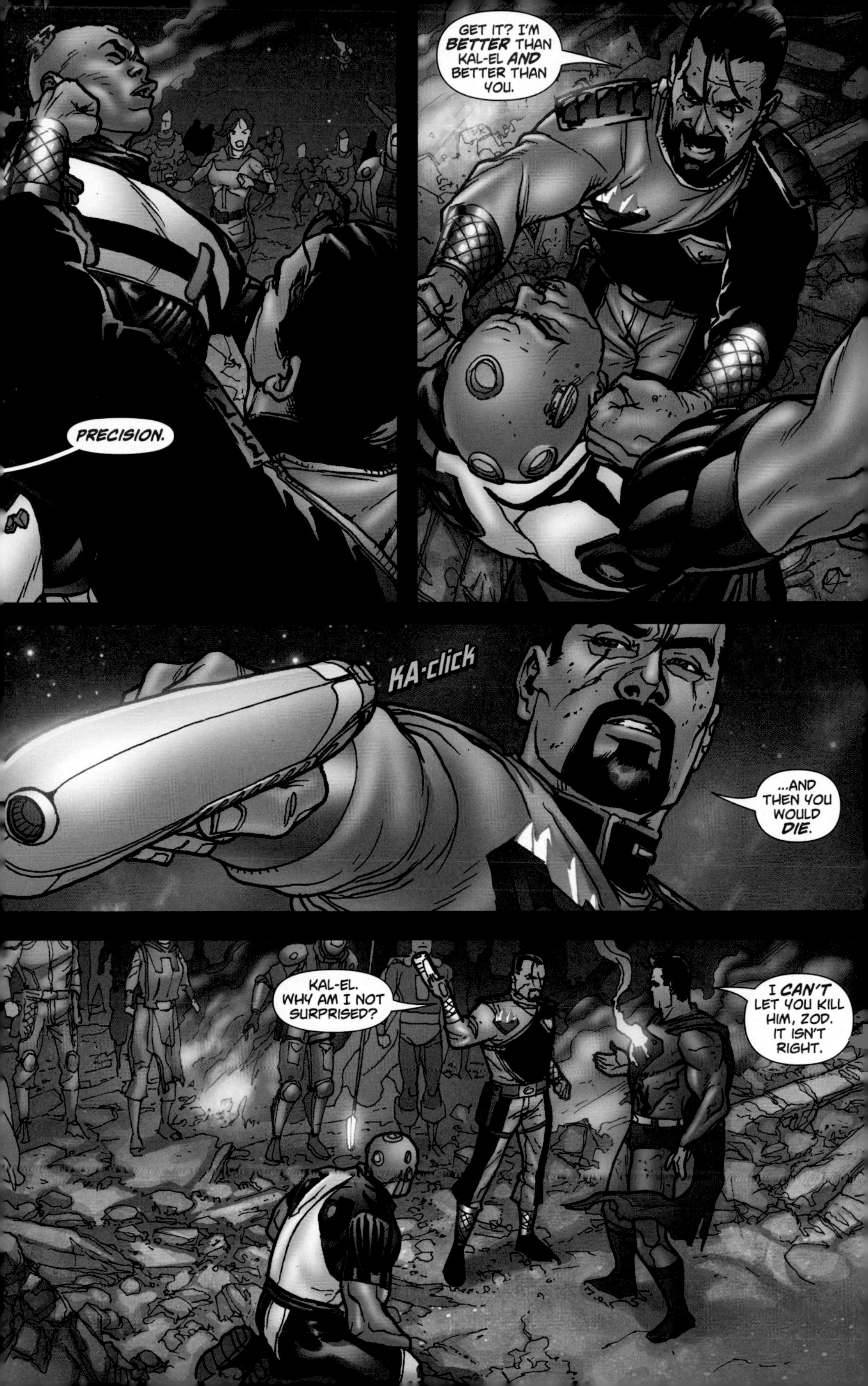
PRECISION.
GET IT? I'M BETTER THAN KAL-EL AND BETTER THAN YOU.
KA-click
...AND THEN YOU WOULD DIE.
KAL-EL. WHY AM I NOT SURPRISED?
I CAN'T LET YOU KILL HIM, ZOD. IT ISN'T RIGHT.

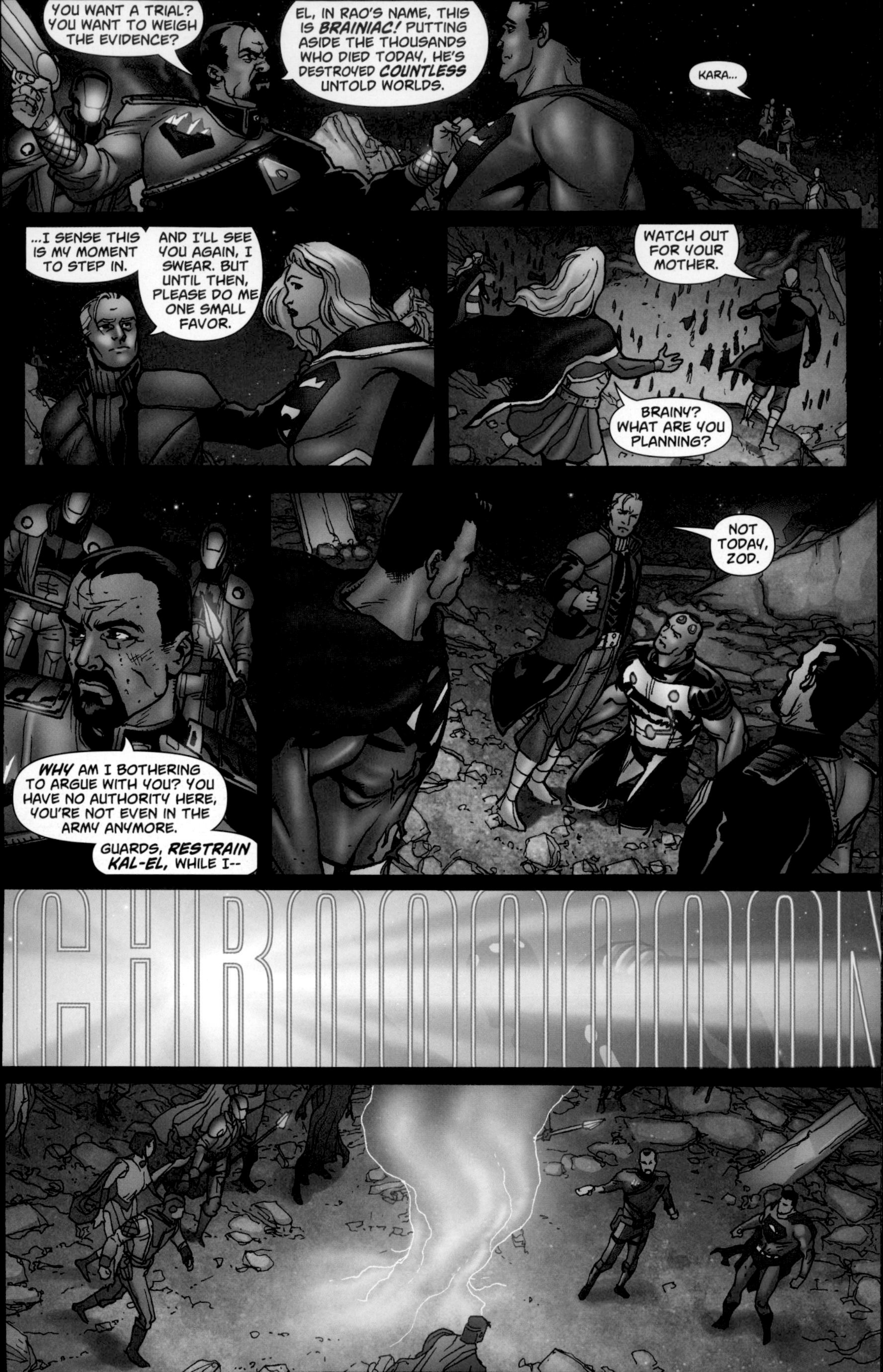
YOU WANT A TRIAL? YOU WANT TO WEIGH THE EVIDENCE?
EL, IN RAO'S NAME, THIS IS BRAINIAC! PUTTING ASIDE THE THOUSANDS WHO DIED TODAY, HE'S DESTROYED COUNTLESS UNTOLD WORLDS.
KARA...
...I SENSE THIS IS MY MOMENT TO STEP IN.
AND I'LL SEE YOU AGAIN, I SWEAR. BUT UNTIL THEN, PLEASE DO ME ONE SMALL FAVOR.
WATCH OUT FOR YOUR MOTHER.
BRAINY? WHAT ARE YOU PLANNING?
WHY AM I BOTHERING TO ARGUE WITH YOU? YOU HAVE NO AUTHORITY HERE, YOU'RE NOT EVEN IN THE ARMY ANYMORE.
GUARDS, RESTRAIN KAL-EL, WHILE I--
NOT TODAY, ZOD.
CHROOOOOON

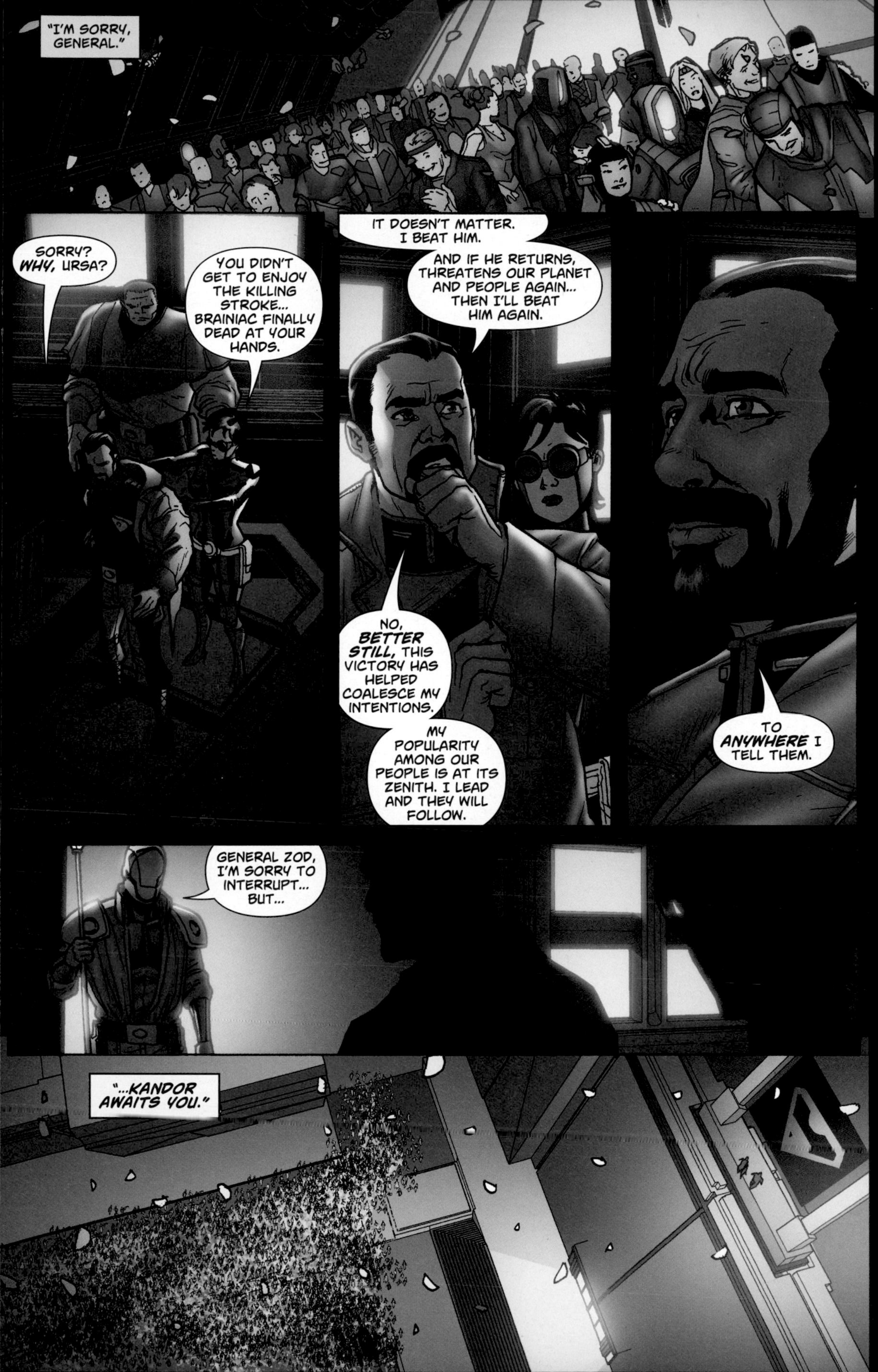
"I'M SORRY, GENERAL."
SORRY? WHY, URSA?
YOU DIDN'T GET TO ENJOY THE KILLING STROKE... BRAINIAC FINALLY DEAD AT YOUR HANDS.
IT DOESN'T MATTER. I BEAT HIM.
AND IF HE RETURNS, THREATENS OUR PLANET AND PEOPLE AGAIN... THEN I'LL BEAT HIM AGAIN.
NO, BETTER STILL, THIS VICTORY HAS HELPED COALESCE MY INTENTIONS.
MY POPULARITY AMONG OUR PEOPLE IS AT ITS ZENITH. I LEAD AND THEY WILL FOLLOW.
TO ANYWHERE I TELL THEM.
GENERAL ZOD, I'M SORRY TO INTERRUPT... BUT...
"...KANDOR AWAITS YOU."

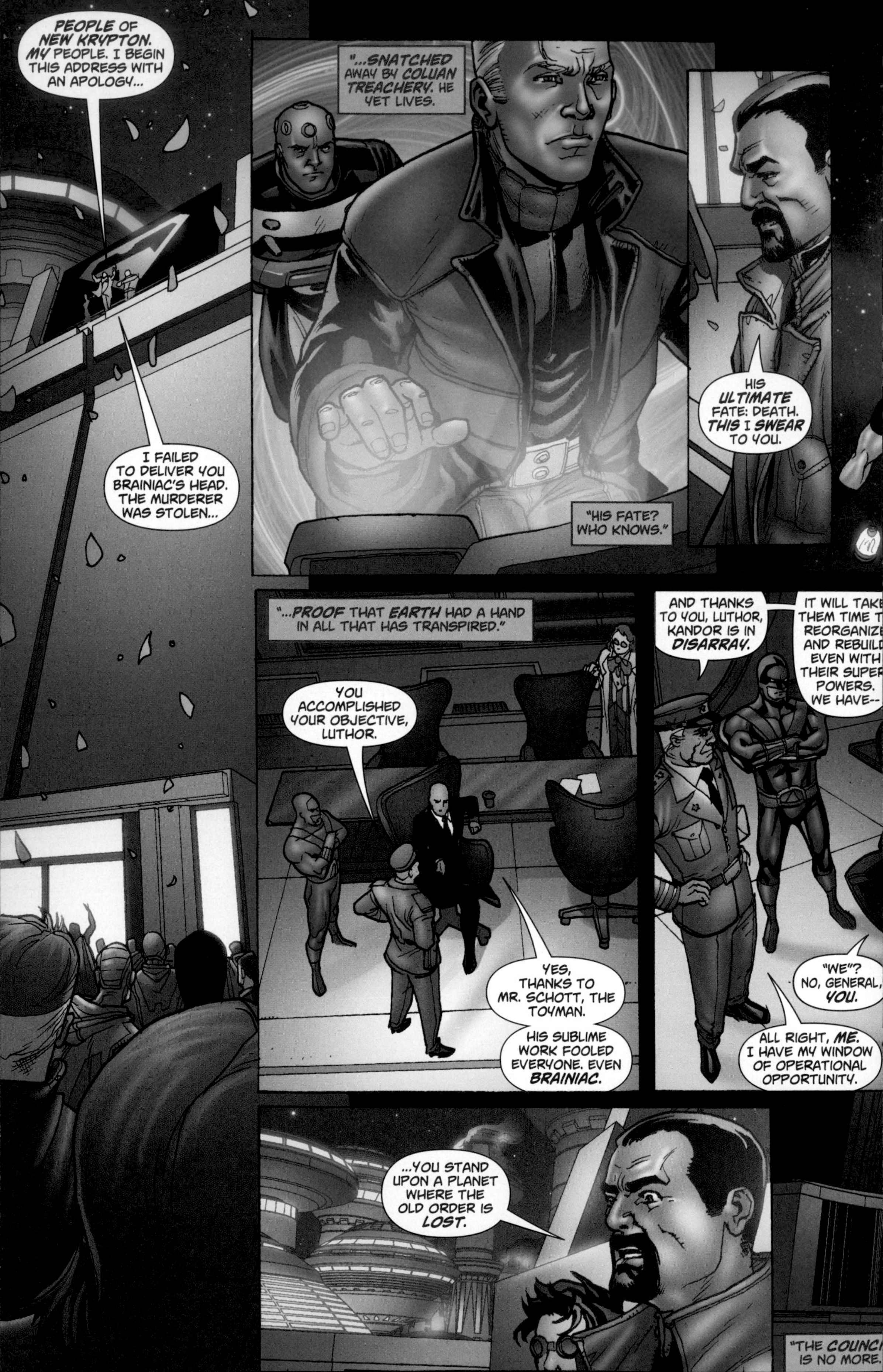
PEOPLE OF NEW KRYPTON. MY PEOPLE. I BEGIN THIS ADDRESS WITH AN APOLOGY...
I FAILED TO DELIVER YOU BRAINIAC'S HEAD. THE MURDERER WAS STOLEN...
"...SNATCHED AWAY BY COLUAN TREACHERY. HE YET LIVES.
"HIS FATE? WHO KNOWS."
HIS ULTIMATE FATE: DEATH. THIS I SWEAR TO YOU.
"...PROOF THAT EARTH HAD A HAND IN ALL THAT HAS TRANSPIRED."
YOU ACCOMPLISHED YOUR OBJECTIVE, LUTHOR.
YES, THANKS TO MR. SCHOTT, THE TOYMAN.
HIS SUBLIME WORK FOOLED EVERYONE. EVEN BRAINIAC.
AND THANKS TO YOU, LUTHOR, KANDOR IS IN DISARRAY.
IT WILL TAKE THEM TIME TO REORGANIZE AND REBUILD EVEN WITH THEIR SUPER POWERS. WE HAVE--
"WE"? NO, GENERAL, YOU.
ALL RIGHT, ME. I HAVE MY WINDOW OF OPERATIONAL OPPORTUNITY.
...YOU STAND UPON A PLANET WHERE THE OLD ORDER IS LOST.
"THE COUNCIL IS NO MORE.

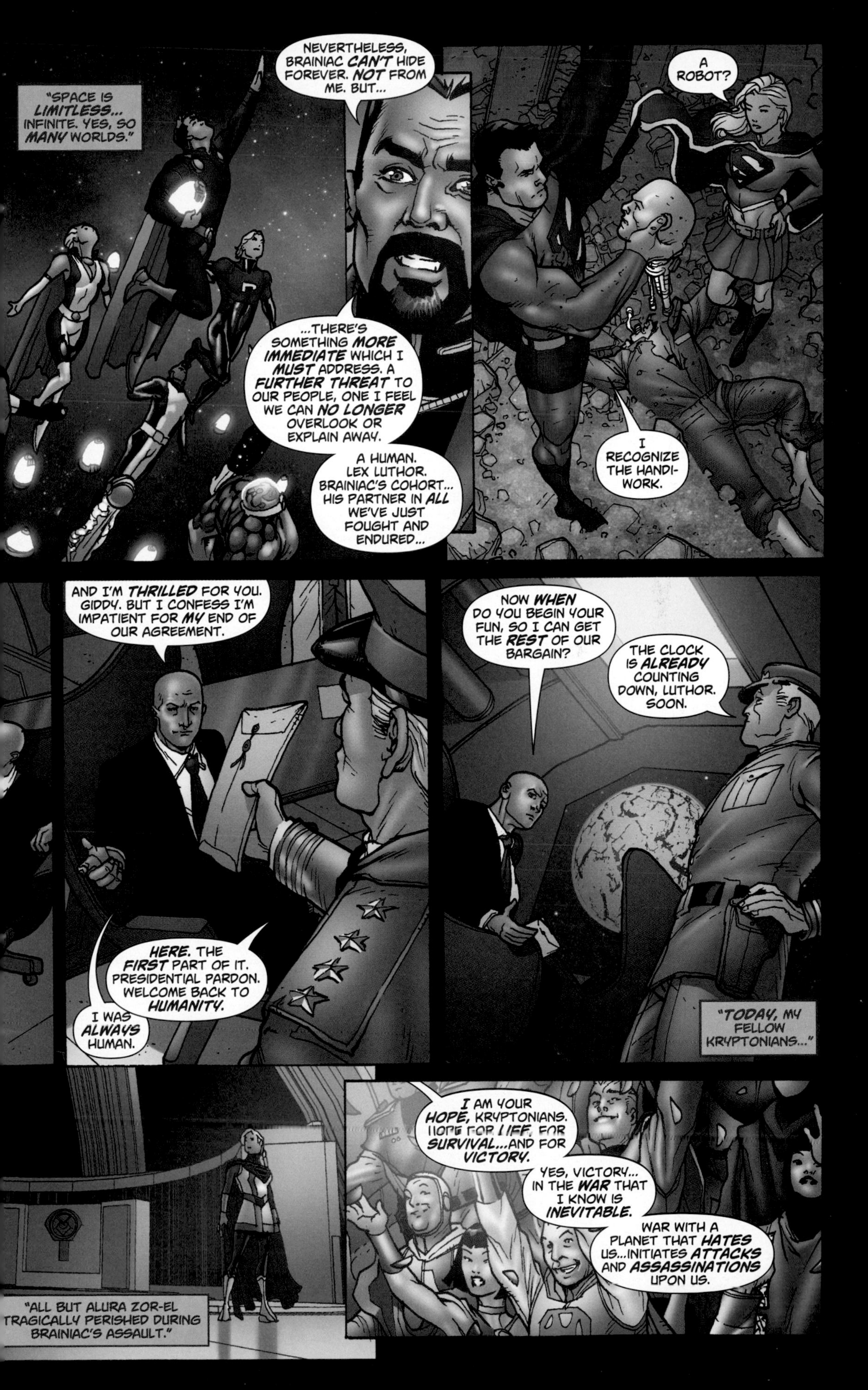
"SPACE IS LIMITLESS... INFINITE. YES, SO MANY WORLDS."
NEVERTHELESS, BRAINIAC CAN'T HIDE FOREVER. NOT FROM ME. BUT...
...THERE'S SOMETHING MORE IMMEDIATE WHICH I MUST ADDRESS. A FURTHER THREAT TO OUR PEOPLE, ONE I FEEL WE CAN NO LONGER OVERLOOK OR EXPLAIN AWAY.
A HUMAN. LEX LUTHOR. BRAINIAC'S COHORT... HIS PARTNER IN ALL WE'VE JUST FOUGHT AND ENDURED...
A ROBOT?
I RECOGNIZE THE HANDI-WORK.
AND I'M THRILLED FOR YOU. GIDDY. BUT I CONFESS I'M IMPATIENT FOR MY END OF OUR AGREEMENT.
HERE. THE FIRST PART OF IT. PRESIDENTIAL PARDON. WELCOME BACK TO HUMANITY.
I WAS ALWAYS HUMAN.
NOW WHEN DO YOU BEGIN YOUR FUN, SO I CAN GET THE REST OF OUR BARGAIN?
THE CLOCK IS ALREADY COUNTING DOWN, LUTHOR. SOON.
"TODAY, MY FELLOW KRYPTONIANS..."
"ALL BUT ALURA ZOR-EL TRAGICALLY PERISHED DURING BRAINIAC'S ASSAULT."
I AM YOUR HOPE, KRYPTONIANS. HOPE FOR LIFE, FOR SURVIVAL...AND FOR VICTORY.
YES, VICTORY... IN THE WAR THAT I KNOW IS INEVITABLE.
WAR WITH A PLANET THAT HATES US...INITIATES ATTACKS AND ASSASSINATIONS UPON US.

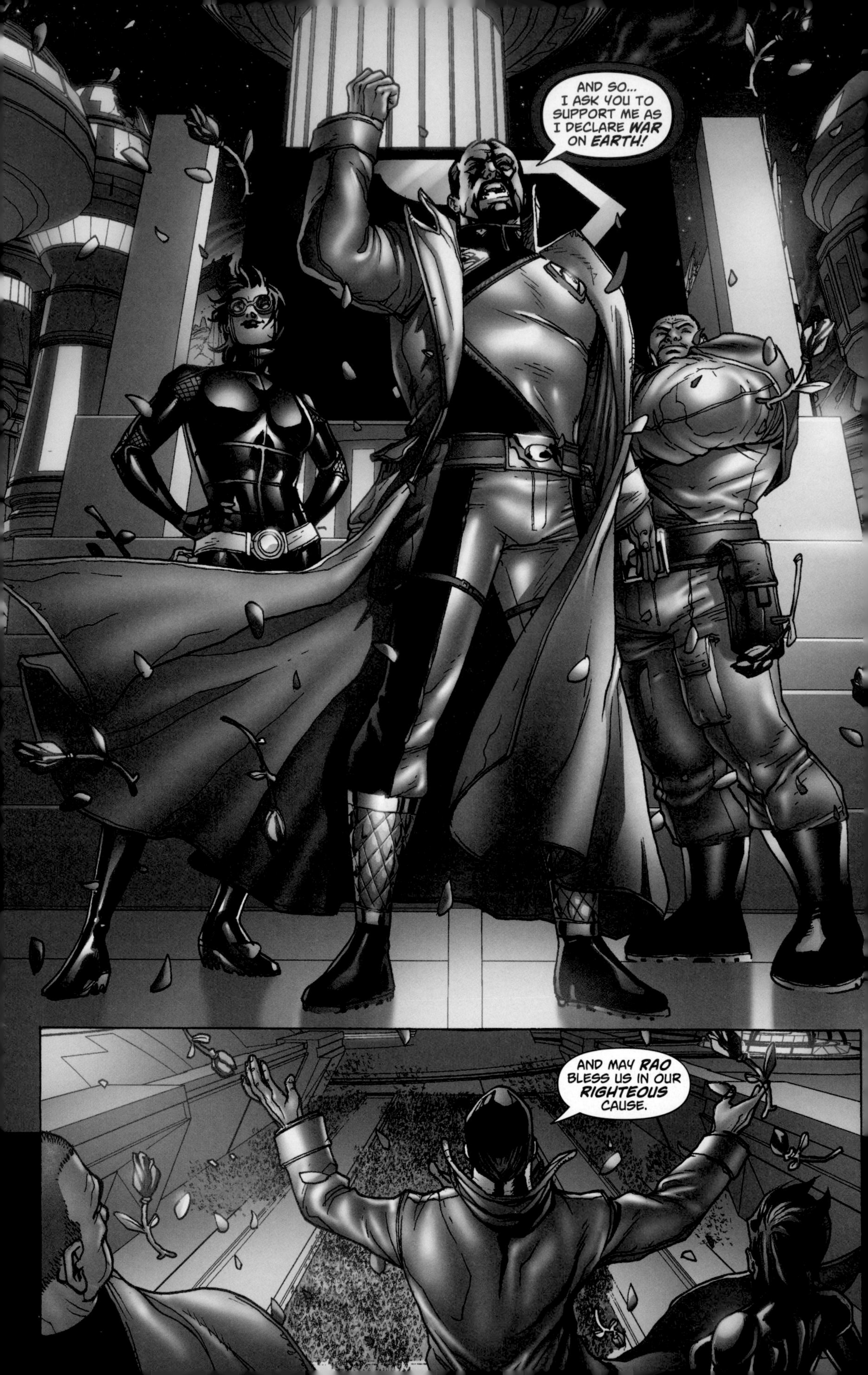
AND SO... I ASK YOU TO SUPPORT ME AS I DECLARE WAR ON EARTH!
AND MAY RAO BLESS US IN OUR RIGHTEOUS CAUSE.

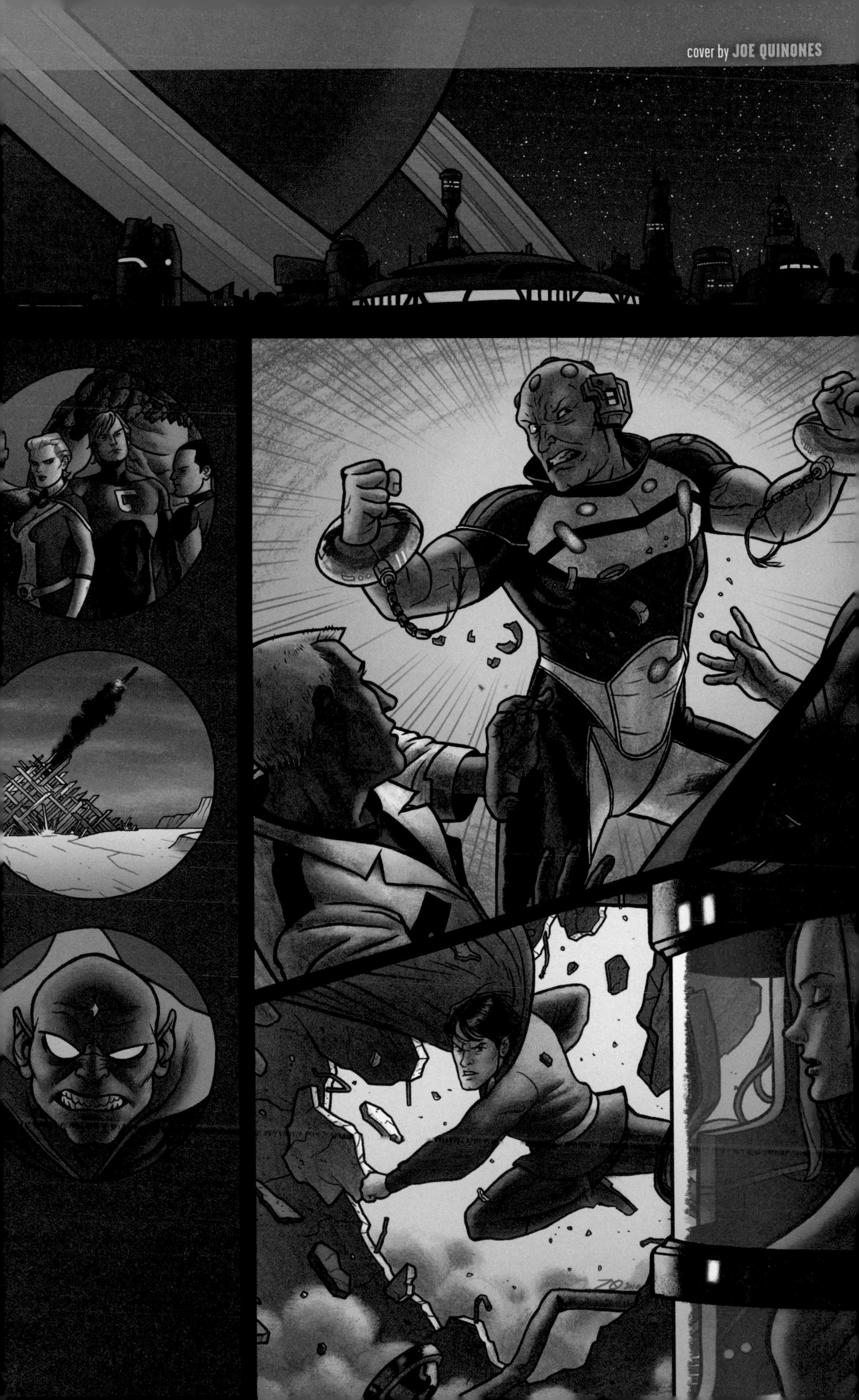
cover by JOE QUINONES

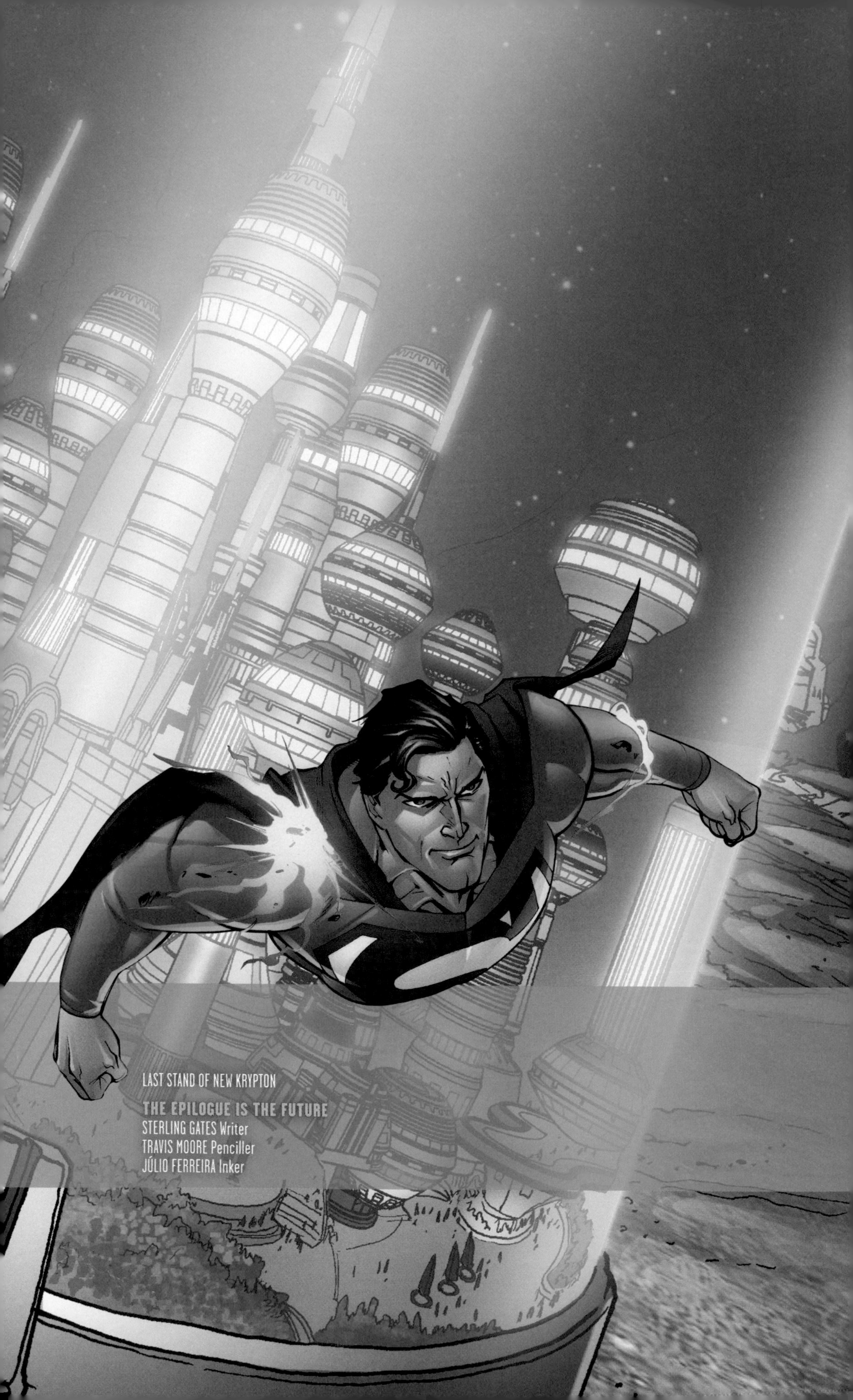

LAST STAND OF NEW KRYPTON

THE EPILOGUE IS THE FUTURE

STERLING GATES Writer
TRAVIS MOORE Penciller
JÚLIO FERREIRA Inker

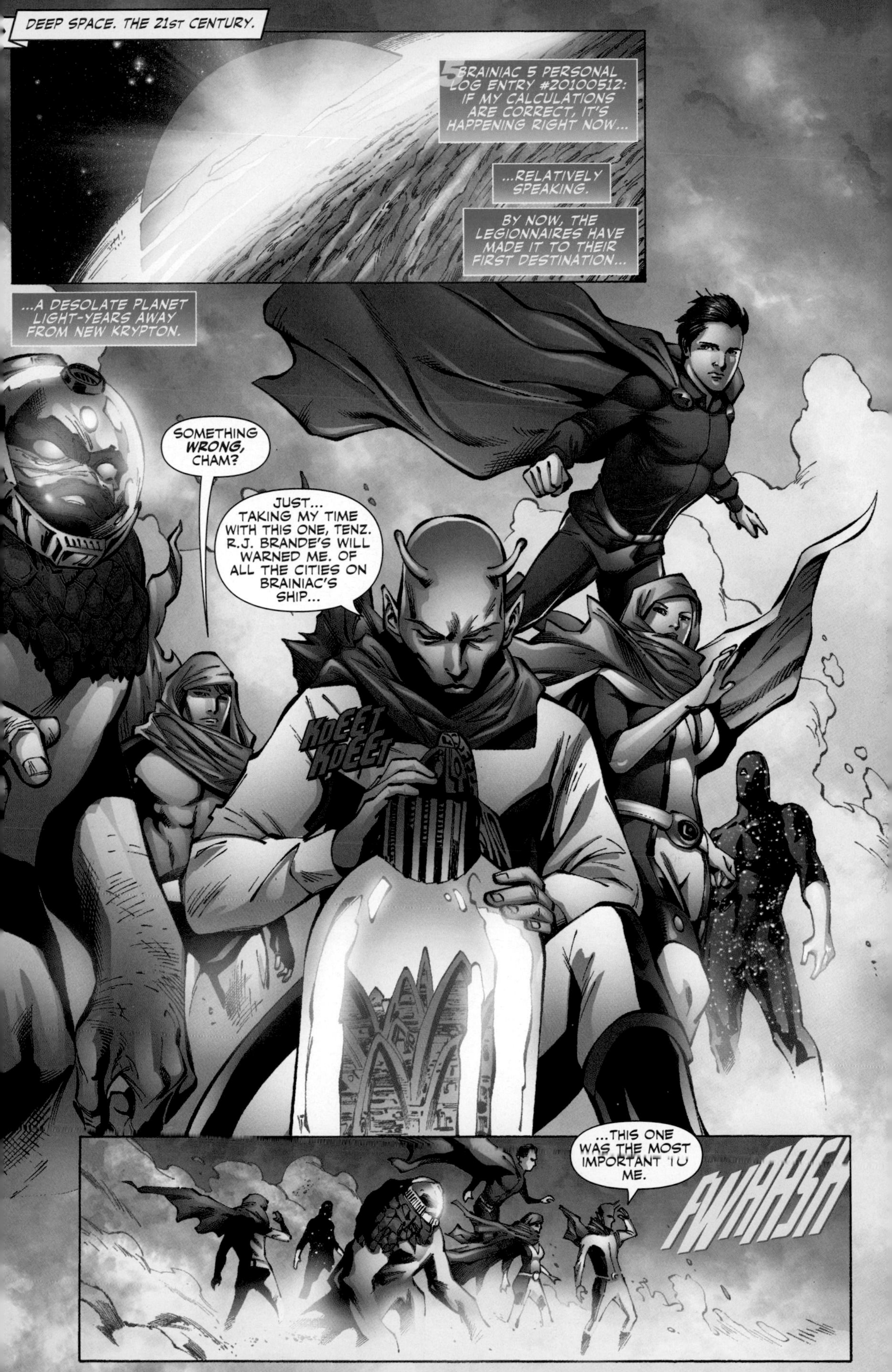
DEEP SPACE. THE 21ST CENTURY.
BRAINIAC 5 PERSONAL LOG ENTRY #20100512: IF MY CALCULATIONS ARE CORRECT, IT'S HAPPENING RIGHT NOW...
...RELATIVELY SPEAKING.
BY NOW, THE LEGIONNAIRES HAVE MADE IT TO THEIR FIRST DESTINATION...
...A DESOLATE PLANET LIGHT-YEARS AWAY FROM NEW KRYPTON.
SOMETHING *WRONG*, CHAM?
JUST... TAKING MY TIME WITH THIS ONE, TENZ. R.J. BRANDE'S WILL WARNED ME. OF ALL THE CITIES ON BRAINIAC'S SHIP...
KDEET KDEET
...THIS ONE WAS THE MOST IMPORTANT TO ME.
FWAASH

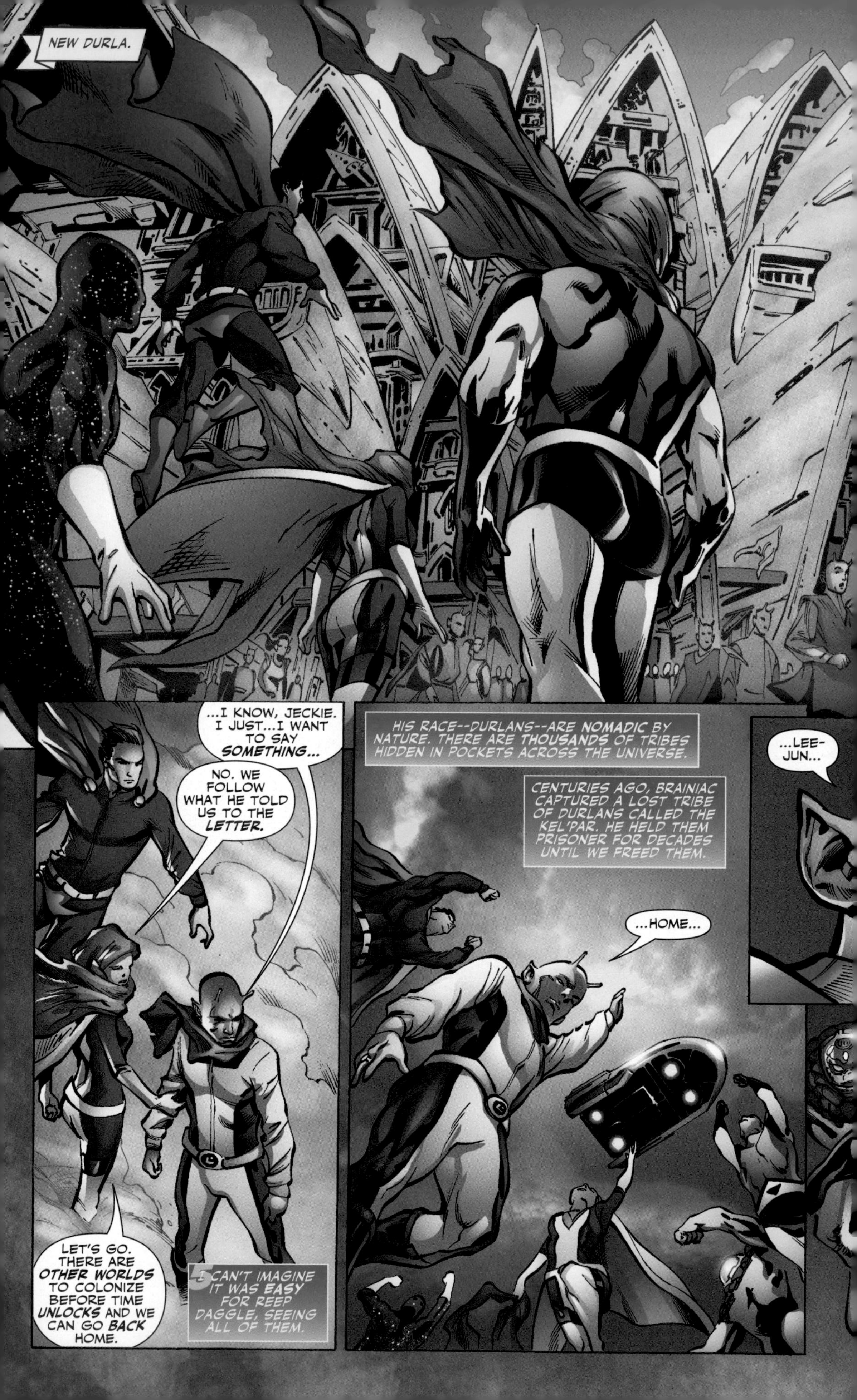
NEW DURLA.
...I KNOW, JECKIE. I JUST...I WANT TO SAY SOMETHING...
NO. WE FOLLOW WHAT HE TOLD US TO THE LETTER.
LET'S GO. THERE ARE OTHER WORLDS TO COLONIZE BEFORE TIME UNLOCKS AND WE CAN GO BACK HOME.
I CAN'T IMAGINE IT WAS EASY FOR REEP DAGGLE, SEEING ALL OF THEM.
HIS RACE--DURLANS--ARE NOMADIC BY NATURE. THERE ARE THOUSANDS OF TRIBES HIDDEN IN POCKETS ACROSS THE UNIVERSE.
CENTURIES AGO, BRAINIAC CAPTURED A LOST TRIBE OF DURLANS CALLED THE KEL'PAR. HE HELD THEM PRISONER FOR DECADES UNTIL WE FREED THEM.
...HOME...
...LEE-JUN...

WHO ARE YOU?!

WE ARE THE LEGION. AND WE--

CHAM.

YOU *READ* BRANDE'S WILL. WE'RE NOT ALLOWED TO SPEAK TO *ANYONE.*

ONE OF THOSE DURLANS WAS QUELTOP DAGGLE.

CHAMELEON BOY'S ANCESTOR.

THAT'S WHY R.J. BRANDE SENT THE LEGIONNAIRES BACK HERE, TO THIS TIME PERIOD.

IF WE DIDN'T SAVE THE LIFE OF QUELTOP, IN NINE HUNDRED YEARS' TIME, THERE WOULD'VE BEEN NO REN DAGGLE.

REN DAGGLE...WHO EVENTUALLY BECAME R.J. BRANDE, THE MAN WHO FATHERED BOTH REEP AND THE LEGION OF SUPER-HEROES.

THAT'S WHY THE LEGION'S MISSION WAS SO IMPORTANT. IT WAS A MISSION WE'D *ALWAYS* UNDERTAKEN. A TIME LOOP...

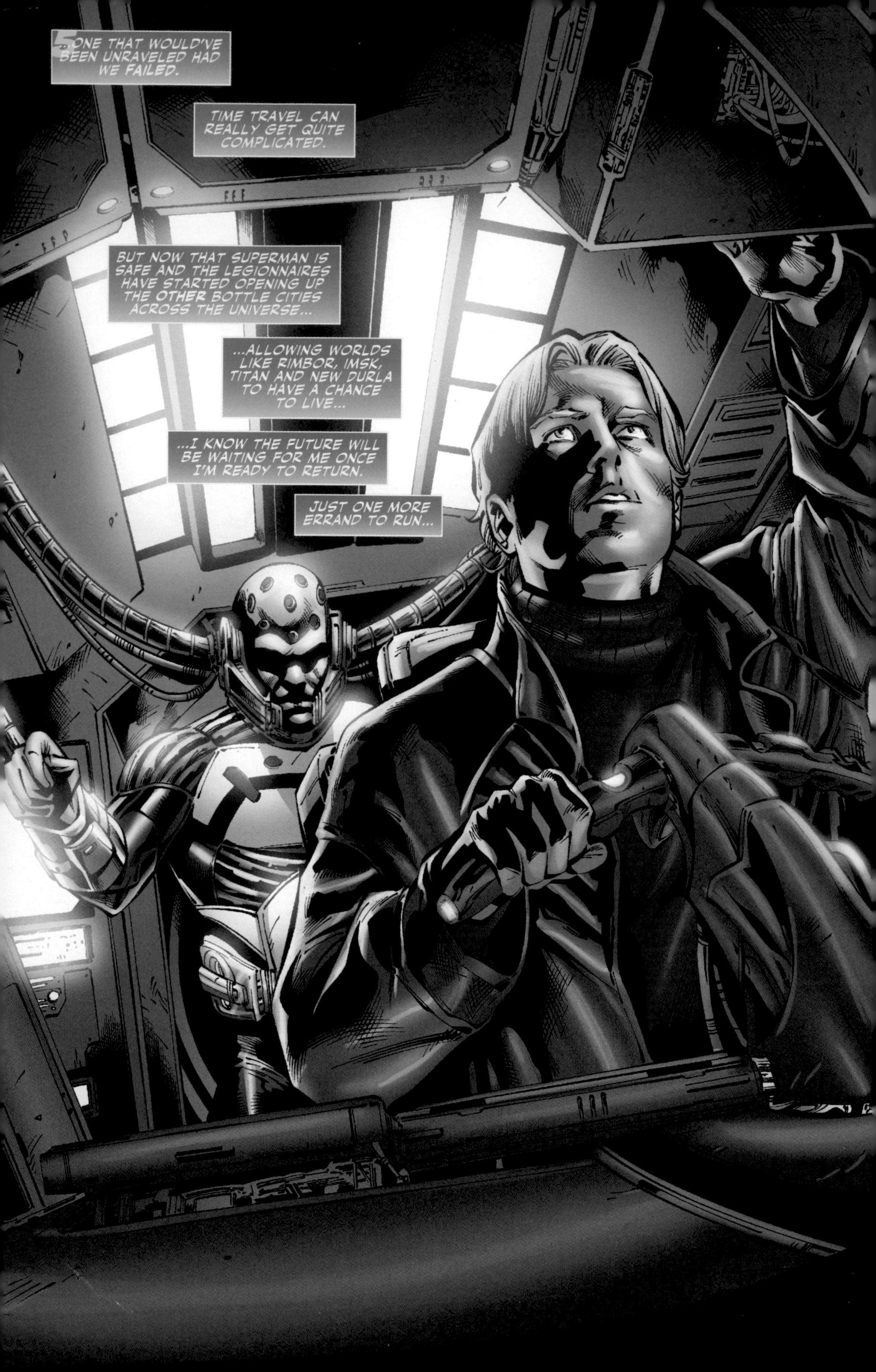
5
ONE THAT WOULD'VE BEEN UNRAVELED HAD WE FAILED.
TIME TRAVEL CAN REALLY GET QUITE COMPLICATED.
BUT NOW THAT SUPERMAN IS SAFE AND THE LEGIONNAIRES HAVE STARTED OPENING UP THE OTHER BOTTLE CITIES ACROSS THE UNIVERSE...
...ALLOWING WORLDS LIKE RIMBOR, IMSK, TITAN AND NEW DURLA TO HAVE A CHANCE TO LIVE...
...I KNOW THE FUTURE WILL BE WAITING FOR ME ONCE I'M READY TO RETURN.
JUST ONE MORE ERRAND TO RUN...

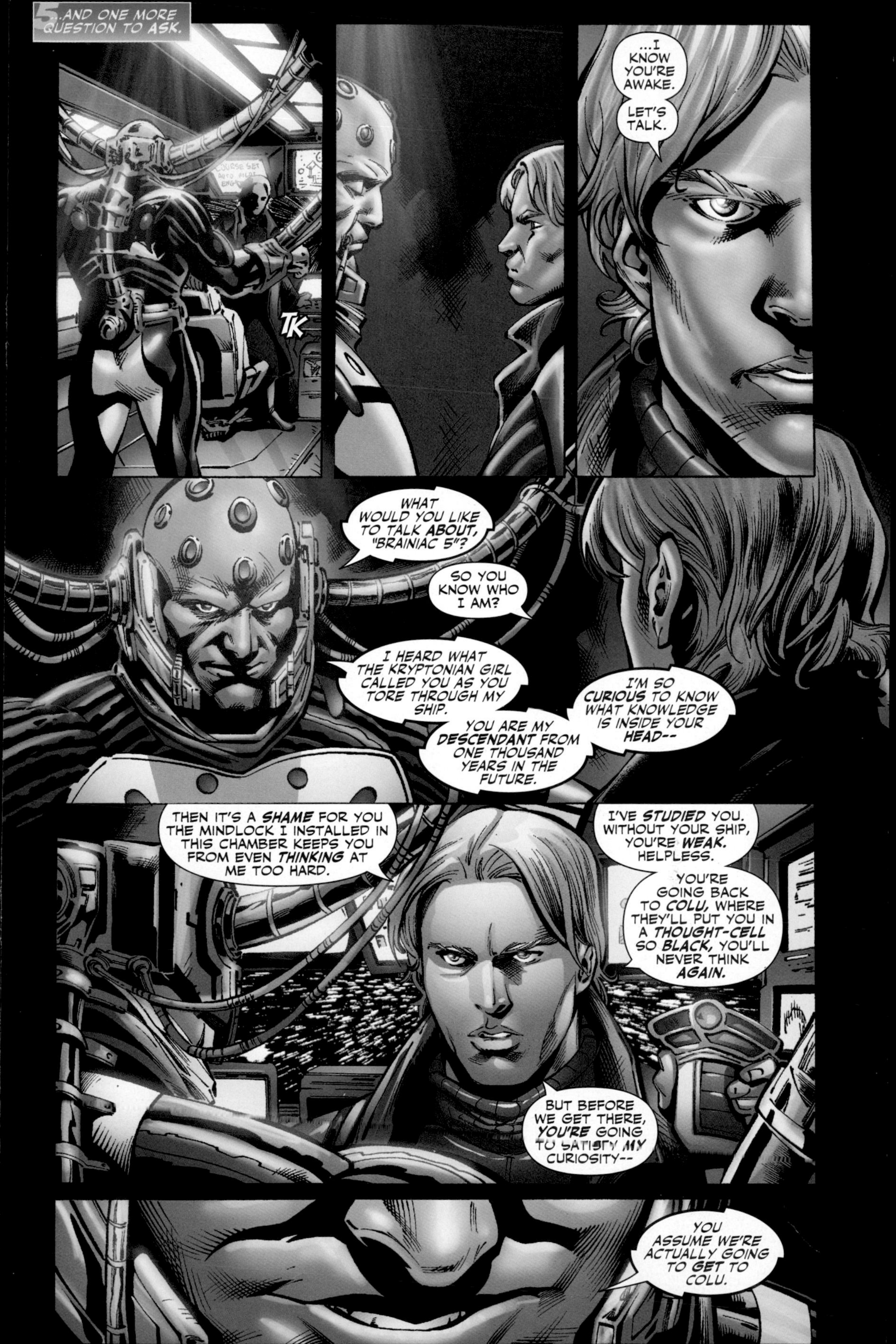
5 ...AND ONE MORE QUESTION TO ASK.
TK
...I KNOW YOU'RE AWAKE.
LET'S TALK.
WHAT WOULD YOU LIKE TO TALK ABOUT, "BRAINIAC 5"?
SO YOU KNOW WHO I AM?
I HEARD WHAT THE KRYPTONIAN GIRL CALLED YOU AS YOU TORE THROUGH MY SHIP.
YOU ARE MY DESCENDANT FROM ONE THOUSAND YEARS IN THE FUTURE.
I'M SO CURIOUS TO KNOW WHAT KNOWLEDGE IS INSIDE YOUR HEAD--
THEN IT'S A SHAME FOR YOU THE MINDLOCK I INSTALLED IN THIS CHAMBER KEEPS YOU FROM EVEN THINKING AT ME TOO HARD.
I'VE STUDIED YOU. WITHOUT YOUR SHIP, YOU'RE WEAK. HELPLESS.
YOU'RE GOING BACK TO COLU, WHERE THEY'LL PUT YOU IN A THOUGHT-CELL SO BLACK, YOU'LL NEVER THINK AGAIN.
BUT BEFORE WE GET THERE, YOU'RE GOING TO SATISFY MY CURIOSITY--
YOU ASSUME WE'RE ACTUALLY GOING TO GET TO COLU.

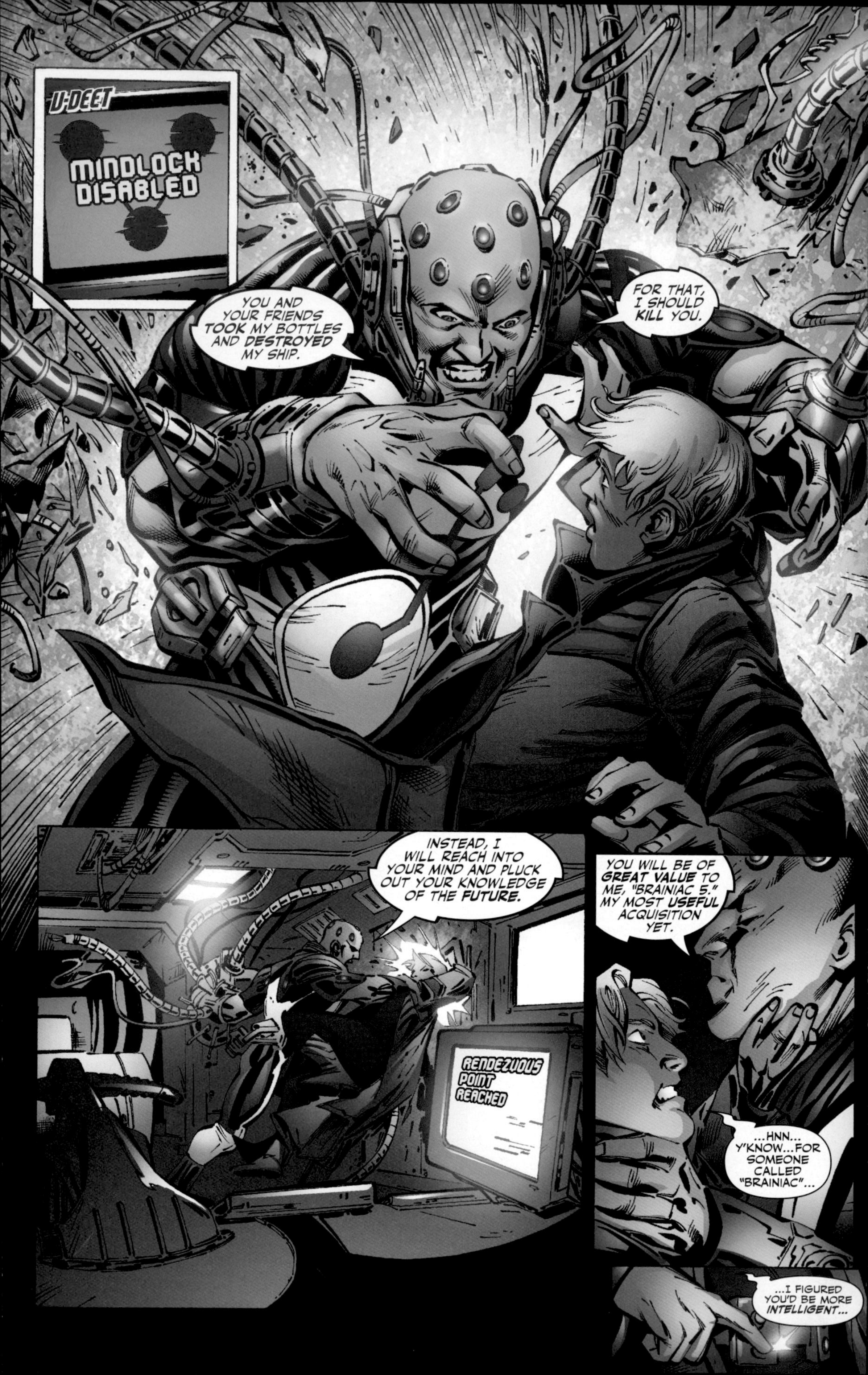
U-DEET
MINDLOCK DISABLED
YOU AND YOUR FRIENDS TOOK MY BOTTLES AND DESTROYED MY SHIP.
FOR THAT, I SHOULD KILL YOU.
INSTEAD, I WILL REACH INTO YOUR MIND AND PLUCK OUT YOUR KNOWLEDGE OF THE FUTURE.
RENDEZVOUS POINT REACHED
YOU WILL BE OF GREAT VALUE TO ME, "BRAINIAC 5." MY MOST USEFUL ACQUISITION YET.
...HNN... Y'KNOW...FOR SOMEONE CALLED "BRAINIAC"...
...I FIGURED YOU'D BE MORE INTELLIGENT...

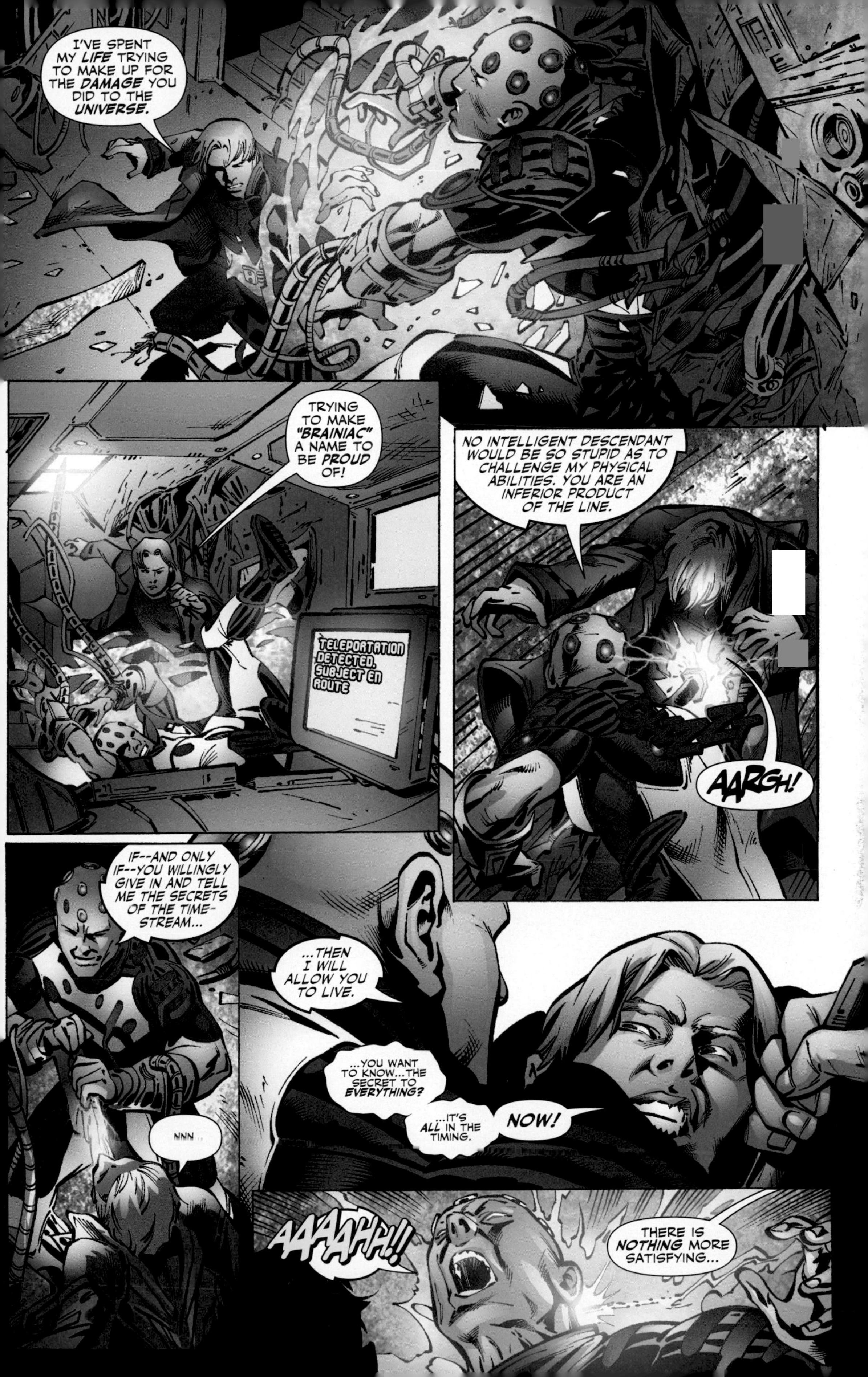
I'VE SPENT MY LIFE TRYING TO MAKE UP FOR THE DAMAGE YOU DID TO THE UNIVERSE.
TRYING TO MAKE "BRAINIAC" A NAME TO BE PROUD OF!
TELEPORTATION DETECTED. SUBJECT EN ROUTE
NO INTELLIGENT DESCENDANT WOULD BE SO STUPID AS TO CHALLENGE MY PHYSICAL ABILITIES. YOU ARE AN INFERIOR PRODUCT OF THE LINE.
AARGH!
IF--AND ONLY IF--YOU WILLINGLY GIVE IN AND TELL ME THE SECRETS OF THE TIME-STREAM...
NNN...
...THEN I WILL ALLOW YOU TO LIVE.
...YOU WANT TO KNOW...THE SECRET TO EVERYTHING?
...IT'S ALL IN THE TIMING.
NOW!
AAAAHH!!
THERE IS NOTHING MORE SATISFYING...

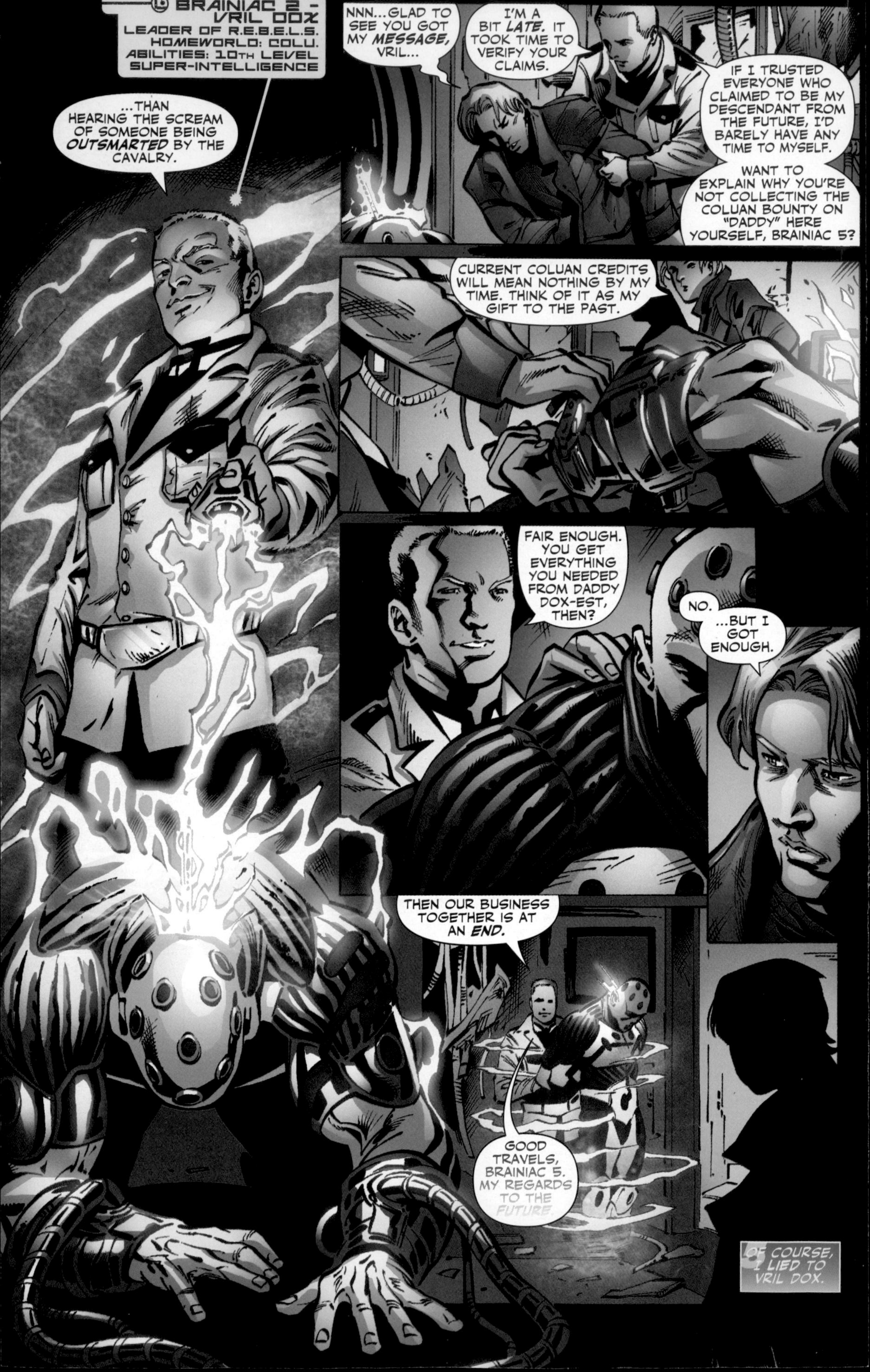
BRAINIAC 2 - VRIL DOX
LEADER OF R.E.B.E.L.S. HOMEWORLD: COLU. ABILITIES: 10TH LEVEL SUPER-INTELLIGENCE
...THAN HEARING THE SCREAM OF SOMEONE BEING OUTSMARTED BY THE CAVALRY.
NNN...GLAD TO SEE YOU GOT MY MESSAGE, VRIL...
I'M A BIT LATE. IT TOOK TIME TO VERIFY YOUR CLAIMS.
IF I TRUSTED EVERYONE WHO CLAIMED TO BE MY DESCENDANT FROM THE FUTURE, I'D BARELY HAVE ANY TIME TO MYSELF.
WANT TO EXPLAIN WHY YOU'RE NOT COLLECTING THE COLUAN BOUNTY ON "DADDY" HERE YOURSELF, BRAINIAC 5?
CURRENT COLUAN CREDITS WILL MEAN NOTHING BY MY TIME. THINK OF IT AS MY GIFT TO THE PAST.
FAIR ENOUGH. YOU GET EVERYTHING YOU NEEDED FROM DADDY DOX-EST, THEN?
NO.
...BUT I GOT ENOUGH.
THEN OUR BUSINESS TOGETHER IS AT AN END.
GOOD TRAVELS, BRAINIAC 5. MY REGARDS TO THE FUTURE.
OF COURSE, I LIED TO VRIL DOX.

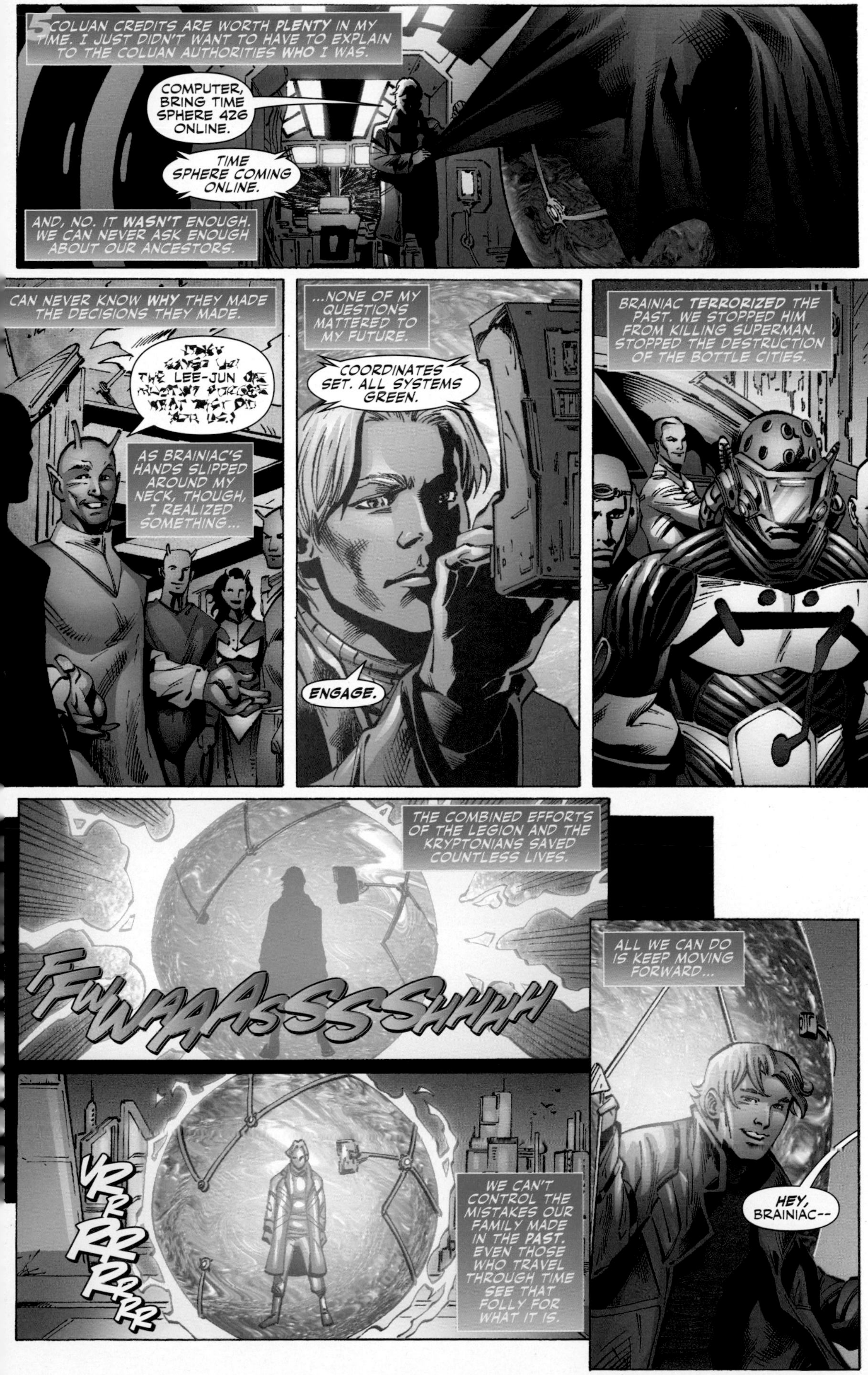
COLUAN CREDITS ARE WORTH PLENTY IN MY TIME. I JUST DIDN'T WANT TO HAVE TO EXPLAIN TO THE COLUAN AUTHORITIES WHO I WAS.
COMPUTER, BRING TIME SPHERE 426 ONLINE.
TIME SPHERE COMING ONLINE.
AND, NO. IT WASN'T ENOUGH. WE CAN NEVER ASK ENOUGH ABOUT OUR ANCESTORS.
CAN NEVER KNOW WHY THEY MADE THE DECISIONS THEY MADE.
THE LEE-JUN
AS BRAINIAC'S HANDS SLIPPED AROUND MY NECK, THOUGH, I REALIZED SOMETHING...
...NONE OF MY QUESTIONS MATTERED TO MY FUTURE.
COORDINATES SET. ALL SYSTEMS GREEN.
ENGAGE.
BRAINIAC TERRORIZED THE PAST. WE STOPPED HIM FROM KILLING SUPERMAN. STOPPED THE DESTRUCTION OF THE BOTTLE CITIES.
THE COMBINED EFFORTS OF THE LEGION AND THE KRYPTONIANS SAVED COUNTLESS LIVES.
FFWWAAAASSSSSHHHH
VRRRRRRRRR
WE CAN'T CONTROL THE MISTAKES OUR FAMILY MADE IN THE PAST. EVEN THOSE WHO TRAVEL THROUGH TIME SEE THAT FOLLY FOR WHAT IT IS.
ALL WE CAN DO IS KEEP MOVING FORWARD...
HEY, BRAINIAC--

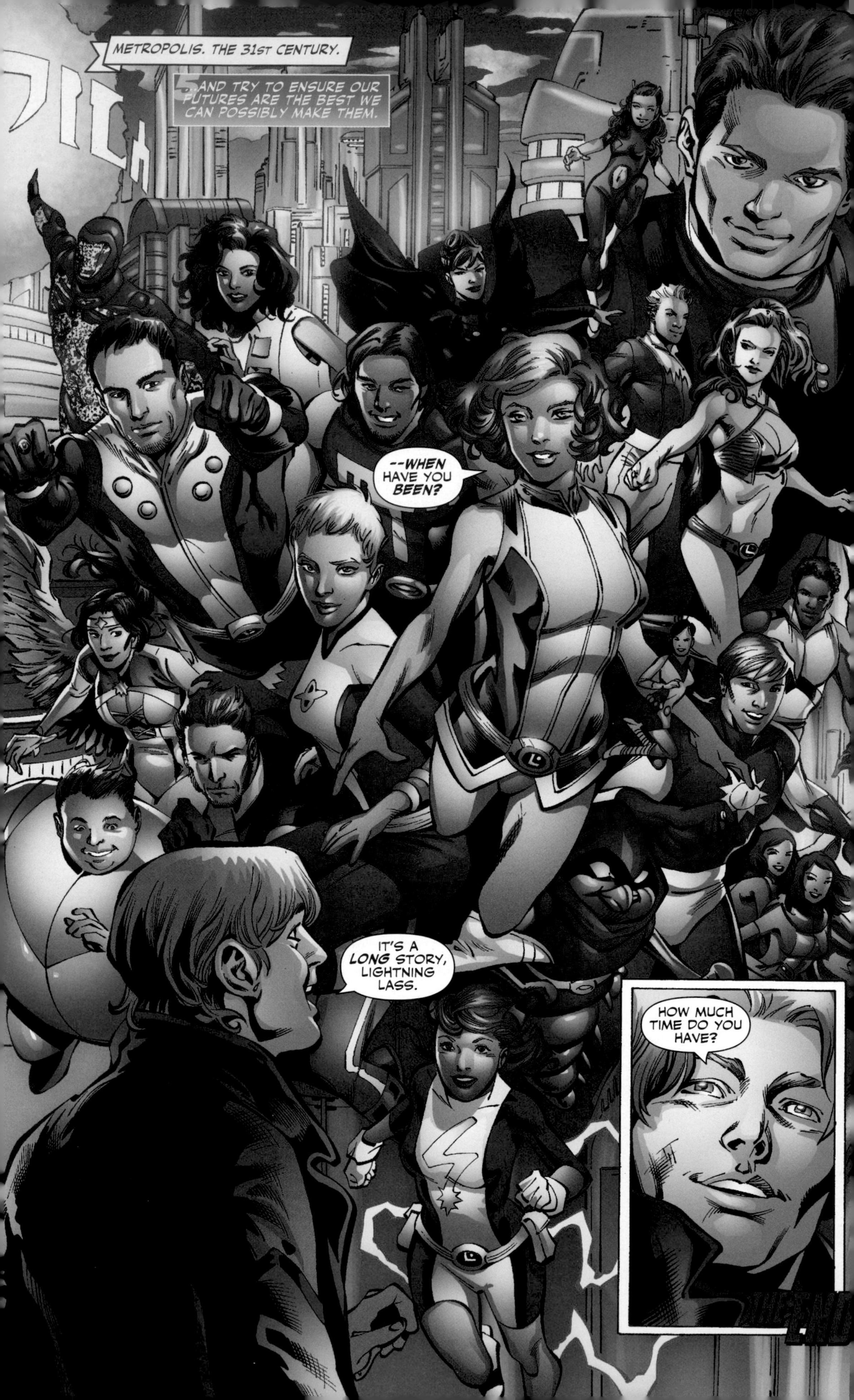
METROPOLIS. THE 31ST CENTURY.
...AND TRY TO ENSURE OUR FUTURES ARE THE BEST WE CAN POSSIBLY MAKE THEM.
--WHEN HAVE YOU BEEN?
IT'S A LONG STORY, LIGHTNING LASS.
HOW MUCH TIME DO YOU HAVE?

AFTERWARDS: AN AFTERWORD
BY STERLING GATES

"And so...I ask you to support me as I declare WAR on EARTH!" - General Zod

Well, that doesn't seem like a good thing, now, does it?

As you've no doubt surmised from General Zod's declaration of war at the end of LAST STAND OF NEW KRYPTON, the volume you're holding in your hands isn't the final act in the New Krypton saga. No, Super-Reader, you've got one more volume to go -- the ominously titled SUPERMAN: WAR OF THE SUPERMEN, also written by James Robinson and myself. But before you head over there, I'd like to say a few words about the story you've just read.

I think New Krypton is an incredible place. Only in the DC Universe would you find a planet full of super-powered people just like our Man of Steel, all of them terrified of the alien despot who once kidnapped and bottled them, Brainiac. Think about it: 100,000 aliens with heat vision are all suffering from post-traumatic stress disorder! That's a powder keg just waiting to go up!

By the time editor Matt Idelson asked me to come on board and write the SUPERGIRL monthly book, Geoff Johns and James Robinson had already worked out a lot of how New Krypton would work. The first thing they designed was the Guild system, which would take all of the disparate versions of Kryptonians that had been seen before and turning them into one slightly fractured — but still working — society. Supergirl's mother Alura would do her best to lead all of the Guilds, backed by the new High Council and counter-balanced by a military headed up by one of Superman's worst enemies, General Zod. Huge dramatic potential with high stakes there, with Superman and Supergirl caught in the middle.

• • •

One day, James called me and asked if I'd be interested in co-writing a story called "Brainiac and the Legion of Super-Heroes." It would start with the New Kryptonians facing off against their own personal bogeyman, Brainiac, in a battle that would determine the fate of another of DC's best concepts: the Legion of Super-Heroes. If our heroes fell, not only would New Krypton be destroyed, the future would cease to exist!

I was listening. I love the Legion of Super-Heroes just as much as I love Superman. Pitting Superman, Zod, the PTSD-suffering New Kryptonians, and the Legion of Super-Heroes against Brainiac and Lex Luthor? Hoo boy, was I all over that.

James and I plotted our story in late fall 2009, utilizing all of the elements that he and Geoff had already started seeding throughout the Super-books (Geoff was in full-on "Blackest Night" mode by this point, so he had to leave the Super-books behind). Soon after starting, the title of our crossover was changed to "The Last Stand of New Krypton," a title I adored. It evoked danger! Action! Suspense! Since both the Legion and Supergirl had seen some drastic continuity changes over the years, I wanted to take this opportunity to try to restore some of the more classic elements of Kara's relationship with the Legion and with Brainiac.

James wanted to tell a big Mon-El story over the course of it, connecting him back to the Legion, and we were both very concerned with finding a way to make the New Kryptonians stars in their own right as they rose up to help Superman stop the threat.

Throughout writing this story, James and I kept talking about how this was first and foremost a story about the New Kryptonians and their fears, and about how none of the Guilds would unite under any one person. The High Council and Alura had failed them all, as had Supergirl's attempts at unification. Obviously, they needed a hero to unite them...

...and they got one in General Zod, the man who almost kills Brainiac in the streets. The New Kryptonians are driven toward Zod's leadership over the course of Last Stand, and it's Zod — not our hero, Superman — who "wins" the hearts of the people at the end. It's a dark and unexpected ending for a Superman story, and it leads to another very dark and tragic Superman tale.

• • •

There are a few moments I'm particularly proud of across the two volumes of Last Stand, including the Military Guild member who puts the gun to his head once he sees that the city of Kandor has been rebottled, the little Kryptonian girl who can't turn off her super-hearing, and the wife of the man killed in Brainiac's opening attack coming back at the end to fry Brainiac with heat vision. I loved the way Pete Woods drew her face as she looks at Brainiac and says "Get him." Chilling stuff.

While I can't speak for James, I know I had a wonderful time co-writing this crossover with him and working with our phenomenal art teams. Pete Woods, Jamal Igle, Travis Moore, Ivan Rodriguez, Bernard Chang, Eduardo Pansica, Javier Pina, and Julian Lopez all did beautiful jobs, and my hats are off to all of them.

So. Going forward. The Legion have saved their worlds, ensuring the future. Supergirl met Brainiac 5, the man who could end up being the love of her life. Superboy got to see what a Kryptonian planet would look like, and Superman saw his friends and family unite to help save his world. Everyone got a little something out of this story, didn't they?

Oh, and General Zod got *exactly* what he wanted: With Brainiac defeated (and made to kneel before Zod!), the people of New Krypton would now follow him anywhere...

...including into a war with the planet Earth.

I hope you enjoyed SUPERMAN: THE LAST STAND OF NEW KRYPTON, Super-Reader. Get ready for the next (and final) volume in the New Krypton saga, as the 100-Minute War begins!

SJG
Los Angeles, October 2010

ADVENTURE COMICS 10 variant by **BERNARD CHANG**

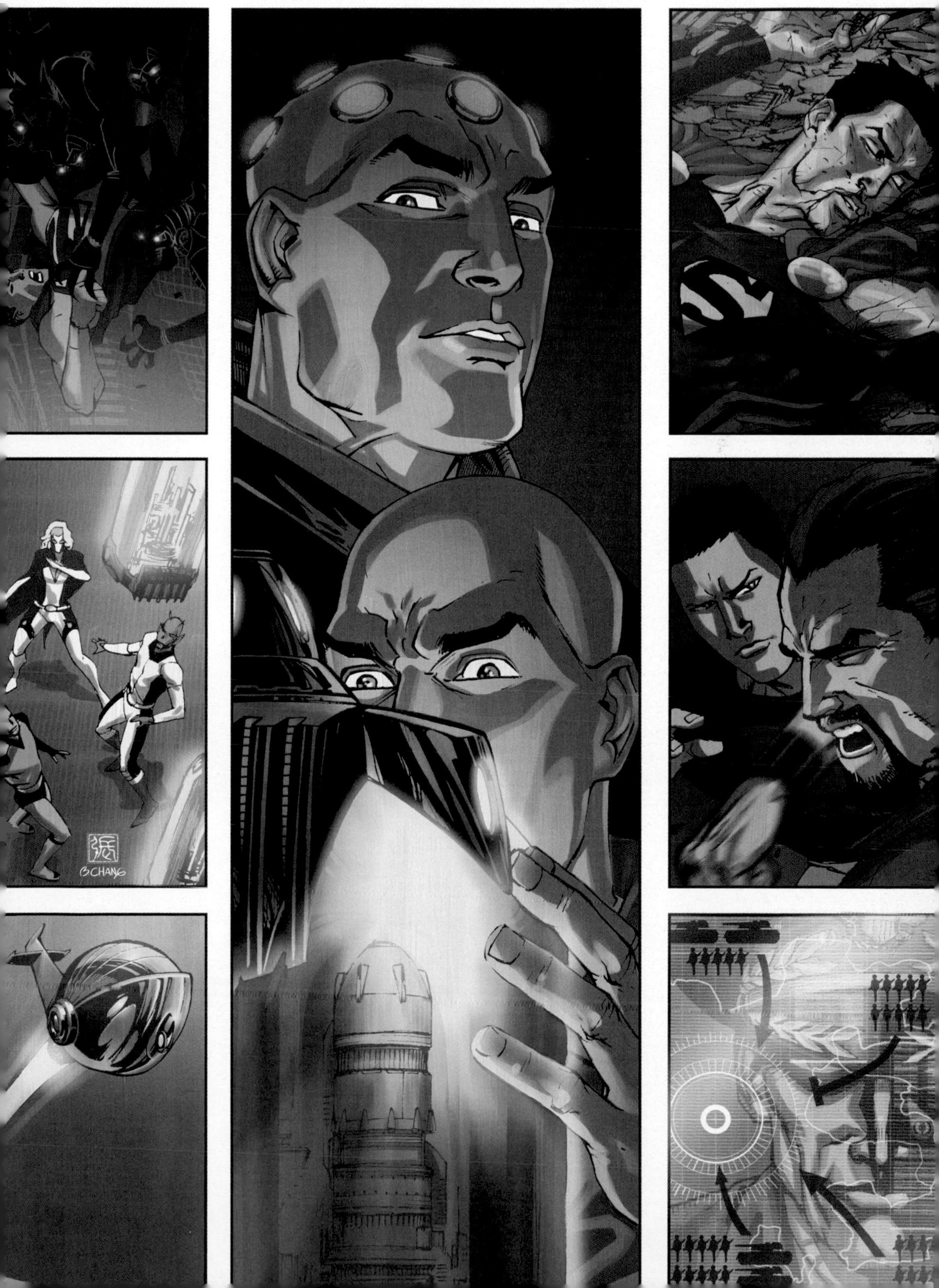

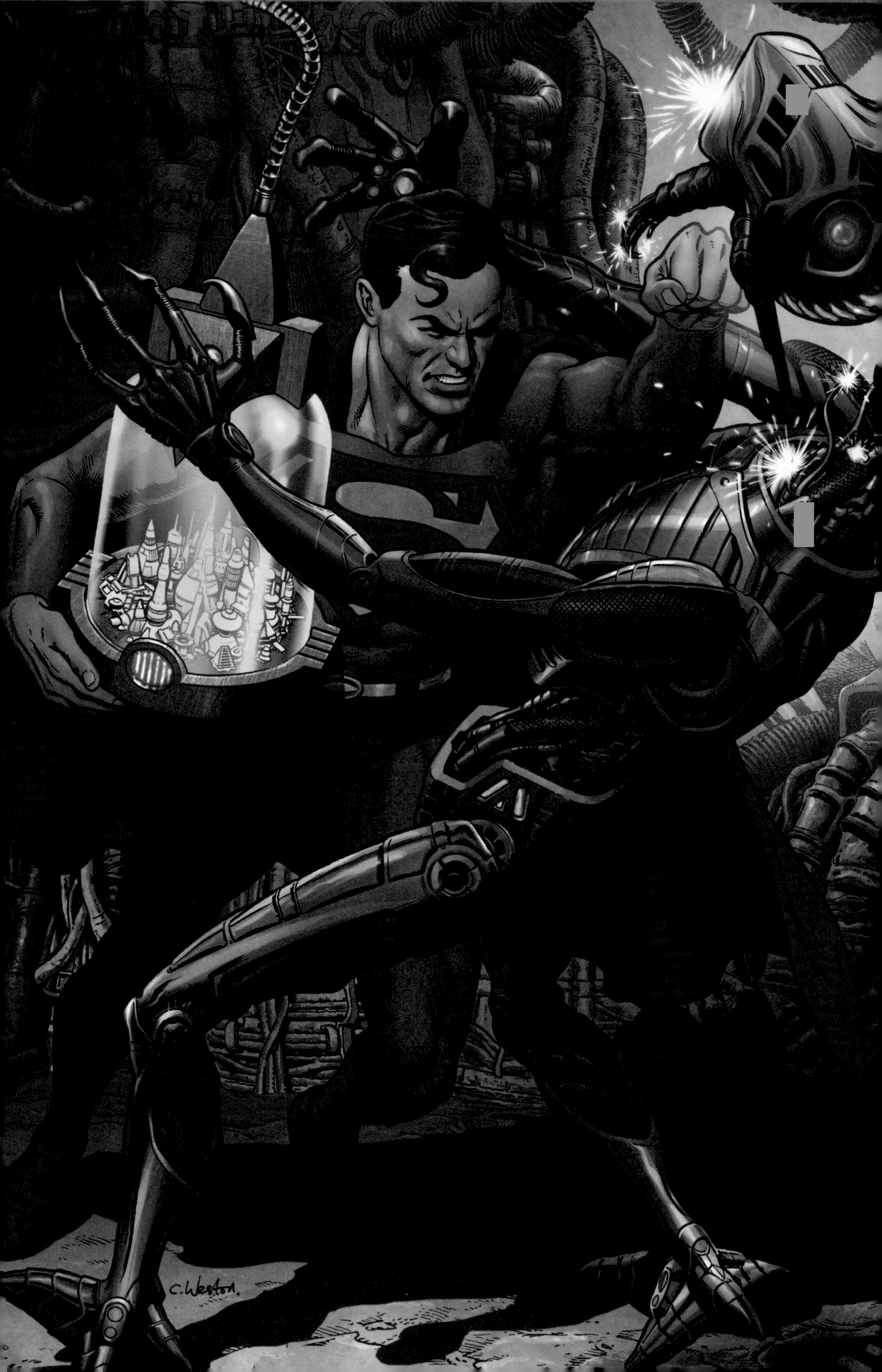
C. Weston.

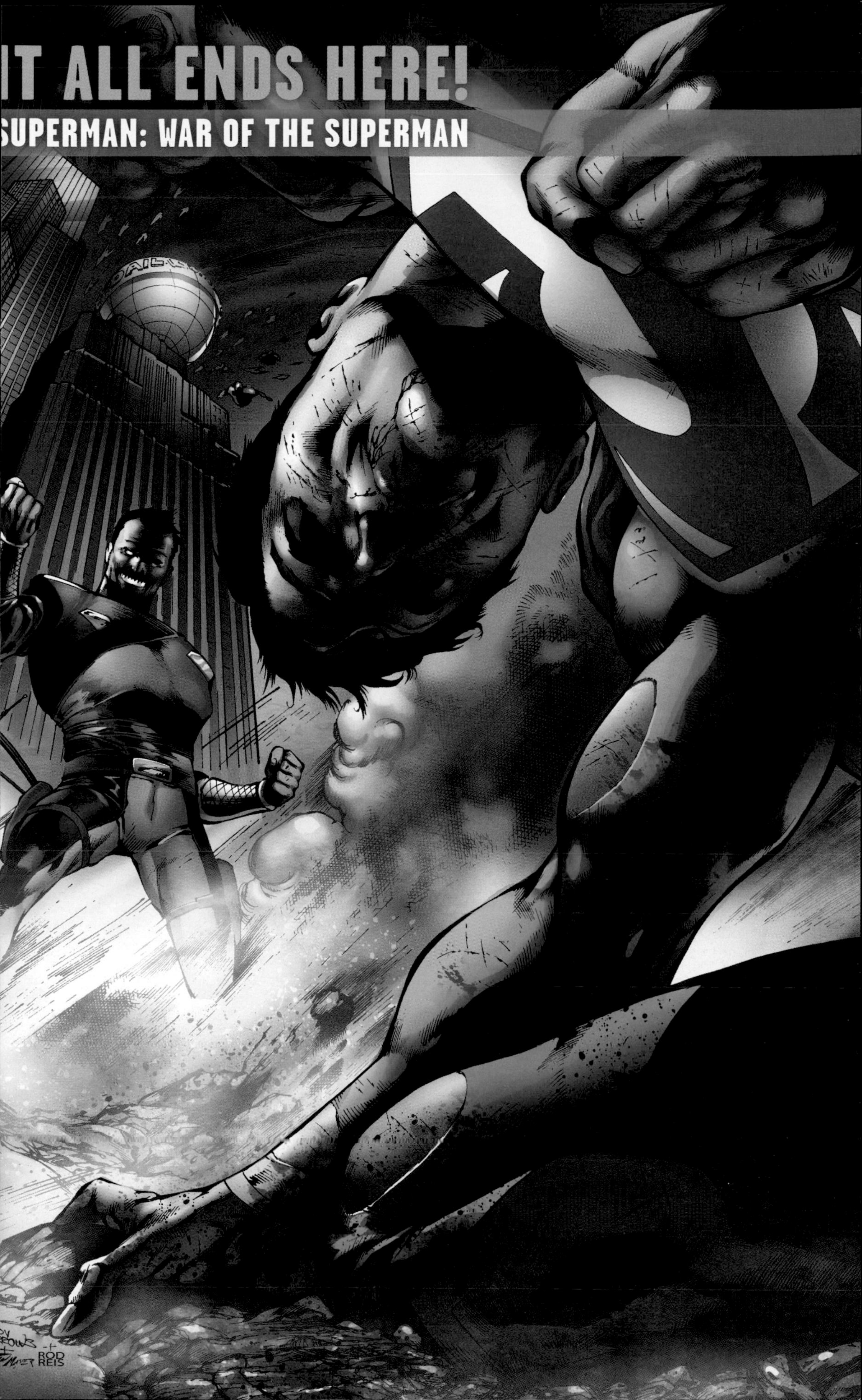
IT ALL ENDS HERE!
SUPERMAN: WAR OF THE SUPERMAN
ROD REIS

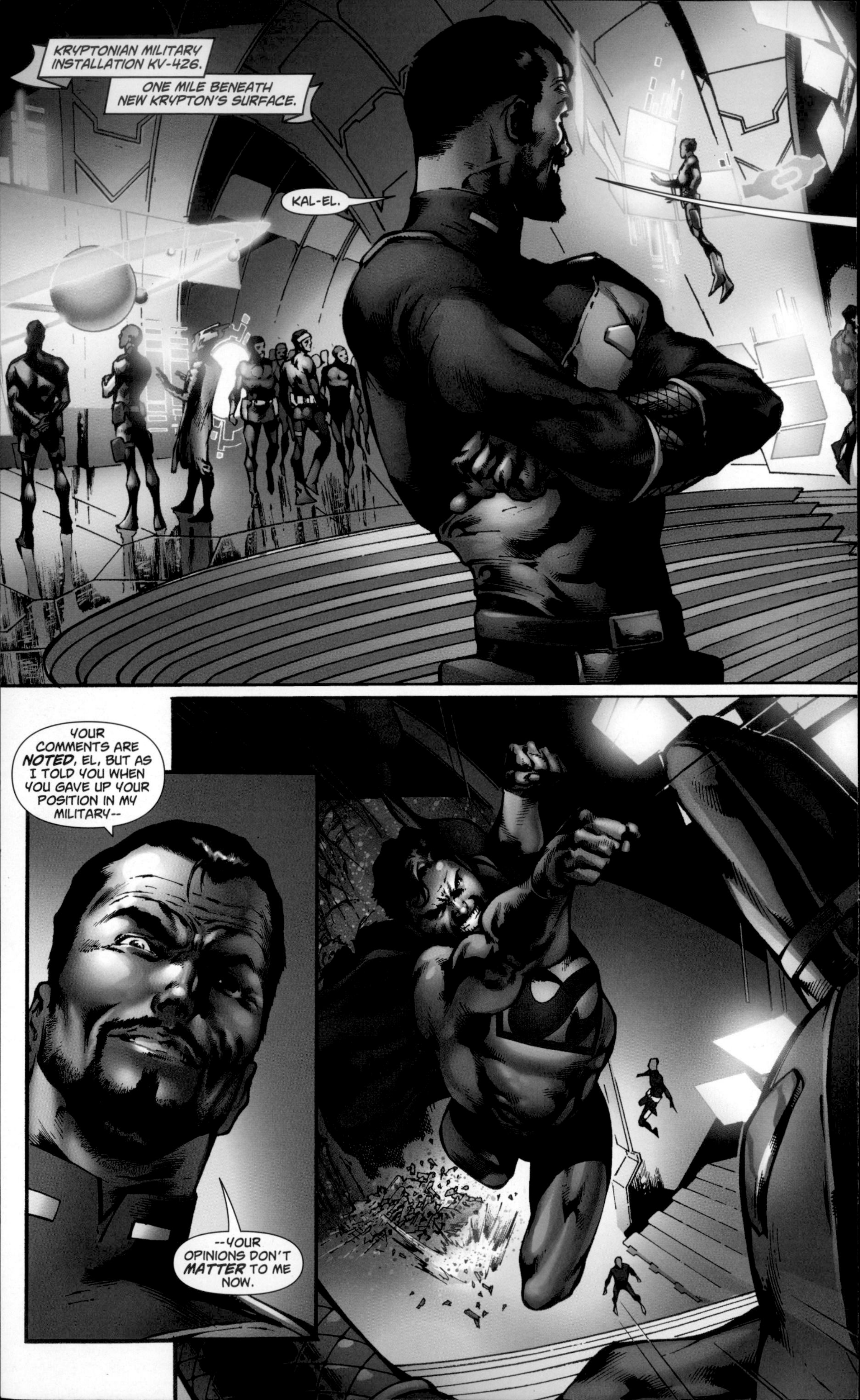
KRYPTONIAN MILITARY INSTALLATION KV-426.
ONE MILE BENEATH NEW KRYPTON'S SURFACE.
KAL-EL.
YOUR COMMENTS ARE NOTED, EL, BUT AS I TOLD YOU WHEN YOU GAVE UP YOUR POSITION IN MY MILITARY--
--YOUR OPINIONS DON'T MATTER TO ME NOW.

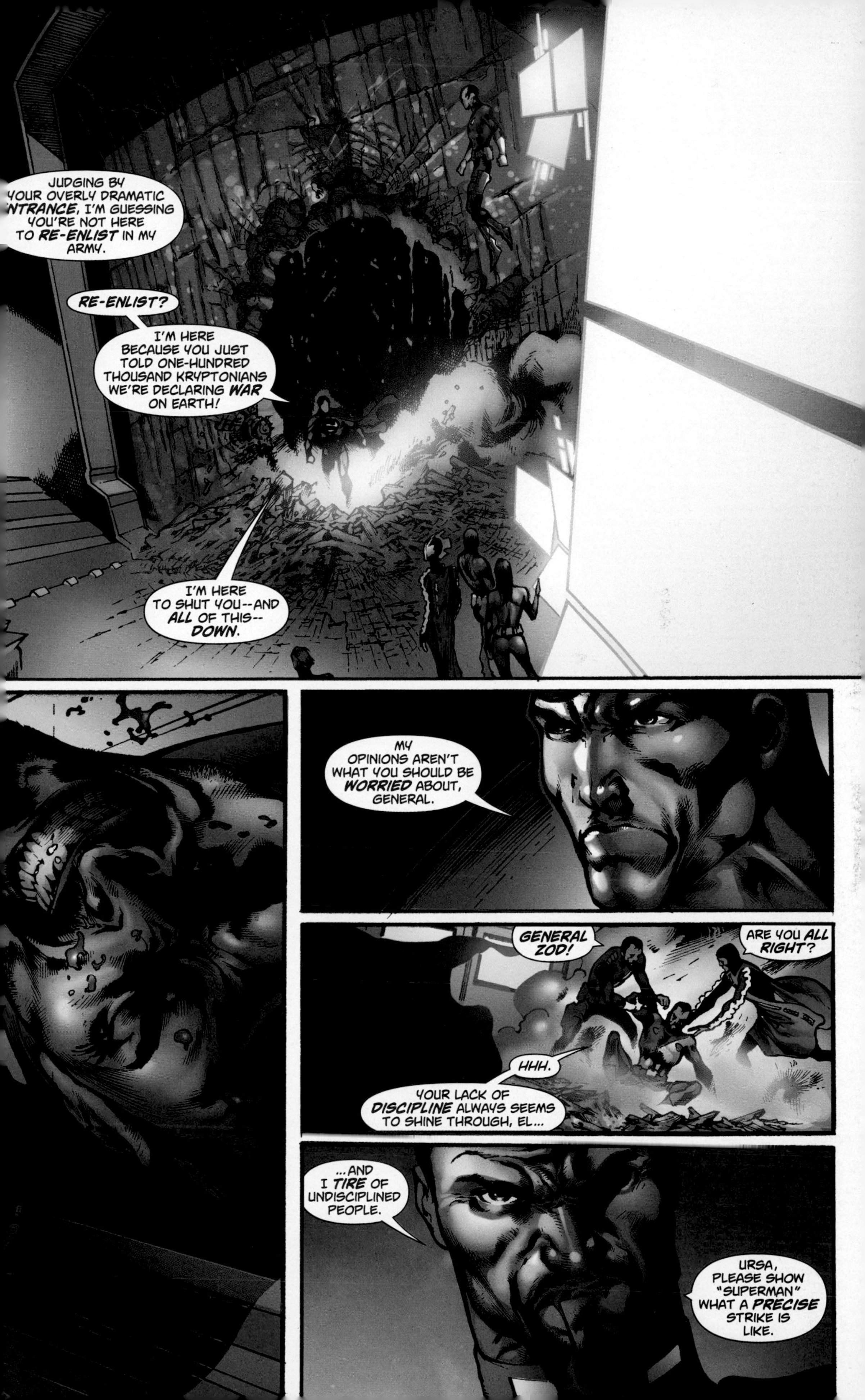
JUDGING BY YOUR OVERLY DRAMATIC ENTRANCE, I'M GUESSING YOU'RE NOT HERE TO RE-ENLIST IN MY ARMY.
RE-ENLIST?
I'M HERE BECAUSE YOU JUST TOLD ONE-HUNDRED THOUSAND KRYPTONIANS WE'RE DECLARING WAR ON EARTH!
I'M HERE TO SHUT YOU--AND ALL OF THIS--DOWN.
MY OPINIONS AREN'T WHAT YOU SHOULD BE WORRIED ABOUT, GENERAL.
GENERAL ZOD!
ARE YOU ALL RIGHT?
HHH.
YOUR LACK OF DISCIPLINE ALWAYS SEEMS TO SHINE THROUGH, EL...
...AND I TIRE OF UNDISCIPLINED PEOPLE.
URSA, PLEASE SHOW "SUPERMAN" WHAT A PRECISE STRIKE IS LIKE.

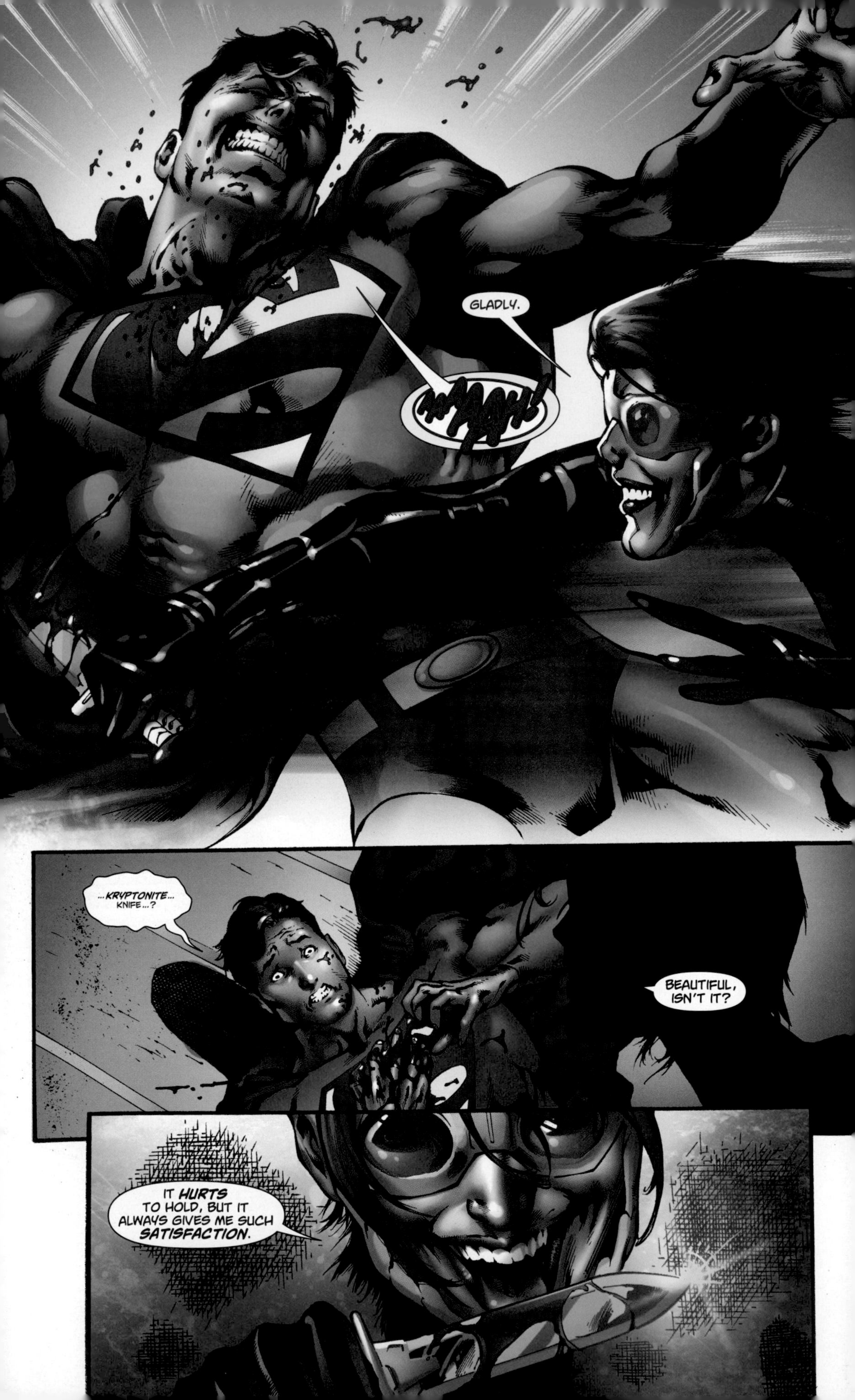
GLADLY.
AAAAGH!
...KRYPTONITE... KNIFE...?
BEAUTIFUL, ISN'T IT?
IT HURTS TO HOLD, BUT IT ALWAYS GIVES ME SUCH SATISFACTION.

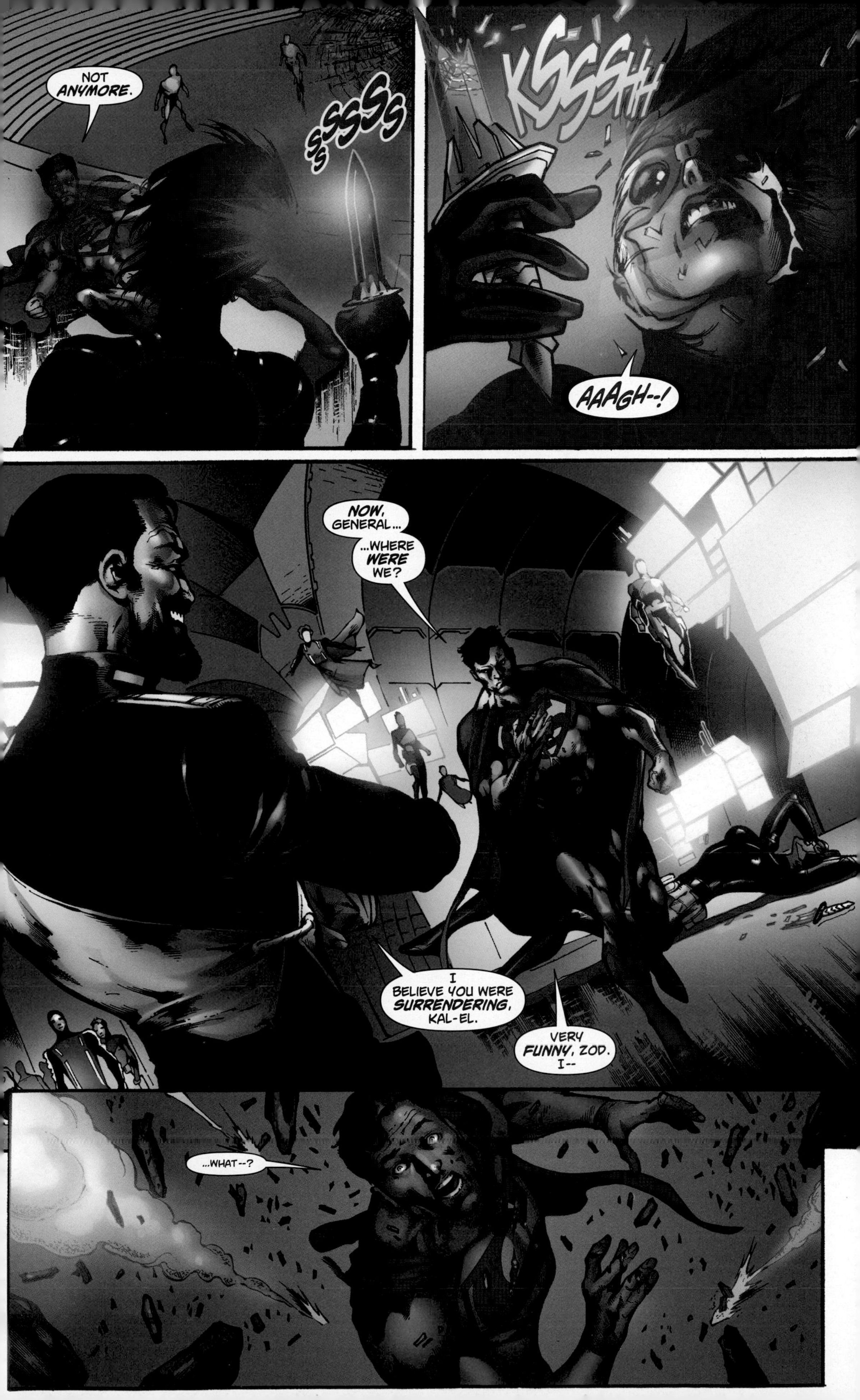
NOT ANYMORE.
SSSSSS
KSSSHH
AAAGH--!
NOW, GENERAL...
...WHERE WERE WE?
I BELIEVE YOU WERE SURRENDERING, KAL-EL.
VERY FUNNY, ZOD. I--
...WHAT--?

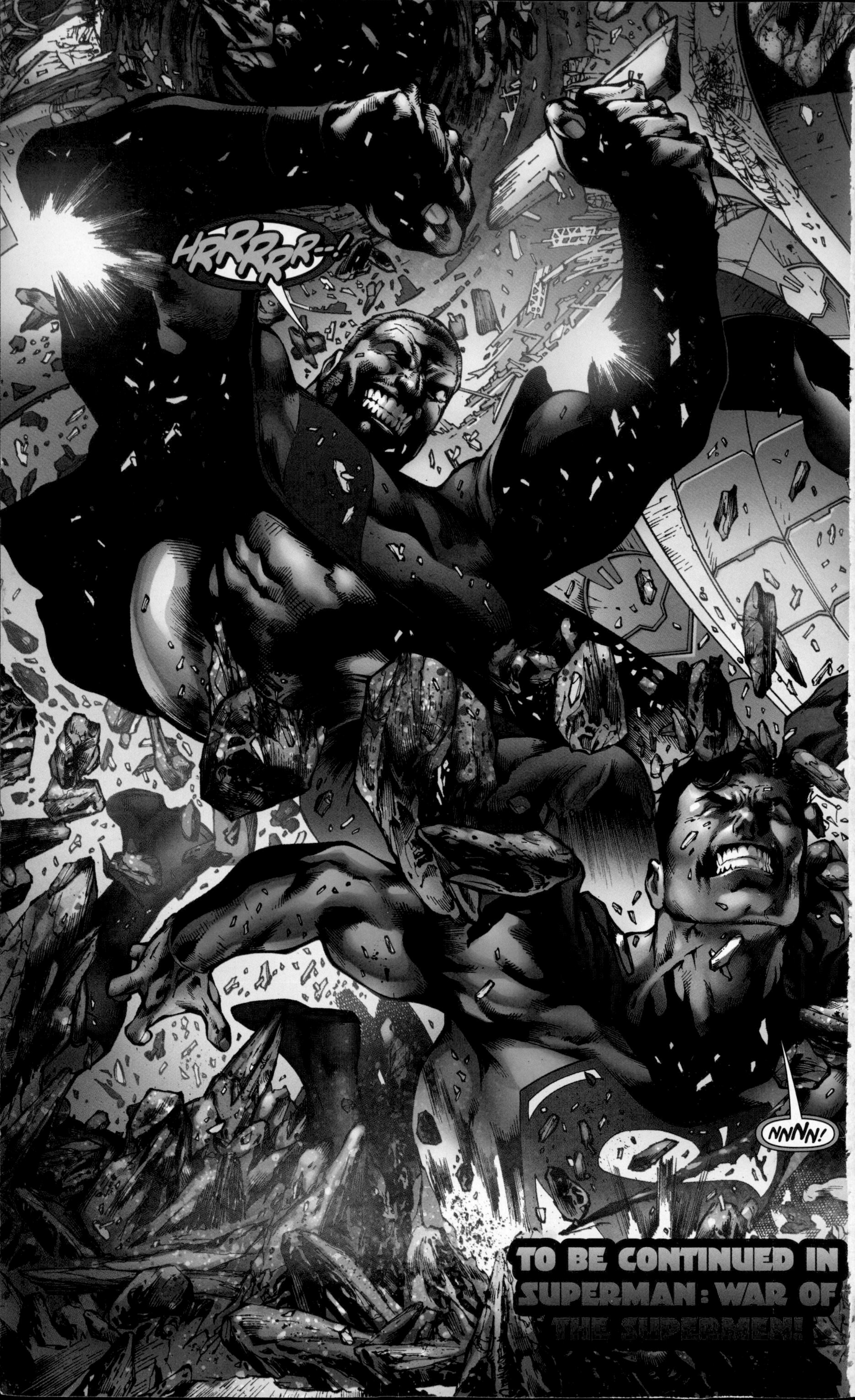
HRRRRR--!
NNNN!
TO BE CONTINUED IN SUPERMAN: WAR OF THE SUPERMEN!